A NEW TESTAMENT JOURNEY

Encounter and know the extraordinary God of the Bible
A simple plan that reads a chapter of the bible each
weekday of the year

CONTENTS

WELCOME TO "A NEW TESTAMENT JOURNEY"

I really want you to read the bible; to enjoy the incredible book and to have your life changed by it.

As I've reflected on why some see God doing extraordinary things through them and others always seem to be disappointed, I have found that the habit of seeking daily encounters with God to be the marked differential. People who build a habit of opening their bible every day (and try to find God there) - even if it is for a tiny amount of time - seem to move forwards with God. Those who don't build this habit tend to struggle.

I live in a highly diverse church community. We have many first generation immigrants; some of the materially and relationally poorest people in our city. I think of some who are in emergency housing, without income, without a family network, without an understanding of how UK systems work. And yet they are thriving. They abound in joy. They hug me and shine light into my life. And they do it to pretty much everyone they meet. I think of others who carry so much privilege and have material things that their grandparents would only have dreamed about. And yet they seem to be on the edge of a cliff emotionally, mentally, spiritually, relationally. There are, of course, many and complex factors at work in all of our lives, but time and again I notice that daily encounters with God are a dramatic differential.

And, of course, we should expect it to be so. Jesus said that those who hear his words and practise them are like those who build their house on the rock. Those who don't will fall apart in the storms.

The scriptures are the counsel of heaven, they are the path of life, they contain all we need to equip us for a life that is good. The scriptures are even - in this mysterious phrase - from the breath of God; like a daily breathing out of the Creator into his creation. And so this book is written to help ordinary "christians" build that habit of daily encounters. This book is written to help you build a rhythm of receiving from your Redeemer. Please do use it for that; it will change your life.

This book is intentionally provocative. I have sought to bring in a flavour of the shocking manner of Ezekiel-the-maniac, or Paul-the-riot-starter or even Jesus himself; the one the masses were delighted to kill. I mean, if we are actually going to encounter

God it should probably put out our hip or silence us for months or make us fall down as if dead, never to be the same. I hope this envisions you and makes you thirst for what is real. Perhaps you have previously found the bible boring... I hope this could never be that.

This book is also intentionally grubby. I have tried to celebrate the earthiness of the Christian faith that gets lost in the manicured musings of many middle-of-the-road writers. The disciples were unschooled and ordinary. They argued and attacked people with swords and sold everything they had and wept on others shoulders. Jesus touched lepers, wrestled demons, ate with sinners. Most shockingly of all Jesus exposed people's shame in front of the crowds and then offered them glorious redemption or gutting rebuke in an equally public square. I hope that the grubbiness of the writing makes you see how the bible really speaks into your real-world life, meeting you there (not just in a well-groomed worship space), marinating majesty into your mundane Monday to Saturday.

Finally, I've tried to embrace (rather than overlook) the mysterious complexity of much of the New Testament. Some comments on some days fly in multiple directions all at once and probably fail to get anywhere much into any of them. I'm big enough to accept that. Very Smart People have been arguing for centuries about what Paul has put in his paragraphs. I suspect I am not going to land neat answers in 300 words. And more than that,I don't believe our "goal" in reading the New Testament should be to land neat summaries of every passage, every time we come to it. Neat summaries can often stand in the way of that. Instead we come to each passage to meet Jesus there. We come to encounter the One who is always so far beyond knowledge, who lives in unapproachable light and yet who approaches us in love and tells us Truth in undistilled form. God cannot be boxed. But he can be known if we let him show us himself.

And so I'm praying that this book changes your life. I really believe it can. Not because I write good. But because it helps you build a habit of tabernacling with your Lord. It helps you hear Wisdom and, through the drip-drip of wisdom's whispers it helps you start to walk in Wisdom's ways. This book will help you build a friendship with the Father, it will help you be filled with the Spirit and - if you try to reflect and respond to the writings - it will mean you start to sort-of-resemble the Son.

HOW IT WORKS

It's a simple plan, it's a fresh plan. We'll read one chapter of the New Testament every weekday, along with the accompanying devotional and reflection question.

If you do this Monday to Friday each week, with weekends to reflect and catch up, you can work through the whole of the New Testament in a calendar year.

I've organised the readings to start with Luke and Acts, and then work around different books according to author and theme, encountering every letter, before finishing with Revelation in December. It's amazing - one chapter each weekday and that will take us all the way through.

We will run through the New Testament in this way:

Luke, Acts, 1 Timothy, 2 Timothy, Titus, Philemon
Mark, Romans, 1 Corinthians, 2 Corinthians, Galatians, Ephesians, Philippians, Colossians, 1 Thessalonians, 2 Thessalonians
Matthew, Hebrews, James, 1 Peter, 2 Peter
John, 1 John, 2 John, 3 John, Jude, Revelation

If you think well on these words, you will turn around in twelve months time and find your feet are on the Rock. I pray God does wonders in your life as you meet him in this book.

Tom Thompson
January 2023

📖 LUKE 1

Dr Luke would have known what careful was. He wants you to know how carefully he has thought about what he has written. He wants to convince you that in the midst of this oppressive and struggling world God has drawn close to accomplish things so tremendous that they make you want to sing Ave Maria. This is the bare-faced-cheek of the New Testament faith - that the angelic visitations and the miracles, the life interruptions and prophetic declarations are not just fleeting fancies from a fairy tale. God actually did this stuff back in history. God came to common people and invaded them with his mercy. The sun of righteousness really can rise over people like you and me. Jesus really does bring mercy and favour to undeserving people. So, let's start this journey with a question; will you let him? Zechariah nearly missed it, he silently assumed that his situation was one of those exceptions that God can't change. It took a long stint of silence for God to turn Zechariah around. In that Zechariah mirrored the whole nation of Israel - God put them through 400 years of silence to help them learn to really trust in him. I think sometimes it can be in our silence where God can most awaken us to his plans. Sometimes the assumptions that most hamstring us and hem us in are hidden to us until the suffering of silence exposes them. Silence makes us yearn for the light of God to shine into our darkness. It makes us long for the invasion of God into the most barren parts of our lives. In silence we become ready for the rich and deep and wide salvation of our God, no matter how crazy it sounds. When God comes, he comes with tender mercy. He releases favour. He rewrites destinies. He made faithless Zechariah the father of John the baptist - the one Jesus called the greatest of all born men. What might he do for you?

QUESTION FOR REFLECTION

Are there any areas of your life that you - like Zechariah - have assumed God's goodness will not touch?

📖 LUKE 2

When we think about Luke and Acts as a two-part epic it adds an extra shot of caffeine to our bible beverage. At the start of Luke we see the heavenly host, Simeon and Anna prophesying that Jesus will reach all the nations, we see the Holy Spirit falling on people in the temple courts. We see Jesus growing in wisdom and stature and in favour with God and the people. And then at the start of Acts we see Jesus prophesying that the early church will carry his gospel to all the world. We see the Holy Spirit fall on people in the temple courts and we then see the church grow in wisdom and stature and in favour with God and the people. What careful Dr Luke is showing through this structure is that where Jesus went, the church follows. What Jesus did, the church did. Luke wants us to realise that Jesus came as King of the long awaited Kingdom of God. And we - as Spirit-filled kingdom people - must continue to do all our King started. The Spirit anointed Jesus as King and this very same Spirit lives in the church, anointing us for Kingdom ministry. The caffeine in this bible beverage should send shock waves through our weary bodies. We should expect to keep on doing the stuff Jesus did. Time and again Luke demonstrates how the salvation of God is for us, for now, ushering us into a new way of life... if we allow it to. What the Spirit is doing could so easily be missed. Think about how the Spirit "moves" Simeon to go into the temple courts so that he would come across Mary, Joseph and Jesus (2:25-27). This was what Simeon had been waiting his whole life for and yet, he could so easily have missed this mysterious "moving" and just done some shopping instead. We saw it in chapter 1 and we see it again in chapter 2. God loves to come close. His tender mercy is being poured out. His favour is a free-flowing fountain. But it doesn't hit us round the head. We have to pick up the cup to drink, we have to be alert to the movings of the Spirit, we have to seek earnestly for Jesus and store up in our hearts the things that he says. We can be weary travellers, we can be working the lowest paid jobs, we can be an old man on our deathbed, or a long-term widow. We can even be anxious parents. All we need to do is come to Jesus and let him be our King. If we do that, not only will we be drawn into delights of salvation but we will even end up doing so much of what Jesus did.

QUESTION FOR REFLECTION

What would it feel like for the Spirit to "move" you like He moved Simeon?

📖 LUKE 3

The message John the Baptiser brought was astonishingly powerful. It shows us the fundamentals of the message of the Kingdom. John headlined with in-your-face demands for repentance. John looked at people's census responses, John looked at people's bible reading plans, John heard people talking about their Christian heritage... and he spat half-digested locusts on them. "That isn't enough" he cried, "you can't just claim a Christian inheritance or copy certain Christian practices; you have to be cut to the heart, you have to want to kill the sin in you and to live a new life for God." This was an unadulterated demand to be baptised in the Spirit or to face the coming wrath. Talk about being beaten with a winnowing stick! But John didn't stop there. He had got in people's faces once but then he went and got in their faces a whole nother time. He pointed at his hearers and called them serpents and he pointed at the stones and called them children. He railed against the idea that you could presume others out of the kingdom; citizenship was through God's work alone. God could make citizens out of some ancient pieces of rock if he wanted to and so he could certainly make them out of Gentiles too. Any hint of excluding others from God's favour just because of their upbringing would make John bite like a camel. So we see in John's message the mega-themes of the Kingdom; life-change empowered by the Holy Spirit and the mercy of God being poured out on all the nations. The Kingdom is a life of generosity and integrity only possible with Holy Spirit. And the Kingdom is a life of explicit openness to the whole people of the world. Oh how I want those Kingdom themes to define my life. How does that happen? Luke is keen to show that it doesn't come by us listening to great preachers. Like a mallet that is used by a chef to tenderise the steak and then is put back into the drawer, John is swiftly sidelined from the narrative. Jesus is left front and centre; the Son who is deeply loved by God. It is only by being baptised by him in his Spirit that we can even begin to live a truly Kingdom Life. So if you want to live a life of generosity and integrity and see a global impact flow out of your fingers, nothing matters more than you coming to the Son.

QUESTION FOR REFLECTION

Do you feel like Jesus has baptised you with his Spirit?

📖 LUKE 4

I don't know about you, but one of my big three temptations has never been to jump off the top of a building to force God to catch me. What's going on here? Jesus' temptations only make sense when we realise that the Wilderness is where Jesus confronts Satan over the destiny of the earth. Jesus goes into the wilderness a bit like David goes to Goliath; mano-a-mano to fight for the land. Jesus has - just like David - been anointed as King and has - just like Israel - been commissioned to release salvation to every family across the earth. This brings Jesus into unresolvable conflict with earth's current landlord; Satan. Satan uses three tactics to try to avoid the battle he knows he can't win. The first tactic Satan uses is to try to convince Jesus there isn't a battle to fight at all. Forget this fasting lark; just tuck into some food and enjoy the fruit of the earth. Jesus bats that away by quoting from Deuteronomy; God's people have a mission to follow and if it takes some pain; let it be so. In the second temptation Satan pushes Jesus to agree to a "win-win" truce; Jesus gets most of what he wants as long as Satan gets to stay in post. Again Jesus quotes from Deuteronomy. God must be the only King of this earth. No power-sharing deal can even be considered. And then we get to this weird temple temptation. Perhaps the most subtle temptation of all is for us to fight the battle against Satan but to do it our way. If the devil can tempt Jesus to jump from the top of the temple he will "kind of be doing what God wants" (face death in Jerusalem) but he will be doing it in his own, easier and quicker way. This is the temptation to say Jesus is your King but then to pursue life in whatever way you think best. If Satan can make us think we are doing something good, even while he is drawing us away from how God wants us to do it, then that actually is a victory for Satan; he has prevented the King of the Kingdom from being fully in charge here on earth. What Jesus fights for in the Wilderness is intimate obedience to the Father in every single thing. The key to Kingdom expansion is intimate obedience to the Father. And so this chapter shows us that the biggest fight of your life will be whether you can persist in loving obedience to God even when times are tough. Satan will try to take you anywhere but loving obedience to the Father, because he knows that in loving obedience God becomes your King. And when God becomes King, Satan's head will be crushed and his reign will be no more.

QUESTION FOR REFLECTION

What would greater loving obedience to the Father look like in your life?

📖 LUKE 5

What did Jesus mean when he said to the paralysed man "Your sins are forgiven"? Surely he can't mean the man's paralysis was a punishment from God that would be removed when forgiveness is released? Sadly so many of us secretly think that that is what God is like. The conundrum is unpicked when we realise that we often have far too narrow an understanding of sin, and therefore far too narrow a view of Jesus' saving work. The modern concept of sin - if it exists at all - suggests you can point at a person and say a specific act was a sin and another specific act wasn't. It is an individualistic fault-focused idea. But Jesus talks about Sin like a Kingdom. Sin is a manifestation of Satan's power that holds people in exile from God and corrupts them from the inside out. For Jesus, therefore, forgiveness is to plunder a person out of Satan's foul influence; to forgive a man is to re-birth him as a member of God's great community. Jesus' forgiveness of the paralysed man (and of you) is therefore not about Jesus pretending his evil actions never occurred but it is releasing the man from his sin-defined destiny and commanding him to walk into new life in the community of the redeemed. The stories about the fishermen and the tax collector are therefore one and the same as the paralysed man. Each of them are delivered from destinies drudging towards death and are reborn into a life defined by the Life of the Messiah. Jesus came to liberate people from the lord of this earth by making him their Lord instead. That is what forgiveness means. If we lifted the bonnet of your view of repentance, what would we find? Would it be a nitpicking, narky moan not to commit acts of sin, or would it be beckoning to rehabilitation and belonging; to movement and to membership. I want the church again to be known for liberating the lost, for inviting distraught and wounded people into the kingdom of kindness where they can find new rhythms and new destinies in intimate obedience to their God. I want to be someone who, like my Lord, gives remarkable, generous invitations to the new life of walking each day in the goodness of our God.

QUESTION FOR REFLECTION

What would be different if you were filled with all the goodness of God?

📖 LUKE 6

Jesus' claim to be Lord of the Sabbath is pretty mega. Sabbath observance was a crucial and eternal aspect of being God's people, so it's no wonder that the Pharisees took exception to Jesus trampling all over it. From the Pharisees' perspective, Jesus was taking a chainsaw to the supporting branch of their tree house called Torah. False Prophets like him needed to be killed. But what they missed - what they ultimately refused to even consider - was that Jesus was the planter of the Torah tree and the builder of the original tree-house. Jesus' redefining of Sabbath (with the Old Testament precedent of King David) was really a restoring of God's original intent for the structure. A major theme in the Early Church's understanding of Jesus was that he came to bring a fresh re-interpretation of all God had already revealed. The twelve apostles don't replace Israel (they were already part of Israel!) but they do symbolise the re-creating of Israel that God had always wanted, and Jesus was now providing. In the same way Jesus doesn't just ditch sabbath, instead he shows sabbath to be the provision by God for his people to lean into the nurture of God. God wanted Sabbath to be a day of formation - where the "sons of the Most High" would remind themselves of the Mercy of the Most High... and thereby become more merciful themselves. God wants a people defined by Sabbath; who abound in mercy, who even love their enemies, who are a tree bearing beautiful fruit. Is that what Sabbath is for me? A non-negotiable commitment in my life to lean into God's provision and to infuse myself with God's mercy? I worry how much I live the praxis of our culture's religion; "always on" productivity. I find myself driven by the idol of efficiency. I try to solve my problems with a bit more effort, or a bit more information. Or I just scroll my phone because... well... I can? I fear I have gone to the opposite extreme of the pharisees' rigid rules on rest, but with the same effect; I miss the nurturing mercy of God and I have little reserves left to show his mercy to others. But - here is the good news - Jesus came to help people like me and you. If we allow him to be our teacher his blessing of rest can rest upon us. If we let Jesus's kindness and mercy be our portion, if we allow his nurturing sabbath to soak into our soul, we will become a really good tree and we will bear really good fruit.

QUESTION FOR REFLECTION

How are you intentionally leaning into the mercy and nurture of the Most High?

📖 LUKE 7

If I was round a friend's house and a sex worker wandered in and started caressing my feet I suspect I would feel a tad uncomfortable. If she then started sobbing and lathing me in perfume I would be gathering up my stuff and skedaddling for the exit. The fact that Jesus sits, relaxed and smiling while this excruciating scene is unfolding is an astonishing display of his security. The fact that Jesus then praises this woman and rebukes the much more sensibly-behaved diners is shocking to say the least. Who really behaves like this? Who do you know who actually changes people's lives while they nibble their tiramisu? When we allow these stories about Jesus to come to life in our imagination we realise there was something about Jesus' shalom-filled presence that caused people's true natures to be exposed. The way he did stuff - the way he treated people - caused their most polished presentations of themselves to crack apart and their deepest secrets to be laid bare. And then, when the exposure had been made, Jesus would issue a stunning act of forgiveness or an equally stunning call to repent. Jesus seemed happy to challenge the proud because they might actually listen and then they would come to life. But Jesus really delighted when humble hearts were laid bare before him because it enabled him to pour the healing of the Spirit into their salivating souls. Jesus drew people close so he could actually change their lives. Indeed, when John the Baptist started to doubt that Jesus had really brought the Kingdom, it was the changed lives that Jesus pointed to as evidence of his Kingship. And this is why we love Jesus, isn't it? Not because he is comfortable to be around; he isn't… but because he changes us. And he wants to keep on changing us. We come ashamed, exposed, wrenched apart by our lives. And then he looks at us with love, speaks a word of forgiveness and washes away our shame. And at times it is others that Jesus wants to change through us. Jesus trusts us enough to give us precious moments when someone's deepest self is exposed so he can use our grace-imbued words, our love-defined response to usher them into new life. What Luke wants us to realise is that this person after person transformation - this grubby work of seeing people's shame and seeing it washed away - is the highest pinnacle of ministry of the Kingdom. Jesus loves to change people's lives.

QUESTION FOR REFLECTION

Have you exposed your deepest shame to Jesus? What does he say to you about it?

📖 LUKE 8

Unless loads of them had had an argument with Peter (cf John 18) I don't think there were many of Jesus' listeners who had no ears. So when Jesus said "those who have ears, let them hear" he was probably making a profound point. And his point was probably this - that listening is important, but hearing is even more so. Lots of people listened to the parable of the sower, lots of people saw Jesus taking out the lamp and putting it on a stand. But not that many people really heard what he was saying. Most of the crowds, in fact, slotted Jesus' sayings into boxes formed by their narrow assumptions - and either applauded him or rejected him based on whether he seemed to "feed" their view of life or to "resonate" with what they felt deep down. But few of them gave to Jesus what he was asking for; few of them really heard him. To hear Jesus is to allow him to form us, it is to fight to understand what he is actually saying, how it is different from what we thought, and what implications such a mindset change would have for our lives. To hear Jesus is to cede authority to him; to place more trust in his opinions and perspectives than we place in those we received from our community or those we hear online. To hear Jesus is to move beyond just looking for what "resonates" with us and to allow every single thing he says to rework us and to redefine us. Those who do that become incredibly fruitful; crazily so. Those who do that become brothers and sisters and even mothers of the Messiah. This probably takes a bit of thinking about. We live in an age, and even in a Christian culture, with so much noise around us all the time that we have got used to listening to everything but "hearing" barely anything. Even these New Testament Journey readings can be stuff we "bash through" to achieve a goal. Sit and think for a moment. When was the last time we actually just let Jesus be foreign and unfamiliar and fresh to us? When was the last time we sat and imagined and considered who this guy really was and how our life would look if we really took him at his word? Or, to put these questions another way - the gospel way - hear this; the route to you becoming a people who brings deliverance to others is now open. It is now possible for you to become a ridiculously fruitful person bringing others back from the dead and calming storms in their lives. All you need to do is listen to Jesus and then really hear what he says.

QUESTION FOR REFLECTION

What is one thing you have really "heard" from Jesus this month? How has this redefined the way you live and think?

📖 LUKE 9

The Jesus journey is reaching a critical point; patterns have been set, eyes have been opened, hearts have been captured. And so it is the time for the lightning fire of pure revelation to be injected into the mix. It is not the lightning fire of judgement as Israel may have expected; judgement of the Romans, judgement of the gluttons and drunkards who littered Jewish society. Instead the lightning fire is the news of Jesus' departure. Often it is entrances that are glorious, it is arrivals that stir the crowds. But with Jesus it is his departure that excites figures no less great than Moses and Elijah. The glorious splendour of Jesus is not that he comes with a sword but that he departs to leave his Spirit. His desire, at this stage in proceedings, is not to establish an earthly power that draws lines around itself and opens fire on the outsiders. His desire is to depart so that his house can be opened to all. His desire is that service and humility, welcome and permission can be released in his people through the work of his Holy Spirit. We live on the receiving end of this desire. Our glorious inheritance is of a departed king. But our king has left his presence behind him. Our King has left his presence to transform us from self-obsessed, hostile-minded individuals into generous, life enhancing communities who bring hope and transformation to his fallen world. I so much want to be part of one of those communities. I yearn for church to be like Jesus died for it to be. And, when I think about this, I realise that church can be like that - that the Presence in me is strong enough to use me as a catalyst to spark such a church into being. That same presence lies in you; the power is in our hands. Will we scrabble around for chances to confess Christ, to feed the hungry, to serve kids, to deny ourselves. Or will we keep on taking our hand off the plough? Will we let self-respect or the opposition of others or a lack of comfort cause us to forfeit our very selves? O Jesus please make me worthy of your kingdom. Please make me great in your kingdom. Please let me be one who doesn't taste death until I really see the Kingdom of God manifested in our midst.

QUESTION FOR REFLECTION

What would it look like for the Kingdom to be established in the midst of your life circumstances?

📖 LUKE 10

We are pretty much halfway through Luke now and he has laid out ample evidence of Jesus' personality (birth, baptism, miracles, transfiguration) and his plan (Luke 4 "The Spirit of the Lord is upon me..., sending out of the 12). We must mark as read that Jesus is the Humble Empowered One who empowers people to humbly spread all the fruit of his salvation all across the globe. Assuming that case has been made, Luke begins to expose the key distinctives Christians need to cling to if we are indeed to be the Kingdom. We have already noted Jesus' penchant for people who persevere; for people who don't easily take their hand off the plough of showing mercy to others. Part-time practitioners need not apply. In this chapter (and leaking into the next) we find Jesus going on about the one thing that is needed; the distinctive behind all the distinctives. Thank the Lord, it is not the house-work! With the anecdote about Martha and Mary, Jesus elevates the call to intimacy with God above everything else. Intimate obedience to the Father is the Kingdom. In this gospel Luke is careful to show Jesus repeatedly popping off to pray. In Acts, Luke shows the church repeatedly stopping everything to pray. What more is there to say about this? Jesus prayed with intimacy and dependence and Jesus wants his followers to pray with intimacy and dependence. Scratch that; it's a statement that is too general and easy to wriggle away from. Let's try this; Jesus wants me to pray with intimacy and dependence; he wants me to learn to live in intimacy with him, free from stress and worry about many things. He wants the same for you. He wants this kind of prayer to be the distinctive of our lives. He wants this for us because it is the best thing; it is what it is to be truly human. Oh God, please would you teach us to pray.

QUESTION FOR REFLECTION

What simple, achievable step could you take to upgrade your prayer life and grow in intimacy with God?

📖 LUKE 11

How do we, as followers of the King, access the power of the King? What is your answer to it? Some try suits and smoke machines, some shouting or total spontaneity. Many of us just copy what the latest "power church" seems to be doing. And most of us - if we are honest - lack power. This is what many have called "the open secret of the Western church". It seems to me like it is time for a change? When Jesus cast out those demons he was flagging up to everyone that God has got the devil licked. God's finger - just his finger! - could bind the Strong Man and plunder all his house. So when, in this context, Jesus told us all to pray "your Kingdom come" he showed us all that we can - with our wrinkly, grubby and very puny fingers - somehow act with the finger of God. He showed us that when we ask for the Kingdom to come we should expect to overcome the devil and divide up all his plunder. What this actually means is that the power is in his Presence. We access the power through simply and repeatedly coming to the One who owns the kingdom and the power and the glory forever and for ever and forever. God's Power is accessed through humble requests made direct to the loving Father. The Power is in God's Presence. It is as straightforward as that. This is the true story of grace. Now before you check out thinking "I've tried that", it is worth also looking at what Jesus says about "the lamp of the body". What this seems to imply is that the power grows stronger in us as the presence goes deeper in us. The kind of prayer Jesus is advocating is formed by the kind of "hearing" that he advocated in chapter 10. Anyone, anywhere, can see the power flow through them when they allow the presence and priority of God to fill them and redefine them. And part of the priority of God - part of "lived prayer" is to plunder the Devil's house. And so, next time you have a chance to minister in the power of the Kingdom - take it. And as you stand with a hand on a shoulder remind yourself whose hand is with your hand. Look for the finger of God and release the power that His Finger carries. Don't use a strange voice, or shout or doubt, don't even think about yourself at all. Just fix your eyes on Jesus - on His Presence - and do what you think he wants you to do; say what you think he wants you to say. And, while it might take time to learn it, even as you begin, you will see the power of God dividing up plunder between you and the person you pray for.

QUESTION FOR REFLECTION

How could you increase the number of people you lay your hands on and pray for?

📖 LUKE 12

If we just had the gospel of Luke and none of the rest of the New Testament it would be difficult to own much stuff and feel happy. The way Luke puts his gospel together, and the quotes of Jesus that Luke majors on, speak very strongly of the dangers of wealth. And we Christians have been struggling with them ever since. Like a bit of fluff in a bath, I repeatedly struggle to get a grip on my greed. I think I have it in my hand and then see it once more floating gleefully on the top of the water. The temptation is to give up and just accept that greed will always be there. But Luke ferociously advocates a generous life completely free from worries about bigger barns, new wardrobes or weekly shops. How can it be? Can you and I really grasp this kind of life? Well, for Luke, the nub of our salvation isn't actually to focus on possessions or money but to reconsider what "life" actually means. For Jesus, "life" is synonymous with His Kingdom. Life is the loving nurture of the Father. Life is the clothed, counted and cared for submission to the master. Oh what a wise and joyful thing it would be to have this kind of life. Don't you want it? Imagine never having to worry about money again. Jesus seems to have actually believed his followers could grasp this kind of life. He speaks like he expects us all to enjoy this way of living. So how do we have it? We seek it. And that means doing things differently. We give attention to adverts about the character of the Father more than adverts on the latest item in the shops. We look at the trees and the birds more than new clothes or new restaurants. We carry an awareness that the "pagan world" around us will relentlessly nudge us towards hypocrisy. And so we deliberately build watchfulness into our week. We replace the barrage of information and the "scrolling down" of smart phones with bible and silence, with worship and waiting. And we practise giving things away and selling stuff we like. Not because the stuff is bad but because Real Life is better. We confess and practise heresy towards materialism so that we can enjoy the bounty of Kingdom. That is Life, as Jesus defines it.

QUESTION FOR REFLECTION

What one thing could you give to someone to express the loving generosity of the Father?

📖 LUKE 13

The Pharisees were happy to care for their animals and (just over in the next chapter) to have rich and delicious food made and served to them on a sabbath. They were happy to enjoy the friends and the fruit of their elevated position on the Sabbath. Yet on the Sabbath they denied a wretched woman her first scrap of hope. That, in microcosm, is what Jesus despised about the kingdom the Pharisees ruled over. Jesus is undeniably clear on this - his kingdom is not like that. In Jesus' Kingdom any status, any authority, any riches are used like yeast to leaven dough, they grow like mustard trees so birds can perch in their branches. Jesus comes and embodies this Kingdom. He puts his reputation to one side so he can heal a crippled woman. He stands up for the slandered... and he wants his people to do the same. I'm convicted by this. I realise how often I have - like those hypocrites - been delighted with visible virtue but a bit too busy to show sacrificial service to someone smaller than me. I realise how often I have - like Jerusalem - been at the centre of all kinds of religious activity and yet acted with very little compassion. Jesus invites me - and you - to change. He wants us to take whatever authority we have, to gather together all the status we possess and pour them out on the last, the least and the lost. This might mean befriending the ugly (probably best not to tell them that is your strategy), or the long hard slog of growing our own disciples instead of hopping off to enjoy the worship at the big established church next door. Or it might mean cooking a meal for a new mother, spending years investing in kids or helping an immigrant fill out official forms. All of these may seem a bit "narrow"; a bit restrictive. But these kinds of actions are the fruit that Jesus looks for on the fig tree. These are the kinds of hidden and small actions that will become enormous and significant at the resurrection of the righteous. Living this kind of Kingdom lifestyle may not sound as fun as "just receiving", "you being you" or "chasing your dream" but in the End it is Jesus' Kingdom that will last and flourish and fill everything in every way. The other kingdom - you know the self-centered, self-promoting one that loves to be seen - doesn't end that way and Jesus weeps over all who refuse to leave it behind.

QUESTION FOR REFLECTION

What authority or position do you hold? Who could you serve with it?

📖 LUKE 14

I wouldn't want Dr Luke as my GP; it seems that everything he says is so harsh. You need to choose the lowliest seats. You need to invite people to dinner who can't pay you back. You have to carry your cross and hate your wife and children. It is impossible for a rich man to inherit eternal life. Matthew and Mark record these sayings in gentler formats - why did Dr Luke opt for such an abrasive bedside manner? Well, Luke, with his straight-talking, shows that the very things that have wreaked destruction on the early church are the things that Jesus had warned against all along. If only Ananias and Sapphira had counted the cost of the "narrow door" before their catastrophe of clinging to cash. If only the Judaisers in Galatia had mulled over Jesus' parable of the Kingdom Banquet before they arrogantly annulled the validity of grace gifted to gentiles. Luke is like an elderly GP who has seen it all before, has heard every trick in the book and who can't be fooled by any of our clever explanations. Luke knows that sin so often sneaks through our defences and subtly convinces us that some other thing must have caused the loss of our salty flavour. No. It will be pride. No. It will be an old view of yourself. No. it will be you trying to get approval from the wrong people in the wrong way. And, in this sense, Luke is a brilliant doctor because the prescription he is giving is direct from our Maker himself. All through his ministry Jesus asked people to really hear him. All through his ministry Jesus warned people about the "yeast of the pharisees" and of the evil that comes from within. Jesus urged people to trust him when he pointed the finger at the real source of their sorrows. He urged them to relentlessly put into practice every remedy that he prescribed. Jesus knew it wouldn't be easy - that's why he called it "carrying our cross". But he also knew the result of it would be delightful, like building a tower, like winning a war or like feasting on a great banquet that never will run dry. If you want easy words then look elsewhere. But if you want the words of life, Luke's gospel will do you well.

QUESTION FOR REFLECTION

Are there any places other than God that you gain your approval?

📖 LUKE 15

These awesome stories. In them Jesus unfolds his robe and exposes huge, dazzling treasures about the personality and intention of God. They truly are brilliant aren't they? But something I had not spotted before - the fresh bread for me in this today - is that the three parables in ch15 and then Jesus' teachings all the way through to 17:10 are all in response to the mumbling groans of the pharisees about Jesus spending time with sinners. Jesus - who so often is tight-lipped and enigmatic in his responses to questions - releases a barrage of assertions when it comes to this topic. He's like the guy you poke on social media who then replies with an essay; "and another thing...". And so I find myself reviewing the way I have so often read these deeply beautiful and astonishing parables. So often I've seen myself as the lost coin, as the lost sheep as the son being given the fattened calf. Or I've seen them as a stimulus to evangelism; to wanting to see new people come to faith and discipleship. Both of these readings are valid and edifying. And yet I think the thrust of Jesus' argument is targeted on a subtly different place, at least when we see the flow of his argument as it moves from chapter 15 into 16 and 17. Jesus' passion is not just that I rejoice when sinners come to faith but that I accept God as a God who eats with sinners. I worship a God who eats with sinners. When you think about that; it is a bonkers thing for a holy God to do. Eating together takes time. Eating together includes reclining and making casual conversation. Eating together is shared vulnerability, when guards are dropped and honest opinions exposed. And our God does that with sinners. I so often lurch from seeing God as demanding and utterly holy - calling me to take up my cross and to reject "the world"; into seeing God as warm and cuddly - a relaxed and care-free socialite laughing his way through banquets. And yet, in these chapters of Luke we are told we must hold both views of God at the same time. We must look beyond human inclinations for God to be either / or and instead learn both to recline with him as prodigal father and to be rebuked by him as the convicting parable-writer. And, somehow, through the work of the Spirit, to be people who similarly embody the oxymoronic nature of our gracious, holy faith.

QUESTION FOR REFLECTION

Imagine yourself as an observer, watching the father meet the prodigal son and then holding an expensive feast with him. How do you respond emotionally to these scenes?

📖 LUKE 16

Has Jesus gone loopy? Has he eaten some bad fish and started advocating criminal behaviour? Jesus is telling the shrewd manager story not because he wants people to be dishonest but because he wants to shock people into seeing what shrewdness really is. Shrewdness realises the temporary nature of a situation, it recognises there are but a few moments to exploit it and it is ruthless in doing so. Jesus is speaking into the fleeting nature of this life compared to the eternal nature of his coming Kingdom. He is urging his people to be unimpressed by anything we own or achieve in this life, and to fervently and ruthlessly sacrifice it for our own eternal gain. I wonder if you read that right? Do things for your own eternal gain. Jesus has no problem with self-interest. He just has a major problem with his children seeking benefit in places where there isn't any; he doesn't want us frittering our inheritance on the alluring but fleeting fancies of money and status in this life. This nuance is really important as it shows the blooming, flourishing goodness of God. God does not want us to be ascetics by acting as if everything we want or enjoy is bad. That denies God as creator of the world and the designer of us. (Full-on asceticism is actually the root of the lie that the serpent told Eve back in Genesis 3.) But God doesn't want us to be hedonists either. Hedonistic Christians assume that God's presence will bring great pleasure and riches to them in every moment. An ascetic would rejoice in the poverty his master was inflicting upon him. A hedonist would be crushed by it. But the shrewd servant sees it as an opportunity. Shrewd servants spot possibilities. All the time. Even when things are going up the famous creek. This parable is Jesus' unashamed appeal for us to get better at spotting possibilities, especially with the use of our money. Jesus wants us to look at our bank account differently. Every penny in there can be invested in getting stuff back in the coming Age. Jesus wants us to win favour and befriend and to donate for the sake of future reward. To our "christian" culture it almost seems shameless. But Jesus says it is clued-up, effective, dynamic living. So which will you choose? The limp "selfless" "christian" view or the shrewd, opportunity-obsessed call of Christ? The choice is yours. I hope you'll be shrewd.

QUESTION FOR REFLECTION

If you had £50 in spare cash, how could you use it to gain friends for yourself?

📖 LUKE 17

Jesus is perplexed by the 9 non-returning lepers not because they lacked gratitude but because they failed to see who he is. Their lottery numbers came up… and they forgot to cash in the ticket. How could they have been so blind? These 9 lepers have been wasting away outside of the city, cut off from all prospects and relationships, permanently ringing a bell and saying "unclean, unclean" and watching their body decay before their eyes. Now they can live again - they are healthy and can marry and gain employment, they can rejoice and converse with others. But; if they are really smart; they will realise how much more they can find if they simply return to Jesus. The nine have received a tiny off-cut of grace and have been too thick or too distracted to come back to get the whole meal. Our cultural narrative tells us to be like the nine. It encourages us that we can live our dreams and be happy if we can just get free from the oppression of X. X might be the expectations of society, X might be a particular government or a particular relationship or a particular group of people who make us live a lie. X might even be a physical illness or a mental health issue. Our culture tells us all we need is to throw off that one thing and then "you be you" and you can step out into a life of unadulterated bliss. Jesus is puzzled by that idea. He knows we are oppressed by external factors like leprosy and he wants to set us free from them. But he knows we can only then thrive in our new found freedom when we have our hearts formed by him by sitting under his teaching. The life of bliss - what Jesus called "blessedness" - is found in Jesus' Kingdom when we make Jesus our King. How amazing would it be to copy the clever former-leper? What if when we snag a nice feeling from Jesus we follow the logic so that when we feel lonely, rather than trying to feel good about ourselves, we come to Jesus and receive affirmation beyond belief? What if when we stumble across an answered prayer for provision, we choose to move beyond hoarding our stuff for our goals, and instead open up our purses in generosity and trust God that he knows what we need? What if we decided to interact with Jesus not just to take temporary tonics but to lean into his long-lasting, life-transforming leadership? What if we chose to trust Jesus not just to give us delightful moments of deliverance but also to also lead us into the slower and equally delicious renovation of our hearts?

QUESTION FOR REFLECTION

What aspect of your heart is Jesus wanting to renovate? How could you let him do that?

📖 LUKE 18

There is only room for one big man in the kingdom, and that spot is already taken. Jesus seems to be particularly rigid about this. I'm feeling a little uneasy about all the people I've flattered or assured of their importance to God. On one level that was probably right; to utter the love of the Father to his trembling children. He does, after all, care astonishingly about every single person. But on another level, if we always make the kingdom about us it can start to make us think that God not only wants us but needs us. That God not only needs us but is lucky to have us. And then it isn't long before we start saying to ourselves that if God keeps on overlooking our demands he will lose out on us all together; like a snotty-nosed servant we will pack up our stuff and head off to another master who we think will be more grateful. I fear that too many people I have seen walk away from Jesus have done so because they felt that they had 'tried him out' and he 'hadn't delivered the goods'. I wonder how different their stories would have been if, rather than deciding to 'try God out' they had actually let God be the boss and they had tried to serve his plans. I wonder how different their stories would have been if they had daily prayed "Jesus, have mercy on me. Have mercy on me; a sinner. I'm just a child. I'm just here to learn." It is this latter degrading level of humility that Jesus is advocating in this chapter. He, in his love, wants us to realise that we are just babies. We are babies, fortunate to be growing up in the greatest house in all the kingdom. Jesus showed people that God sees stuff we have no clue about. God is working on things we are utterly blind to and it is really quite silly when we want to tell him what to do. God is Only Wise. When it comes to what is best for the world God scores 100% and most of us might get one question right... if we are lucky and the marking is generous. Our perspectives on ourselves are so small and our track records are so poor that the greatest expression of God's love for us is to have his voice take priority over our own. Yes - that is what Jesus is saying to us - that the Kingdom only works when we let Jesus be King and that means we, in turn, choose simply to obey. Jesus is keen that we - all of us - see ourselves as spare change in the pocket of God trusting his love and his wisdom to spend us wherever he likes.

QUESTION FOR REFLECTION

If you gave Jesus total control over your life, what might you do differently?

📖 LUKE 19

This is where we can peer inside the head of Jesus and see how he understood himself. By giving himself the title "Son of Man" Jesus was stepping into the prophetic tradition of Daniel 7, claiming to have divine authority to smash the corrupt kingdom that was ruining people's lives. In Jesus day most people thought that meant Israel as a whole, or an individual representing them, overthrowing the Romans and reclaiming the land. Nobody - except for Jesus - thought the Son of Man would peer up trees to chat to short sinners and then go and eat at their house. Jesus demonstrated that the true enemy kingdom that needed defeating was not the Roman one but the Kingdom of Satan. And Jesus demonstrated that the authority of God to tear down that kingdom was not expressed through global warfare but through acts of love and invitation to broken individuals. In this way Jesus shows the authority of God in this Age does not look like Solomon; enthroned in glorious splendour, all his human enemies humbled before his extensive armies, receiving notable guests who are overwhelmed by his wisdom and greatness. No, the authority of God in this Age looks like the pre-coronation David, skirting around the edges of the land, welcoming odds and sods into his band of merry men and liberating people from their captivity to the enemy. Jesus seeks and saves the lost. This is something I have to keep coming back to about Jesus. Yes he is more magnificent and powerful and glorious than I have ever glimpsed. Yes he is the center of all history, victorious, unshakable, the only big man in the Kingdom. But he doesn't sit on a throne expecting people to always come to him. He doesn't sit with a divining rod in his hand assessing our worth and only responding if we match up. Jesus seeks and saves. Jesus gets off his throne (not losing any of his authority or power in the process) and comes looking for us. He comes looking for you. And then when he finds us he peers up at us and asks us what we are doing. He asks if he can eat with us. He whispers such insightful, unexpected questions that it makes us want to repay everything, overpay everything, give back anything we owe just for the staggering joy of having him remain in our lives. I want my vision of Jesus to match his vision of himself; the One given All Authority to smash up Satan's Kingdom who casually eats and chats with people no-one likes.

QUESTION FOR REFLECTION

How could you expand your vision of Jesus to include his immense authority to smash evil.

📖 LUKE 20

The parable of the Tenants is where Jesus brings to a cataclysmic crescendo his confrontation with the temple leaders. Jesus insults their integrity, intelligence and insight. Can you imagine the looks on their faces as he announces to all that the temple leaders are going to be killed by God, crushed by the one they reject, punished most severely? Why couldn't he just leave them alone? Well, as Christians today we have grown up seeing the cross mainly as the atoning work of Jesus to provide us forgiveness for our sins. Amen and Amen. The cross definitely does that. But what Jesus emphasises in this parable is that the cross is part of God's plan to actually get some fruit out of his people. God wants his people to provide him with a harvest of worship and righteousness and blessing to the nations. And they just aren't doing that. So Jesus comes not just to "forgive sins", but to highlight the utter bankruptcy of the current leaders of creation. The Coming of the Son of Man both seeks and saves sinners and shows the stubborn selfishness of stewards who desperately need to be sacked. We have to have both in our vision of Jesus if we are going to know the real him. Chapter 19 shows us the utter generosity and kindness of Jesus to those who have done wrong. But if we just have a "Chapter 19 Jesus" we can never explain why anyone would want to kill him. Chapter 20 shows Jesus determined to bring an end to hypocrites ruling over creation. In Chapter 20 we see Jesus as the one who knows that a shake up and a clearing out is required if a brighter future is going to be born. Jesus' parable points to his death being a "final day" for an old way of being human and a "first day" of a new humanity where goodness and order could be re-established all over the earth. This new humanity would be centered around Jesus, would be filled with his Spirit and would deliver up far greater fruitfulness to our God. And so, as we read these passion parables Jesus causes us to ask - has his atoning work not only taken away our shame but also made us live better? Beyond receiving forgiveness of sins from Jesus, are we actually now bearing delicious fruit to God?

QUESTION FOR REFLECTION

Do you more often imagine Jesus eating with sinners or causing others to hate him so much that they want to kill him?

📖 LUKE 21

This is a tricky chapter. It is OK if it feels like stepping onto a rickety rope bridge over a deep gorge… But there are some reliable planks here that we can stand on. It is always helpful to set a passage in a context, and the context for this passage is that Jesus has come to Jerusalem to launch a whole new humanity. The widow's mite illustrates in miniature what Jesus is doing; he is turning upside down usual judgements about things; stuff that looks impressive can mean nothing to God; stuff that looks tiny can end up being the greatest. And so Jesus must have rolled his eyes when his disciples - even after hearing all of this - started going on about how impressive the temple is; "Have I really taught you nothing??!!". Jesus then lays it out for his disciples in much more detail than before. The temple has become like a visible, impressive offering that means nothing to God. It will be smashed up as a symbol of God's punishment of the Tenants of the Vineyard. That smashing up will be painful and lots of dust will fly around; people will faint, apprehensive of the terror. But at the same time he reassures them that they will be like widows who have given all they have to God, they will be noticed by him and given protection by him. These small ones will become the "others" who take ownership of the Vineyard; they will in fact be the ones to raise their heads and on whom the Kingdom will come near. This is the big story Jesus is telling. Now I realise that most of us have grown up thinking that the Big Story about the Return of the Son of Man is Jesus' second coming and so we have assumed this chapter must be about that. It may include some references to that but Jesus says this will all play out within the generation of the disciples (v32) and so that future event isn't what most of it is about. Indeed, if we make this chapter just about The Second Coming we could end up making the same mistake the disciples did - to think God must be most interested in impressive things like Beautiful Temples and Second Comings and miss how Jesus saw us receiving his Kingdom, manifesting his Kingdom, giving everything we have for his Kingdom was actually what he meant by him coming in his glory. If Jesus teaches us anything we must realise the immense importance the Son of Man placed on his New Humanity. And we may finally understand that when we - like the widow - give everything to God it's one of the greatest things in history in the eyes of our God.

QUESTION FOR REFLECTION

How might God respond to you if you gave more to him?

📖 LUKE 22

My grandfather used to go on and on about these two swords (v 38) saying that they proved Jesus wanted to be a violent revolutionary. What a load of tosh (may my grandfather rest in peace). We really can't take a single verse and give it more weight than all the other verses of the New Testament. Even if we just read on a few more verses we see Jesus standing Peter down when he actually uses the sword. In context, the sword comment was one more way that Jesus was warning his followers to be ready and alert. Tribulation was coming. A better bone to gnaw on in this passage is how Jesus treats Peter. How Jesus looks-straight-at-Peter. Gulp. Poor old Peter must have soiled his toga when he realised the depth of his shamefacedness. From that point on he could never have doubted the basis of any future engagement with Jesus - epic portions of grace. And yet the funny thing is that we don't even get told what Jesus' look was. I'm not entirely sure why that is, but perhaps it is because it is less important than the fact that Jesus looked at all. Jesus had more than enough to be getting along with and yet his mind was on his followers. Jesus already knew that Peter would betray him and yet he didn't take that knowledge and whack Peter with it. Rather, he used it to focus his attention on Peter, turning his aspect towards him in the moment of his greatest betrayal. Isn't that wonderful? Jesus chooses to give himself particularly to those who are goofing up and bankrupting themselves. This is the way of the Kingdom that he has bestowed on us. Jesus doesn't blandly say that everything is OK but he does show he is there, watching, aware of our plight and dropping hints of the redemption that he is wanting to bring. This is the covenant that he signed with his blood. If you have bankrupted yourself you need to know that he watched you do it. You need to know that he is watching you now. You need to know that the same epic proportions of grace that were served up to Peter are available for you too. Look at Jesus looking at you. Get on your face and receive the sweet forgiveness his broken body offers to you. Receive his kingdom, and then go be a disciple who gives the same service to others that Jesus has given to you.

QUESTION FOR REFLECTION

Who do you know who has really messed up? How could you minister Jesus' grace to them?

📖 LUKE 23

As the gospel reaches boiling point we find a single message emerging from the flames. The essence of Jesus, the central claim about this extraordinary individual is that he is king. The assembly accuses him of it, Pilate grills him on it and Jesus confesses it. What the assembly just can't accept and Pilate can't grasp is that Jesus is not just king with a small 'k' but King of the New Creation that is dawning on the earth. This King's reign and dominion has arrived and it will know no end. Jesus is King. But, just in case we presume the New Creation King is like the current earthly kings, Luke conjoins Jesus' greatest declaration of his Kingship with Jesus' greatest demonstration of his love. In this chapter we gaze with wonder upon the unfathomable depths of his love. Every paragraph is buckling under the weight of Jesus' compassion and care. Jesus has been tortured and ridiculed, put through agony and humiliation and yet he turns to the women - He turns to them! - and desperate to see them saved he urges them to weep and prepare for the coming troubles. Surely He should have been fixed on saving himself from his own troubles? But love showed him another way and he chose it. As they batter the metal through his flesh he asks his Father not to spare himself the pain but to spare the hammer-bearers the agony of their own actions. When nobodies claim superiority over him he doesn't vilify them or curse them but ignores them. And when a criminal submits to Him He promises him the greatest future anyone could ever desire. And that is not even to mention the actual act of dying. Greater love have no King than this; that he lay down his life for his subjects. Whoever we are, whatever we have done Jesus - the King - responds to us with monstrous volumes of love. His rule longs to see us do well, his throne is turned towards us and his aspect is open wide. He is the King of Kings but, my goodness does he love his subjects. He loves us and he loves us and he loves us till days have no end.

QUESTION FOR REFLECTION

What does it feel like to be loved so much by Jesus?

📖 LUKE 24

All over this chapter we encounter the bewildering unexpectedness of Jesus rising from the dead. I thought crucifixion and resurrection went together like burger and chips but it seems that wasn't always so. The women see an empty tomb and meet the angels but don't seem to quite grasp it. Peter sees the strips of cloth but cannot join the dots. The disciples seemed even less with it, walking around gloomy, licking their wounds. And this should cause us to think; do we really understand the resurrection? Do we really understand how utterly shocking and unusually world shifting it was? The disciples thought God was all about rescuing Israel from the Romans and that he would resurrect all righteous ones once that victory was completed. But Jesus died without killing a single centurion and then he rose from the grave when the Day of Resurrection was nowhere in sight. This surprise took the disciples a long time to get their heads around. I still don't think I've got my head around it... even though for a long time I assumed I knew what it meant. Jesus describes himself fulfilling all the scriptures had truly taught. He speaks of the Kingdom and he urges the disciples to wait for the Spirit. It seems that the new possibility the resurrection enabled was not a few Christians going to heaven when they die but a whole new Spirit-empowered humanity seeking and saving every nation across the earth. This is what Jesus thought he was doing. And that is, in fact, what he started doing. This first ever truly resurrected one continued to seek and save the lost. Jesus, oozing the abundant life of heaven was happy to humbly eat food with a couple of guys who thought that their world had caved in. Isn't that utterly remarkable? Jesus patiently and persistently explained all things to the dishevelled disciples who were acting a bit dumb. Jesus didn't bash them around. Jesus didn't walk off to find some smarter students. Jesus showed what it is to live this new "glorious" humanity; to wait on the Spirit and to happily breathe hope into hapless old humanity. And this - I must admit - is as bewildering to me as Jesus rising from the dead. I finish this gospel marveling at our King. Jesus is so powerful and yet so patient. Jesus is filled with glory and yet his manner is so generous. Jesus is so sure of what is right and yet he is so willing to stay and eat with those who haven't got a clue. I find myself captured by him again. Don't you?. I must admit that my heart is burning within me. And it's my greatest prayer that your heart is burning within you too.

QUESTION FOR REFLECTION

In all of Luke's gospel, what aspect of Jesus' character was most amazing to you?

📖 ACTS 1

This is the book about Jesus' new Humanity seeking and saving Old Humanity. And it starts by laying the foundation stones for how new Humanity makes decisions. What do we do when we don't know what to do? In this first chapter the apostles are like kids gone camping. They start off clueless, staring intently at things with confused looks on their faces. Then slowly they get it together. By the time the chapter is over; they are ready for the wind to come. Jesus and his angels have given them a steer. They told them 3 things. The first thing is to relate to Jesus as Exalted King Of Everything. If in doubt - do what worships Jesus. His resurrection vindicates him as King of Life. So worship him. The second thing is to begin to read the Word differently. The disciples always read the bible. They probably knew it by heart. But now they re-read it as a document fulfilled in the Christ. They plunder the psalms for obscure references to Judas not because they fit their purposes but because they now realise that the Psalms and the Prophets and all the Old Testament are pointers to Jesus. So many people today read the Old Testament as if it is about them. If they read it at all. But the Scriptures are only about us in relation to Jesus. They always place us in Jesus' Story. They pin us in these years between Jesus ascended, glorified in heaven and Jesus descended, glorified on earth. That changes everything. So read the scriptures that way. And the third thing. Oh the delicious third thing is what this book is all about. The Spirit. God's Empowering Presence. He will baptise us and empower us for mission to the ends of the earth. When you don't know what to do; wait for the Spirit. With friends. The rest of the book is simply the outworking of these 3 activities (or rather - it is what God chooses to do when his people perform these 3 activities). The book is what Jesus continued to do through kids who learned how to pitch a tent; kids who started off clueless but did the three things they were told, and all heaven broke loose. Please make these three things the foundation stones for your life.

QUESTION FOR REFLECTION

Which of these 3 foundation stones grabs you most today? What would it look like for you to lean on it more?

📖 ACTS 2

They honoured Jesus as Lord. They re-interpreted the Old Testament as speaking about Jesus. They made space for the Spirit. It is what they had been told to do. It was good religion. But did they - even the ministry-seasoned apostles - expect it to lead to that?! The blowing of the violent wind. The tongues of fire. The jubilant jibber jabber in the Phrygian parlance. The rending of the hearts of the three thousand. The birth of the church was a totally sovereign act; the bequeathing of the Spirit was done at the whim of the Almighty. God took their good religion and made it Heavenly. Oh I want our religion to become heavenly again. A serial frustration in my life is that the Spirit is everything I need and yet I can't control him. He is a Sovereign Act. Being all together in one place to honour Jesus and make space for the Spirit (v1) is good religion. We can replicate that. Peter's sermon reinterpreting the Old Testament being about Jesus pouring out his Spirit (v16-36) is good religion. We can replicate that as well. But what we can't replicate is verses 2-4. We can't replicate the visitation from heaven. That is a Sovereign Act. And the visitation from heaven is the whole deal. Heaven brings the power. Heaven brings the purity. Heaven brings the staggering wonder that is incomprehensibly wonderful. Even as I write this I feel my tear glands swelling with yearning for Holy Spirit to come as he came to them. And I feel my throat going dry with the agony that He comes only if Jesus wants Him to come. I've been in church long enough to know that good religion is indeed good. It has its dodgy moments but on the whole it is good. But I've also been in church long enough to know that nothing really happens without Jesus choosing to pour out Holy Spirit. Luke is telling us that Jesus is willing. Luke is showing us that Jesus' willingness arrived when he was exalted to the Father. So we call on you Jesus; please give us Holy Spirit. Pour out on us a Sovereign Act that sets our good religion on fire. We want to be heavenly like they were.

QUESTION FOR REFLECTION

How much do you want the Holy Spirit?

📖 ACTS 3

I used to think this passage was about Peter's courage. It made me want to be more courageous. That's like focusing on Usain Bolt's shoes. Don't get me wrong; Peter's courage was top notch. But it wasn't Peter's courage (nor his power, nor his godliness) that made the beggar walk. It wasn't his courage that increased the number of male believers to 5000 (4:4). If Peter had anything to do with it at all it was his total obsession with Jesus that enabled him to see the victory. Incredibly, Peter references Jesus at least 16 times in this short chapter. And - this is important - it isn't Jesus' compassion that Peter focuses on; it is his exaltation. Peter doesn't say "because Jesus is very kind I knew he wanted me to show mercy to this cripple". Instead he talks about how Jesus has been raised from the dead and is now exalted as King. Peter pins the moment - the request of the beggar - into Jesus' story. Peter interprets his interaction through the lens of what God has done in Jesus and therefore what Jesus must now be doing in history. It alerts me once again to how small on my horizon are the cross, the resurrection and the ascension of Jesus. For Peter they changed everything. I mean everything. When Peter met a person he saw them as someone living between the Ascension and return of Jesus. He saw them as one of all the peoples on earth who could be blessed now that the Servant has been raised up. He saw them as one on whom the exalted Jesus might send times of refreshing if they would repent and turn to God. Peter sees himself simply as a witness to the coronation of The King; the king who now rules from afar, but whose bounty can be enjoyed if you will only give him your heart. I want to see myself that way. I want the implications of the Ascension to dominate my day. I want to look at people differently; to push a whole now pot of possibilities their way. Ones that are only now available because of the Exaltation of My Lord. Spirit, please come and make Jesus even greater in my mind.

QUESTION FOR REFLECTION

What difference does Jesus' authority make to your life?

📖 ACTS 4

They were family. Pete had all his people with Pete. After his showdown with the Sadducees the text makes clear that Pete and John returned "to their own people". They were a recently assembled rag-tag bunch of individuals and yet so quickly they identified as a "people". It was as a people that they gathered to acknowledge Jesus as Lord and ask him for courage. It was as a people they did a scavenger hunt through the psalms, finding yet more evidence that Jesus was the fulfilment of every promise. It was as a people that they shared possessions so that - as a people - they would not have need. I want to be part of a people. Don't you? In truth we are already in a people - we are part of Pete and Abraham and David's people if we have put our faith in Jesus. So what I mean is that I want to be part of a people who both think and act like a people. I want to do life together with others who want to explore together and seek together and love together. To see an end to the barrage of "I can't make it" messages just as a gathering is starting, or the lack of any contact at all. Instead I long to be part of a people who have had that seismic shift in their subconscious so they no longer think of themselves just as individuals but as individual parts of a people. That is what a Spirit-filled church looks like. And the way the Spirit gives birth to such a thinking is to raise up Josephs who can be renamed Sons of encouragement. These Josephs (more commonly known as Barnabases) are the glue in the church. They give, they smile, they cheer, they reach out, they love. Somehow they buy into being part of a people before the rest of us have even woken up in the morning. They pray for the church over breakfast. They care for the church over coffee and they encourage the church over their evening meal. They are delicious "family builders"; often undervalued, except by Jesus. If you are one of them; we love you. If you want to be one of them; Godspeed to you. And if you know one of them; emulate them. For it is only when we follow their example that the people of Jesus can begin to live like the people of Jesus.

QUESTION FOR REFLECTION

How could you help build a sense of the church being "a people"?

📖 ACTS 5

Like Stan Lee in a Marvel movie, the exalted nature of Jesus pops up somewhere in every instalment of the early church. It really is worth dwelling on. Here we see the apostles declaring that "God exalted (Jesus) to his right hand as Prince and Saviour that he might give repentance and forgiveness of sins to Israel" (v31). The reason God raised Jesus and gave him Spirit-distributing power was to give repentance and forgiveness to a nation. And then to nations. Jesus is appointed Prince with a purpose - to draw more and more people out of sinful living and to establish them as holy; dwelling in worshipful friendship with their God. This pastoral, missionary zeal is the driving motive behind the signs being done by Peter's shadow; Jesus used someone he utterly trusted to demonstrate crazy levels of his power so that tongues would wag and then tongues would repent and then tongues would sing. It wasn't that Jesus was desperate to use a shadow to heal people; as funky as that was. It was that Jesus knew the much-forgiven apostle would use the display of power to issue an invitation to receive forgiveness. It was the forgiveness and the friendship that Jesus wanted. It was the same missionary agenda that activated the annihilation of Annanias. As a well known leader in the Jesus movement Annanias' deception would spread a disease of disrepute if it wasn't duly dealt with. It wasn't Jesus' spite that killed Annanias. It was a decisive act by the Missionary Prince to undercut an act that would abort the advance of his mission. So if you want more power; get with the programme. If you want less frustration of your efforts; turn them towards releasing forgiveness and friendship from the exalted Saviour. Exalt Jesus in your mind. And put yourself in more positions where he can release repentance to others through you. God gives the Holy Spirit to those who obey Jesus (v32). Choose just to do what He says. Choose to follow his call to release repentance to people in your life. Even to those walking just behind you on whom your shadow happens to fall.

QUESTION FOR REFLECTION

What miracles have you seen Jesus do?

📖 ACTS 6

Oh sweet Stephen. We should all pray for Stephens to be raised up in the church. Even better, we could pray to become a Stephen... except for the bit about the stones... Perhaps it is impossible to have one without the other? What Stephen and his pals illustrate is how God is always raising a new crop of leaders to step into service of his mission. The mighty oaks of the apostles look around and find a whole new canopy of foliage emerging around them. Our father is a farmer. He is always growing fresh crop. The big beasts of Peter and John and James had every credential. And yet God sprouts less credentialed people to do what the apostles could not have done. And the big beasts generously laid their hands on them; they made space for the new crop. That didn't just mean waiting on tables; Stephen and Philip and Parmenas (which I thought was a type of cheese?) and the bloke from Antioch spark off a multi-ethnic, Mediterranean-wide expansion of the mission of forgiveness. Oh sweet Stephen. God raised him. Make no mistake about that. But Stephen had invested in the stuff that made him useful to the LORD. He had filled himself with a lot of stuff; the Spirit, wisdom, faith, grace and power. It is interesting that across the New Testament these are things that the church prayed into one another. Stephen seems to have continually placed himself in environments where people prayed wisdom into him, where people prayed grace into him, where people prayed faith into him. If you feel a hint of calling to leadership. If you think you might be some emerging foliage in the mighty forest of God. If you want to be useful to the cause of Jesus Christ then I suggest you fixate yourself on being filled with these things. Place yourself in relationships and in environments where people pray these things into you. Learn all you can. Receive all you can. And then, when responsibility is being handed out, the people who have invested in you will be pleased to choose you. And - more than that - God will be pleased to use you. He will fill you even fuller with his Spirit and will use you to increase the number of disciples in the land.

QUESTION FOR REFLECTION

What are you filling yourself with?

📖 ACTS 7

He called them brothers and fathers. As they dragged him, yelled in his face and smashed him with rocks he prayed forgiveness on their ignorance. And - equally lovingly towards them - he called them stiff necked, uncircumcised in heart and murderers of God's anointed. He did all of this to their faces. He pointed at their wickedness and error while simultaneously opening wide his affections. He imitated Jesus. He imitated the up front, truth-filled, crazily committed grace-filled love of his Lord. It's a love I want so much. Even if it kills me. And, if I'm honest, the fact that it might kill me is what holds me back. I once heard an Anglican Bishop reflecting on how everywhere St Paul went he caused a riot and everywhere the Bishop went he had a cup of tea. Somewhere along the line I also learned to people-please. I learned the lop-sided lope of speaking affection without speaking correction. I learned to be the anaemic approver who made people feel OK about themselves when what they really needed was to repent and receive forgiveness. It's a prevalent disease in the middle class West; most of us curl up in the foetal position if we have to confront people over something small, let alone calling them to repent of being stiff-necked, betrayers and murderers. And so we fail to see heaven open. We serially fail to love people like Jesus did because we serially fail to diagnose their disorder. We think we are being nice but we are actually being like a GP who gives you a pat on the back when you need a new liver. And so Holy Spirit I ask that you will help me imitate Stephen as he imitated Jesus. Not so that I will get killed. Not so that I offend people. But so that I am willing to really love people - to generously embrace them and tell them how they must change. And I ask also that you bring people into my life who will do the same for me. Who will speak the truth in love, who will correct, rebuke and encourage me and help me really know God. Anaemic faith is dead to me now. I want heaven open. And so with both Stephen-like affection and Stephen-like confrontation we must step into the world.

QUESTION FOR REFLECTION

How could you confront someone in a way that also shows them staggering levels of affection?

📖 ACTS 8

"Unless a grain of wheat falls to the ground and dies it remains alone. But if it dies it bears much fruit." Jesus said that. And then Jesus did that; he died and bore the fruit of the Jerusalem church. And then Jesus' followers started doing it; Stephen died and bore the fruit of the multi-tribal church spreading across the world. And Jesus's followers are still doing this. It's not just martyrdom that Jesus uses to bear much fruit; every time a follower dies to themself, the possibility for kingdom germination is unleashed. What Philip and Peter and John did in Samaria was remarkable. It was a death to prejudice that took them into the murky area that Jews would forever associate with hideous idolatry. To place hands on an unclean Samaritan would have been a death of propriety for the disciples. But it bore the abundant fruit of the Spirit baptising the brand new believers. For Philip to start out on the desert road to Gaza would have been an act of death to comfort. To approach a chariot and ask a random stranger "do you understand what you are reading?" would have been an act of death to pride. And yet it birthed the church in Africa. And we are still reaping the immense fruitfulness sprouting from that glorious branch of Jesus' church. And so we must - if we want to be fruitful disciples - learn the practice of letting our life "fall to the ground". It's a practice of perpetually prioritising Jesus; of doing what he asks no matter what it costs. Often it costs our self-respect, or our reputation, or it bites hard at our emotional reserves. The bible never pretends this practice is easy; the church mourned deeply for Stephen. And all through the book of Acts we see the believers bracing themselves under the emotional weight of sharing in Jesus' sufferings. They carried their cross because they were in friendship with the one who God had raised from the dead. They fell to the ground because they knew that God would raise them up; that miracles and great joy and empowering and baptisms would all flow from their simple decisions to do what Jesus had said. The book of Acts testifies to the truth that Jesus told; the church is at its best when it's willing to die like He did.

QUESTION FOR REFLECTION

Are there any "little deaths" Jesus is asking you to make for the sake of his mission and your fruitfulness?

📖 ACTS 9

The production of a music album and listening to that music album are very different things. We can listen with a single click, getting a blended sound that is clean and clear. Reading back on Saul's conversion feels like listening to an album. A single clear narrative comes through in a clean and easy way. A great apostle is turned from terrorist to teacher with the flash of a light. The mission to the Gentiles is born! I used to think that if Holy Spirit was producing an album of God's glory, being part of it would seem straight forward, unambiguous; obvious even. But look at how messy this whole thing is. In this chapter there are so many bit-parts all working away in slightly confused acts of obedience. Many of them were oblivious to how they were contributing to the mega-riff of God's glorification. The companions of Saul were speechless and confused. Ananias was confused. The synagogue attendees were confused. The Jerusalem believers were confused. Saul himself was probably baffled as he bounced from blindness to escaping in a basket to being bundled out of Jerusalem. It feels like the PA cables all over the floor, the guys in dark T-shirts scuttling around plugging things in and multiple musicians stopping and starting their inputs as per the direction of the producer. A huge help to my discipleship has been to learn of the confusion and messiness - the lack of clarity or "big picture vision" - that lingers around the production of Holy Spirit's creations. Obedience in the midst of ambiguity is what Jesus uses best. Holy Spirit works in the mess. Saul was Jesus' chosen instrument to carry his name to the Gentiles and their Kings. But he spent years being bundled around different bunches of the brothers with very little to show for it. You are also Jesus' chosen instrument to carry his name. Holy Spirit will blend beauty and glory through your life if you just stay obedient, if you keep trusting and keep doing what he asks. It might feel all over the place right now but one day - in the Coming Kingdom, or perhaps before - you will be able to look back and, with a single click, hear the clean and clear anthem of Jesus' glory that Holy Spirit has produced in your life.

QUESTION FOR REFLECTION

Amid mess and confusion can you see the hand of God in your life? What is he producing in you?

📖 ACTS 10

Like a football manager being appointed to their dream job or a kid receiving an exciting new toy, Jesus is chomping at the bit to make use of his newly-given position. In his life Jesus was appointed to start plundering Satan's kingdom in the confines of Israel (v38). He did a pretty good job of that. And so after his resurrection Jesus was "promoted" (exalted) to the judge of all of the living and all of the dead (v42)... which took his remit from about one million people to about 107 billion (and counting). With this new dream job Jesus would no longer just focus on the people of Israel but could now release forgiveness, renewal and refreshing to anyone from anywhere who would believe in his name. And so he was chomping at the bit to release this forgiveness to people from very un-Jewish bloodlines living in very un-Jewish environments. Jesus' challenge was that he was also committed to using his church to do the releasing. And they weren't hugely proactive about reaching out to non-Jews. So he gave them a kick. The saving of Cornelius and his whole gathering of relatives and close friends was entirely the work of Jesus. Jesus sends an angel to Cornelius while he is taking a siesta. Jesus startles Peter with the thrice-repeated vision and then when Peter finally gets to Cornelius' house Jesus (rather rudely) interrupts Peter's sermon by sending Holy Spirit before Peter even does an altar call. I have this vision of Jesus pacing up and down saying "just get on with it, would you!" until he eventually gives up waiting and lets Holy Spirit loose to do his thing. Jesus' enthusiasm for expansion is undimmed. All over the world right now he is giving his church a kick and setting up salvations through dreams, visions and angelic visitations. All over the world today Jesus is releasing Holy Spirit upon very unlikely people. So my prayer is this - please let me in on it Jesus. Please let me - like Peter - be visited by angels, be rudely interrupted by your Spirit and used by you to bring whole households to salvation.

QUESTION FOR REFLECTION

Who might Jesus be chomping at the bit to reach out to through you?

📖 ACTS 11

At first glance the circumcised believers seem mean-spirited in their criticism of Peter. Hadn't they heard the Great Commission? Why wouldn't they just "let God be God"? But their caution - and the way Peter reacted to it - led to much greater health for the church. It's a great example for all of us as we live in these days of Holy Spirit governance. One of the blights on the charismatic / pentecostal church has been the closing down of genuine questions about "what the Spirit is doing". Our churches have often been too slow in calling "anointed" leaders to account or asking for explanation of unexpected actions. This chapter, and the Jerusalem Council (in Acts 15) demonstrate a better way. There is no doubt in anyone's mind that the Holy Spirit is the boss. And there is no doubt that Holy Spirit will speak to specific people about specific things at specific times. There is freedom to minister in the power of the Spirit, to take initiative and to make bold prophetic declarations like Agabus did. But there is also an embodied humility humming all across the bee-hives of these early churches. Every member expected to give time and explanation to collaboratively discern what the Spirit is doing. The people criticise Peter but then embark upon collaborative discernment with him. And Peter willingly walks that journey. In great detail Peter lays open his work before them for their consideration, for the body together to determine what the Governor is saying. So, what do we take from this? Well, firstly we should rampantly pursue the leading of Holy Spirit. We must make space for him to be the Governor. But then we must also rampantly pursue collaborative discernment. So avoid a church or ministry where people never take risks under the Spirit. And avoid a church where the leaders don't lay open their decisions for your consideration. And avoid being one of those people who forms an opinion and is unwilling to change it. And avoid being one of those people who takes offence when someone questions them. Avoid those things and - most likely - you will see the Lord's hand doing great things among you.

QUESTION FOR REFLECTION

When you make decisions, how do you do Spirit-filled discernment?

📖 ACTS 12

This is where Luke's narrative of the early church starts to shift away from Peter and move towards Paul. Peter's final moment of glory is… his almost total incomprehension about an angelic visitation and release from prison. Well, I guess our time with him finished more or less how it started. Of course the fact that Luke moves over to focus on Paul doesn't mean God stopped doing crazy stuff through Peter - or indeed any of the other apostles. I would so much love to know what Peter did after this escape, or to have any details at all about how Jesus used Thaddeus and Nathanael and Mary Magdalene. Oh well. I'll find out in the Coming Age. What we do have in this chapter is a clue that the church in Jerusalem began to feel the pressure of persecution as Herod tried to assert his Kingship over Christ's. There is huge help here to understand what God does when his bride is being bullied. The first thing is that God clearly doesn't stop the persecution; James (one of the 3) is executed and the church has to go into hiding. In his wisdom and sovereignty God allows major loss. But God isn't absent either; like a family of meerkats his angels are always around and we occasionally see them popping into view to help a brother or slay a foe. And, like those meerkats, below the surface the work of God is energetic and is expanding as the word does its work. One of the most remarkable things in this time is how the persecuted church willingly gave away Barnabas and Saul and the John we call Mark. What a beautiful thing - to be so devoted to Jesus' cause that you will give away such giants in the faith even while you are still scared and in mourning over the loss of your leader James. That, in fact, seems to have been a defining feature of the Spirit-filled church; they continued in wonder-filled worship and mission even while being whipped, whacked or wounded by the world. That inspires me. Does it you? Wouldn't it be amazing if we also could also abound in sacrificial generosity even when hard pressed or bruised by assaults on every side.

QUESTION FOR REFLECTION

In your hardest moments God is working powerfully; how can you spot his hand more easily?

📖 ACTS 13

The book of Acts can, at times, feel like a rapid train journey passing staggering scenes, each of which deserve a day's visit on their own. So let's hop off the train for a moment and linger on Lucius the Libyan and Manaen who grew up with a silver spoon in his mouth and Simeon called Niger, which means "the black man". These three - together with Paul and Barnabas - are known as prophets and teachers in the church in Antioch. God had somehow taken the diverse tapestry of their lives and stitched them together, building through them a powerhouse leadership team of a multi-ethnic church. I'm sure it must have been intoxicating. We don't know much more about the background of each of these men of the Mediterranean but one thing we do know is that they have learned to become, together, magnificent manifestations of the three foundation stones of the early church. Firstly they have realised that the exaltation of Jesus to Lord of Everything trumped every cultural inheritance they had from the earth. They could each have chosen to do church that was "easy" for them alongside people just like them. But they realised Jesus had been exalted to King of heaven, with Sovereign authority to unite in Him all peoples across the earth. So they put in the work to forge a church with the fusion culture of heaven, becoming a living witness to Jesus uniting all people together under his universal lordship. Secondly they seem to have reinterpreted the Old Testament through the lens of Jesus. Most commentators think Saul and Barnabas regarded Isaiah 66:18-21 as a defining text for "the work that they were called to"; with the journeys they travel on mapping closely to that prophecy. And then, thirdly, we see them honouring the Holy Spirit. Oh this wonderful Spirit who speaks and helps and empowers through the laying on of hands. And so - with just a very brief stop in this scene - we realise what a beautiful, inspiring gem of a church God can build when just a few people choose to take him seriously. We see how living these 3 Kingdom principles, can turn diverse and ordinary people into a powerhouse for God's purposes.

QUESTION FOR REFLECTION

What part could you play in bringing different cultures together in Jesus?

📖 ACTS 14

He had been dragged out of there with a bloodied face, two black eyes and stone marks all over his body. Many had supposed he was dead. So when Paul showed up later and said "it is through many tribulations that we must enter the Kingdom of God" he had some credibility. He also has something to teach us. In recent years we have made "entering the Kingdom" a "salvation-moment" event. With this assumption we can think that after we come to faith, God will look after us as we fairly passively pursue his plans. The sense of kingdom struggle has been sucked out of our story. Paul would be aghast at such an assumption. Paul knew that "entering the Kingdom" was something that did happen at conversion but that it was also an ongoing activity in this life and - most crucially - would only fully occur when Jesus returns, destroys all evil and releases redeeming renewal on all things in creation. Paul wanted all the church of Jesus to know that, until the return of Jesus, she must endure a similar kind of pummelling to what Paul received in Lystra. The aggressive opposition of "the dark powers" is something his churches have to be able to survive and, indeed, fight back against. So, like with a boxer, Paul put a trainer and a cut-man in the corner of each believer. The "trainer" was church leaders (v23); recognised, authorised elders who would protect, encourage and train the believer to fight for the "coming of the Kingdom" that is already available right now. You need a good church leader in your life who inspires you and equips you to expect more, to experience more. The "cut-man" was prayer and fasting; the intentional intercession for deliverance from evil and growth into all maturity. You need people praying for you, by name, with fasting. One of the biggest learning points for me in recent years has been quite how much I need to fight for the fullness of the Kingdom among us. I am slowly learning what it means to live in this chapter of the story that is characterised by struggle. It is through much hardship we must fight against the powers of darkness. But - as Paul shows us - God does very many things among us if we remain faithful in the fight.

QUESTION FOR REFLECTION

What are you fighting and struggling for? How is it being opposed? Who is joining you in prayer?

📖 ACTS 15

Those of us who lead in any environment would do so well to emulate the beautiful instinct of these apostles. They worked hard to spread joy and encouragement. Not only in formal decisions "not to make it difficult" for the churches but also in each interaction of Paul, Barnabas and Barsabbas with the believers. These apostles left a legacy of encouragement and joy. As I mull over this I realise how often my bias is to analysis and how I have - at times - been a bit prone to criticise. I desperately want to lean towards encouragement and strengthening; towards leaving a legacy of encouragement and joy. Surely that is an instinct all of us should desire? Another beautiful instinct of these elders was to sit under the governance of God no matter what it cost. In the early chapters of Acts we saw how the disciples constantly reinterpreted Old Testament passages in the light of Jesus' resurrection. They do this here in a shockingly sacrificial way. The Jerusalem Council was in Jerusalem (hence the name) - the city made Central to Hope by the prophetic promises of Isaiah et al. And the Council was made up of The Apostles. Yet these Jerusalem Apostles were happy to reinterpret the prophecies about "rebuilding David's tent" in such a way that hugely downgraded their own importance. By confirming Gentiles do not need to follow the law they freed all believers from even visiting Jerusalem, let alone submitting every decision to the Jerusalem Apostles. Syrian Saints and Ephesian Evangelists were given over to the governance of God; to Spirit and Scripture, with a general call to be kind-hearted towards other believers. We can all use a catalogue of cunning ruses to keep people under our control. Instead, Could you and I go the way of the apostles? To release, to empower and to allow God to be the governor? Not giving licence to all behaviour but pointing all people to follow God and not us, to make Him increase in their lives, while we slide gently to one side. That sounds good to the Holy Spirit and to me.

QUESTION FOR REFLECTION

How could you conduct yourself to release encouragement and joy into others this week?

📖 ACTS 16

If you and I can learn to make decisions like Paul did, we will do well. Twice he aborts his travel plans simply because Holy Spirit told him not to go. We don't know how Paul received this guidance but I suspect it was a strong feeling or significant lack of peace. After these two cancellations Paul makes new plans to go to Macedonia because of a vision in the night. So three times Paul changes his itinerary because of relatively subjective pieces of guidance. I suspect this intense responsiveness to Holy Spirit was something Paul cultivated through experience; he got better at reading Holy Spirit like a horse rider gradually learns the leans and licks of his steed. But Paul was not just a super-spiritual savant. He decides where to preach based on regular common sense; he goes to where the interested people are likely to be. And then he stays at Lydia's house because she asks him. And he performs the exorcism of the girl because he gets greatly annoyed. He goes to jail because they make him and he sings because he wants to. He stays in the jail because he sniffs an evangelistic opportunity and then he has a little dig at the police because… well I'm still not quite sure I understand that one. In all of these latter decisions Paul seems to be "rolling with it" as he pursues the missionary instructions of Jesus from Matthew 10. He has set out on a course to proclaim the Kingdom, to cast out demons, to forge relationships with people of peace, to suck up personal sacrifice and (as per Mt 28) to give others the chance to get baptised. So we see that Paul has made one big decision that sets the context for all his smaller decisions - he has decided to follow Jesus' call on his life. The pace and place of pursuit of this calling is then something Paul changes and adapts under the guidance of Holy Spirit and the natural instincts that he feels. Paul forges a prolific partnership with Holy Spirit through his obedience to Scripture, his ability to pick up and "read" specific guidance and then his general instinct to just get on with his calling. We would do so well to make decisions in the same way.

QUESTION FOR REFLECTION

What decisions have you changed due to guidance from the Holy Spirit?

📖 ACTS 17

This was the throbbing heart of Paul's appeal to the world; "There is another King, one called Jesus". Move over Caesar (or any other human ruler) - the God who came in Jesus Christ wants to be King. This sounded strange to people, some sneered, some searched it up, some rioted against it, but, for a growing number under Roman rule, it was a glorious invasion. The news that the good and kind Creator had come as Jesus and wanted to sit as the sustaining centre of their lives was lusciously liberating. Caesar was not a great centre of anyone's life. Caesar's modus operandi pushed people into a way of being that was inhibited and dehumanising. In Athens they knew this but they only medicated their madness through sacrifices to idols. They knew there must be "an unknown God" out there somewhere but they simply lit a few candles and carried on as they were. Paul is greatly distressed by this. It must have been like a great chef seeing people grow sick of fast food, but only swapping their brand of ketchup. Paul had tasted the bounty of having Jesus as the nourishing centre of his life and he so desperately wanted all people to come and join his party. This man's mission around the Mediterranean was not just to see many "become Christians" but to change their king. Paul wanted people to move their meal - where they got nourishment, where they looked to for hope for the future and guidance for the present - from the modus operandi of men to the Messiah of God. Which lands it on us; would Paul be distressed if he took a tour around our hearts? Would he see that the prince of Peace is our portion, that Jesus sustains and directs and reigns in the darkest caverns of our soul? Are we feeding on the hopes and truths of Jesus Christ... or are we living life much like everyone else, while lighting a candle to the Christian God? The good and kind Creator wants to be the sole centre of your life. Saying "yes" to that desire is what it really means to believe.

QUESTION FOR REFLECTION

From where do you get your nourishment? Your inspiration? Your guidance about how to do various things in life? Who is your "king"?

📖 ACTS 18

When I read about Priscilla and Aquila I cry. I'm a long way from being like Paul but I have worked in churches for many years now and I've experienced the sweet support of many magnificent couples like them. I can't put into words how grateful I am to such generous giants in the faith. These people are the heroes of the Kingdom. Churches - like the one in Corinth and Ephesus and Rome - are built not so much by the headline preacher but by the hospitality and gentle counsel of faithful, cheerful followers. We don't hear of a "moment of call" for Priscilla and Aquila. They don't get given any title. They just seem to have chosen to excel in love for Jesus' bride. And - as Paul says in Romans 16:3 - this led them to risk their lives to support Paul. We don't know the details of what those risks were but it is just a hint of what it cost Priscilla and Aquila to sustain their support season after season. They chose to love and it cost them dear. That is why I cry - I know how many times couples like these sit around dinner tables in quiet discussions to help explain things more adequately. I know how many times they choose to give a bit more, how many times they labour hard in prayer for wisdom for the church, how many small choices they make to swallow their pride and remain loyal to their leader. They are the pillars of the temple of God. Priscilla is highlighted as a clear example of a female teacher and church leader in the book of Acts. Rightly so. What a debt we owe to this remarkable pioneering woman. But let's make her agenda, rather than her gender, the focus here. She chose to cheerfully serve and serve and serve. It's no wonder Paul took them with him to Ephesus. It's no wonder Paul referenced them first in his letter to the Romans. These guys were utter legends. They were walking manifestations of the grace and truth of Jesus. And you - dear reader - might be like them. You - dear reader - could be like them. You may not make the headlines or receive much praise from people but the Father sees you and he will build his church around you and he will pour his praise upon you for all eternity.

QUESTION FOR REFLECTION

In what ways are you sowing cheerful hospitality and careful counsel into the church of Jesus?

📖 ACTS 19

"When Paul placed his hands on them, the Holy Spirit came and they spoke in tongues and prophesied." Oh the sweet mercy of Jesus. Paul's hands had been a bouncer's hands. They probably wore knuckle dusters and everything. When he used to place his hands on people they couldn't really speak at all; most of them were dead. But that was before Paul met Jesus. Now Paul laid his hands on people to release life. Now Paul's roughed up palms and stubby fingers shared new creation Presence into a few disciples in an obscure corner of an Asian city. With the laying on of hands Paul imparted into the disciples the promise of the Resurrection. They became as much members of God's household as he was. The closed fists that pushed and bashed and biffed people away from Jesus were now open palms, releasing and empowering and giving people God in their Midst. Oh the sweet mercy of Jesus. It is a helpful corrective to remember that even the anointed apostle reached out his hand to touch random believers who didn't really know what they were doing. May we never get too big or too busy to lay hands on random strangers who need a touch from the Lord. And it's a helpful corrective to remember that what Paul really wanted for the Ephesians was for them to receive Holy Spirit. This didn't diminish his commitment to preaching persuasively about the Kingdom. But the essential act of the apostle in Ephesus was a Holy Spirit ministry time. May we never lose "ministry time" as a central practice in our services and small groups or one on one conversations. It was Holy Spirit who distinguished Paul from the Seven sons of Sceva. It was Holy Spirit who empowered the extraordinary miracles of the aprons and hankies. And it was Holy Spirit who convicted the many of their evil deeds and sparked the bonfire of the scrolls of sorcery. The book of Acts began with Jesus pointing his church to Holy Spirit as the empowering presence they needed. Eighteen chapters have confirmed that. Let's be a church whose practices are formed around our constant desire to be empowered as much as they were.

QUESTION FOR REFLECTION

Who have you laid your hands on recently? What did you impart into them?

📖 ACTS 20

The riots, jailbreaks and healing hankies take the headlines but it's the "small-print" of Paul's life that really matters. We know he preached a lot and suffered a massive amount, but was there more to his daily routines than bible and bruises? This chapter gives us a unique insight. Paul spent a huge amount of time travelling. Quite often - as in v13 and back in 19:1 - it seems that Paul chose to walk long distances on his own, letting his travel mates take the quicker ship. This self-enforced "slow time" would have forged deep patterns of prayer into Paul's life. This is a long way from our daily quiet time of 30 minutes. Many of these walks would have taken a week or more; ample time to get real head-space and know a deep replenishing in your soul. When did I last carve out a week with basically nothing to do except walk? Somehow, some time I want to start living that less hurried pace of life I've been feeling called to. Another vital part of this small print is the tears. Paul says that every night for three years he cried as he warned the Ephesians about the wolves who would come (v31). Even if there is some hyperbole in the phrase it is still shockingly apparent that tears were a part of daily life for Paul. He deeply cared for people and he showed them how much he cared. This wasn't the "preachers cry" in the middle of an anointed sermon - this was face to face, day-and-night weeping. I just don't think I cry enough to be a proper disciple. And that's when I think that maybe the two aspects of this small-print are connected? Maybe Paul could love more deeply and expose himself more readily because he had invested hours in the health of his heart. We know he worked hard - every page of his letters testifies to this - but he also nurtured his soul. He flooded his soul with reservoirs of rest so he had amphorae of agape to pour out on people around him. I want to love more. I want to cry more. And so I want to rest more. O Spirit of God, please forge in me rhythms of life that make me deeply useful to you.

QUESTION FOR REFLECTION

What could you intentionally do slower to allow reservoirs of God's rest flood into your soul?

📖 ACTS 21

Here we see what New Testament prophecy looked like. First Agabus hears something from God. We don't get told how he did this but he was obviously well practised in it because he is known as a prophet. Paul - in his letter to the Corinthians - tells ordinary believers to eagerly desire to have the same gift Agabus had. I wonder if you are agitating to be like Agabus? After hearing, Agabus presents the word in a manner that is creative and compelling. I like this; he really thought it was from God after all. But - and this is equally crucial - Paul weighs the word. Paul seems to be happy to accept the core of the word as being from God and, at the same time, to throw out Agabus' (and everyone else's) application of it. Paul doesn't just use his "feelings" to weigh the word; instead he reinterprets it using the biblical truth he knows God has already spoken. Because Jesus went to the cross for his calling, and because Jesus has called Paul to walk as Jesus walked, then he can't interpret a warning of harm as instruction to avoid harm. Instead Paul uses the prophecy as a warning to steel himself for what is soon to come. Then - most interesting of all - we see how the prophecy plays out. Agabus was correct that Paul would be bound, but he was wrong that it was the Jews who would bind Paul; that was done by the Roman soldiers (v33). So Agabus was seeing something clearly from the Lord, but he didn't get all the details correct. This is a vision of New Testament prophecy; the Lord is in it... but it can be a bit messy. Does that messiness put you off? Over and again I've seen people pull back from desiring the gift of prophecy because they don't get everything right, or they struggle to see clearly exactly what God is saying. But that is a travesty; even Agabus saw like in a glass darkly. So I pray we become less bothered by the mess and more willing to "practice" this wonderful gift. It might be there is a Paul with us on a Sunday who is going to face massive challenges this week and who - if they hear our half-correct prophecy - can strengthen themselves in God for all that is to come.

QUESTION FOR REFLECTION

Might you be an Agabus for your church?

📖 ACTS 22

Paul tells people that God did something to him. Isn't that shocking? In our worldview we tend to lean towards materialist explanations for everything; my friend invited me to this and I liked it and so... I saw this talk and it meant something to me... I had a rough time and so I went back to my faith. All of those versions of our stories are true from one perspective but Paul speaks about the other side of the coin; God invaded my life. God acted. God did something to me. I am what I am not because of a logical chain of events on my part but because an impossibility occurred - Jesus came and changed me. The story is one of an active God, moving in love and us getting swept up into his extravagant plans. Paul told that story over and over again as the story of his life. I wonder if you could tell your faith story that way? You may not have a dramatic conversion story quite like Paul's but, if you look for you, I suspect you could tell how God took initiative and invaded your world. I wonder if you can see how the Holy Spirit has changed you and made you part of God's great redemption of the world. I wonder if you have developed sentences and phrases that sum up what God did, why he did it and how He has changed your world? I guarantee that the story is there if you look for it. I guarantee that God wants to help you identify it and write it. It will be a story that speaks of an existence beyond what we can see... it will be a story that majors not on your decisions and actions but on God's decisions and actions, on God's great love and your actions in response. You knowing this story will be important for you. It will honour what God has done in your life and it will strengthen your trust in him. This story will also be important for those around you - it will help them see God as He is and may even give them the desire to have God do the same for them. It is my prayer that you learn to tell your story and that God will use it to bring great glory to his name.

QUESTION FOR REFLECTION

Can you tell your story of faith in a way that majors on what God has done and why he has done it?

📖 ACTS 23

If this was a TV drama we'd get some syrupy mood music, Paul looking up wistfully and a grainy flashback to 9:13 where Ananias prophesied "this man (Paul) is my chosen instrument to carry my name before the Gentiles and their kings". Luke - who fast-forwarded past anointed aprons and 18 explosive months in Corinth - now slackens the pace to slo-mo on some court cases. Either he'd been reading a lot of John Grisham or he saw these chapters as the climactic fulfilment of Jesus' declaration over this disciple. This brings us back to the image we used in chapter 9; listening to music albums can appear effortless, beautiful and blended, while the recording of those albums can be messy, muddled and flat out exhausting. There is no doubt that Paul is slap bang in the centre of Jesus' will for his life. Claudius Lysias, Felix, Festus and Agrippa are a catalogue of Gentile kings before whom Paul appears. This fulfilment of Ananias' prophecy is spine-tingling. But, to Paul, it must have felt close to disaster. To Paul the whole "outworking of God's will" must have felt like it was on a cliff edge, especially when he found out there were 40 very hungry people trying hard to fling him off the cliff. When we read the bible it is so easy to skate over the details - pasting a veneer onto each character of what we think faith should feel like. It becomes one-dimension, boring, and a long way from anything we will ever experience. But if we stop and use our imagination to put ourselves in the shoes of these early disciples we find these pages pulsating with promise. Today might be a day where the detail of life feels contrary, where your popularity feels catastrophic and your very survival seems in question. But God will out. God's promises over your life will hold. God's purposes for your life will be fulfilled - if you continue to remain faithful to him. The neat summaries of our lives will be beautiful and blended, even if the detail of today feels messy, muddled or is flat out exhausting.

QUESTION FOR REFLECTION

What are the promises God has spoken over your life that will certainly come true in the end?

📖 ACTS 24

The content of Paul's discourse with Felix and Drusilla (v25) smashes through our stock description of the gospel. Paul's chosen themes of righteousness, self-control and judgement do not sit easily inside the soft-pedalled gospel that serenades most Sunday services. All we want to say is God loves us so much. And that's it. Paul's discourse smashes that apart. Like a rhino. Paul clearly lived, embodied and preached the love of God. Paul clearly lived, embodied and preached salvation by grace. But Paul equally clearly lived, embodied and preached an awareness of coming judgement, of God requiring righteousness and of the urgent need for all people everywhere to show significant self-control. And this is important. These kinds of passages concern me so much because they feel more alien to our churches than the messages of the latest Netflix series. We have common ground with the Netflix messages about living our dreams, feeling fulfilled and loving our city. But we seem remarkably detached from discourses about the coming judgement and the essential need for self-control, not so that we can live better lives, but so that we have a better judgement day. Even that last phrase might seem repulsive to some. I must admit I nearly choked as I wrote it. But that is because I grew up in the West. One of the richest lessons I've drawn from my growing number of international friends is how much they embody a healthy fear of God; how easily they can talk about the judgement of God as a motivation for good behaviour. They are more naturally with Paul on that one, and I am the outsider. I crave true Kingdom Culture. Not the syncretised blend of Jesus Kingdom and United Kingdom values that seems quite lovely to everyone - everyone except for Jesus. No, I want the real deal; the unvarnished stuff that Paul lived and died for. I know it ruffles more feathers and I know it leaves you open to rebuke - but it is real. It is authentic, it is empowered and it brings great glory to Jesus' name.

QUESTION FOR REFLECTION

What is your emotional reaction to what Paul says about the coming judgement?

📖 ACTS 25

Festus does not come off well in this chapter. He admits that he is holding Paul - a Roman citizen - without any real reason. His speeches feel duplicitous and egocentric. He is a bad Governor. When we talk about being a church like in Acts we tend to mean extraordinary wonders and the deep care for one another's needs. We imagine a church so caught up in Kingdom Come that even the toilets smell like heaven. This is good; the Acts church was overflowing with heaven's presence. But these chapters help us recognise that the early church also operated in a world where Satan is King and his lying nature is manifested in many malignant ways. The church experienced both a bit of heaven and a bit of hell. To expect the same is to really understand the Now and Not Yet of the Kingdom. This fallen world is the arena in which we fight our faith and we need to be wise as serpents and innocent as doves. Paul shows us the wisdom of serpents; he recognises the remit of his calling and focuses his efforts on keeping his ability to pursue that calling. It must have been hugely frustrating for Paul to be held captive by these self-seeking, corrupt officials. Paul could so easily have used his time in prison fixating on the fickle and feckless Festus. He could have become a Very Angry Man who - when given a chance to speak - layed out all his grievances. But if anything, Paul seems to gain even greater clarity on his calling while he watches his life being frittered away by Festus. When he gets his chance to speak he actually uses it to get to Rome. Perhaps that was some of the good that God worked in Paul during those months and months in prison? Perhaps God uses delays in our lives - even delays that are unfair and frustrating - to help us find greater clarity over his calling on our lives. Maybe, sometimes, God uses slow times in our lives to make us do what Jesus chose to do; to withdraw to lonely places to get direction from the Father about the purpose of our lives?

QUESTION FOR REFLECTION

How can frustration and delay help you gain greater clarity on what God is wanting to do with your life?

📖 ACTS 26

It's the word "first" (v23) that tantalises me. That one simple word places us in a story between resurrections. Jesus was first to be resurrected. We (by implication) will be later. I've been fuzzy on these resurrections most of my Christian life. I could sing until the cows came home that Jesus died to forgive sins. I knew the language about heaven. But the resurrections confused me. I thought it was one of those mysteries reserved for the super-prophets. But it isn't. For Paul put it in his basic summaries of the gospel. The Old Testament drama of creation was a script of hope for this earth - of confidence that God would one day fix this earth; he would heal and restore the valleys of Succoth and the hills of Bashan and make everything, everywhere glisteningly new. It spoke in riddles of all the righteous from all of history rising from their graves to enjoy forever the ravishing goodness of this restored earth. This hope was hyperbolically presented, with mystical language about a restored Eden. It was all a bit fuzzy. The Pharisees and Sudducees sharply disagreed over it. And then Jesus rose. In Jesus' defeat of death, breakfast on a beach, warming of hearts, appearing suddenly in rooms, he showed the resurrection was real and would come to all "in Him". In Jesus' unrecognised and yet also recognisable body "the other side of death", we see something of what our future will look like. When the second resurrection takes place; on the day when Eden will be totally restored and extended across every acre of this earth we will all become like Jesus was. On that day all believers - both currently dead and currently alive - will be resurrected together to live forever in the garden city of joy and beauty and light. Paul spoke about that hope as one of the most basic principles of what it was to be a Christian. He joyfully mentioned it to Agrippa while he stood in a Roman court. It was more obviously true to him than pretty much anything else. And that tantalises me. I so much want to be as clear on that hope as Paul was. And I'd love you to be clear on it too.

QUESTION FOR REFLECTION

What will you look like after the resurrection?

📖 ACTS 27

Jesus said something about storms coming. It is dangerous to draw too much out of narrative sections of the bible, but one undeniable truth in this passage is that Paul had his feet on rock well before the ship hit a sand bar and ran aground. The storm came and his house stood firm. We see the same old Paul here as we have seen all through the book of Acts. He is unchanged by challenge; a man of utter integrity. I wonder whether I am such a man. Please Jesus let it be so. I know that it is the rock - rather than the man - who provides the stability. And so this passage - above all else - urges you and I to build our foundations on solid ground while the wind is gentle. Let's keep on pursuing the presence in the New Testament. If we continue to build on the word I suspect we will - like Paul - find a strange compassion growing for the ordinary people around us. The Centurion and the sailors had ignored Paul's advice when in Crete. They were complicit in the imprisonment of Paul. But Paul - at some risk to himself - stepped out in compassion to urge them to eat up and to keep up courage. Reading the word softens our hearts; it helps us love our enemies - and it prompts us to do so even when we don't feel like it. It is a rock. If we continue to build on the word I suspect we would - like Paul - give thanks to God for simple things like bread, even in the middle of horrendous storms. Reading the word inclines our hearts towards gratitude; it writes thanksgiving into our days - or prompts us to do so even when we don't feel like it. It is a rock. And if we continue to build on the word I suspect we would - like Paul - receive prophetic messages from God, perhaps even receiving angelic visitations. The word awakens our hearts to the Spiritual realities; it releases heavenly treasures to us - or prompts us to act like we have those riches even when we don't feel like it. Yes, storms will come in our lives. You might be in the midst of a storm right now. But if we continue to build our house on the rock then we can continue to stand strong and consistent even if we get caught in a storm and are shipwrecked on a beach.

QUESTION FOR REFLECTION

Which part of the bible do you love the most?

📖 ACTS 28

Mission accomplished? On one level, clearly not. On one level you could read this final passage of Acts and figure that Luke had got bored and cut the thing short. But on another level Luke shows Paul has well and truly hit a home run. He has established a robust and flourishing mission right in the centre of the most important city in the world. It's like a businessman who started selling stuff out of the boot of his car but now is doing a brisk trade from a premium premises on Oxford Street. The Way is no longer a marginal sect struggling to gain traction on the fringes of the Mediterranean; it is influencing life and culture all across the Roman Empire. All across the Roman Empire people of every ilk and circumstance can find life in the glorious message of God's grace. So is that it? Is that the end? No! You don't get a premises on Oxford Street so you can settle down and congratulate yourself on your journey. You trade. You welcome anyone who comes to see you and boldly and without hindrance you preach the kingdom of God. This boys-own adventure through the whole book of Acts leaves me keener than ever to really be church. I want to go even further to worship Jesus as ascended King. I want to reinterpret even more of my life through the Jesus-story - to pin myself more and more in the great narrative God is writing in the world. And I want to be much more empowered by the Spirit. I want to be empowered not only to worship and to reinterpret but also to help many, many others worship and reinterpret. I want to see more signs and wonders, and more totally transformed lives. I want my life to be a shopfront; to be a rented space where absolutely anyone can come and see and hear the Kingdom of God and Jesus the Lord. I know some will not believe - hard heartedness will abound in this portion of God's narrative - but others will be convinced. And for those who are convinced, well, they can become part of the most incredible business venture that anyone has ever conceived. People get to be church - to be Kingdom - to be truly human. Oh, what a prospect that is. I'll give my life to that. Like Stephen and Barnabas and Priscilla and Aquila and Paul and Lydia I will risk my life for that. Come Holy Spirit, set me on fire again. Come Holy Spirit, cause your church to once again live up to all you have given us.

QUESTION FOR REFLECTION

What grabbed you most about the book of Acts? What does it make you want to do differently?

📖 1 TIMOTHY 1

I don't think Paul was a cockney. I've not yet seen the verse where he calls Jesus his gov'nor. So when he calls Timothy "my son" it is more than a colloquialism he'd picked up down the market. It was a statement. It really meant something both to him and to Timothy. We are now entering into a raft of "pastoral" letters which bring a potent challenge to my disconnected, boundaried approach to church-life and home life. Paul saw Timothy as his true son in the faith. He invited Timothy into his life like he was the fruit of his loins and the heir to his estate. Paul was deeply committed to Timothy. He had huge affection for him. He was willing to spend himself and give himself to see Timothy advance. And this is such a potent challenge to me because I have to ask myself who is my Timothy? Who have I drawn into my nuclear family to such an extent that they would see themselves as my son (or daughter?). I don't think the Paul/Timothy relationship is meant to be exclusive to celibate apostles or pastors of churches. I think all of us are meant to invite others into our lives for the sake of raising them up. The phrase "raising sons and daughters" has come to mean a lot to me. It speaks of sticking with people through thick and thin, of investing in others over the long haul. It speaks of actually helping others reach their potential. I wonder if you are doing that? I wonder whether you could lean more towards that? In this throw-away, instant age it would be a beautiful thing to be people who see the worst of others, and invest in them all the same. Whatever else comes up in these pastoral epistles I think the overwhelming thrust of them can be summed up in this; will we continue to treat people like distant cousins, or will we draw them in and nurture them like sons?

QUESTION FOR REFLECTION

Do you have a "Timothy"? Who might God be asking you to raise up to their full potential?

📖 1 TIMOTHY 2

I don't know what to do with verses 11-15 which seem to speak into the role of women. Lesley (my wife) and I come back to them regularly to try to understand how to adopt them in our practice. The Greek is difficult and the culture Paul is writing about is very different from our own. But I'm not happy just to ignore the verses or write them off as obsolete. I know this book is Life and Truth for every one in every age. And so I keep coming back to these verses to think on them some more. However - at the same time as that - I mourn the fact that it is these few verses that get all the attention in this delicious chapter. The first few verses are so barn-stormingly brilliant that they could get a standing ovation several times over. I love the fact that God is called Our Saviour. I know it's a phrase we've heard time and time again but isn't it astonishing that His generous commitment towards us is the defining feature of our God? God holds time in his hands but he wants to hold us too. God's aspect could be fixed on the beauty of the stars or the iridescence of His own being and yet, isn't it just crazy, that he turns his regard to us? God spends time thinking about and longing for all kinds of people from all kinds of places to come to Him for cleansing and healing and empowering in his love. God actively chooses to fix his attention on 'them out there', desiring that they will discover what their life is really about. And as people who love our God and who want to become like him there is a clear call to action - to lift up holy hands in prayer; to pray for everyone. Paul sees us coming to the throne-room of our God and gazing upon his splendour and seeing his compassion for the nations and being drawn into that compassion through prayers, intercessions and teaching the true faith. And so we pray for our work-colleagues and our neighbours and our bosses and our politicians and whoever else we come across. We lift them up to God in prayer, pleading for their eyes to be opened to His goodness and their ways to be conformed to his will. It is a magnificent call enabling us to resemble our magnificent God. O Jesus thank you for the privilege of prayer.

QUESTION FOR REFLECTION

Who do you love to pray for?

📖 1 TIMOTHY 3

Leadership is biblical. That's the first thing to assert. Paul whistled around the Mediterranean appointing and anointing leaders and building his churches upon them. Leadership is a noble thing that God always uses to achieve his purposes. If you aren't submitted to an "elder" you are outside of the desires of God for your life. Frothing along, kind of attached to a church and using pick-and-mix teaching online (no matter how good) is always going to lead to immaturity. God does things through leaders and if you want an effective, healthy life, you need an elder sitting over you. The character of that elder will therefore be crucial; if you are going to submit to someone, you really want to be able to trust them! God knows that. That is why, for God, the central requirement for leadership is not great communication skills or creative ideas... but proven character. Paul calls out four different aspects of character that are important - i) hospitality and gentleness, even when opposed, ii) following through on commitments with those closest to them iii) being able to cope with the stresses of life without blowing up over booze or bling and iv) submitting themselves to the leadership of God. Paul only wants people leading who are proven to be like that. It is a sad realisation that pretty much all of the broader church's problems have sprung out of leaders being appointed who don't carry these four characteristics. And - it is a sad fact that if they don't sound like your leader right now... things will end badly for you. Find someone else to follow! But, if you find a church leader / small group leader / mentor who leans towards gentleness and faithfulness, towards self-control and humility before God then you can feel good about submitting to them. In fact, you can feel more than good; from experience I can tell you that if you follow someone like this, you still thrive even when they get things wrong. Even if your leader isn't perfect or might upset you, even if someone else makes a bigger splash on social media or wears snazzier sneakers - if your leader is a person of good character then God will pour blessings into your life through them. God loves good leaders .God always uses good leaders to advance his purposes in people's lives.

QUESTION FOR REFLECTION

Might God be calling you to leadership?

📖 1 TIMOTHY 4

There are some verses in here that are so good you could put them in a cape and mistake them for a superhero. 4:4 is enormous in its scope. 4:8 could inspire a life-time of value. Verses 9 and 10 are obviously important because they are flagged up in Paul's little way "here is a trustworthy saying...". But I want to focus on 4:13 because I think it has something prophetic to speak into the broader church today and, possibly, into our own church. "Until I come, devote yourself to the public reading of scripture, to preaching and to teaching". I fear that preaching and teaching and the bible in general is in danger of being maligned today. I fear that we have begun to think that being Spirit-led walks us away from sermons and that being Spirit-filled means to prioritise spontaneous surges in our soul over the steady staple of scripture. God is not against the former. Even in this section Paul references a ministry time - a spontaneous surge of prophecy - that changed Timothy's life forever. What we are talking about is "both, and". We want both powerful ministry and precise preaching. And we are at risk of losing the latter. I fear that so many "talks" these days pay only passing reference to a passage penned by Providence. I worry that much popular preaching is so light on bible. (And on the flip side I worry that much of the more considered biblical preaching is just a bit empty of doing what the bible actually says.) So that is why 4:13 feels so important today. It tells us that the first priority of a leader is to make sure the bible is read and preached. The bible tells us who God is and how we all find life in him. The bible urges us to continue to make space for the giving of prophecies and the laying on of hands. The bible commands us to worship and take especial care of the poor. The bible points beyond itself in so many ways... and that is why we must keep the bible primary. I wonder if you are doing that? Is the bible getting a good portion in your life? Is the bible getting much time in your small group? The bible is what leaders are called to promote. Because it is Spirit-inspired and Spirit-filled and it is the only true authority on how the Spirit brings life.

QUESTION FOR REFLECTION

What has Jesus been saying to you through the bible recently?

📖 1 TIMOTHY 5

The surprisingly harsh words reserved for those who don't care for their family (5:8) and the surprisingly mundane solution for Timothy's stomach complaints (5:23) remind us that mature Christian living is not just about a "spiritual" arena of life. God is concerned about hunger and diarrhoea as much as holiness and devotions. He is the God of all creation and we can embrace all his creative goodness, even when a slowly strummed guitar can't be heard playing a worship track. In my life I've found it a constant challenge to draw my faith right into the centre of my life and my life right into the centre of my faith. Something in me constantly wants to separate the two. But Paul does not - and that is very liberating. When you are sick, take a paracetamol and offer up a prayer. God provided both and will be delighted to use either. When you miss a quiet time because your kids needed attention then celebrate the worship you have performed by caring for your family. Faith and life can intermingle in surprisingly "unspiritual" ways. So don't start thinking every single thing that sounds "spiritual" is definitely pleasing to God. The epitome of this kind of thinking is in the "random act of kindness" movement which encourages us to scatter stuff on anyone, anywhere with a slightest hint of need. Paul spends much of this chapter speaking against such an idea. Random acts of kindness are better than showing no care at all… but not much better. Instead Paul advises thought and consideration to be used when handing out your care. Some who say they need support are best advised to go get a job, or go live with their relatives, or to stop frittering away cash. Others - and they are obvious when you take the time to look - should be supported long term, not just with a one-off random act but with sustained provision. All of this just seems like common sense, doesn't it? And that is the point of the chapter - don't divorce your mind and your mission, your worship and your wisdom. Our God made all things and so we need to expand our understanding of what is "spiritual". Real faith should filter a sound mind into every fibre of normal life.

QUESTION FOR REFLECTION

Is there a part of God's creation that you could enjoy today?

📖 1 TIMOTHY 6

This letter has been waist high in the river of life, cleaning laundry and washing our sweaty skin. It has focused on the normal stuff of working out salvation as a community in creation. We've dealt with stomach bugs and how to appoint leaders, on deep care for one another, and avoiding vain disputes. This practical advice on life is important to our God. But then we come across verses 6:15-16 and feel like an accidental panhandler finding a nugget of gold. We were in the river to scrub gussets and this treasure showed up. So don't miss it. Don't miss the luscious delights of what this says about our God. Oh the greatness of God. How could he live in a light that is so bright you can't even approach it... and still live in us? How can he have 'might' that goes on forever... and yet listen to our prayers? How on earth can he be immortal and yet invite us to become like him? I shudder at some of these syllables. The mystery and expansiveness of our Saviour sucks air out of me, and then resuscitates me again. Oh the greatness of God... and he cares about me! And that's the thing. In order to live the life that is real life we need to know the context of creation; it belongs to the King who is beyond us and yet is saving us. Don't lose that delight. Being like God and being content is the greatest of all gains. Do you know that? Have you reminded yourself of that? Everything else is naff by comparison. All the jiggery pokery of life is just an assortment of trinkets when divorced from the presence of God. But if we have him, we have the true riches of all creation. Why would we jeopardise that by trying to run after money? Compared to him it is no better than dust. So please don't miss the context of your life. Amongst the clothes washing and the relationship building and the money earning and food eating, keep your eyes on Him, the blessed and only Ruler of this earth. A hulking great vision of God is what brings life and real joy in this world, especially when that unapproachable God reaches out, takes you by the hand and gives you abundant things to enjoy.

QUESTION FOR REFLECTION

How might God want to expand your vision of his greatness and his generosity?

📖 2 TIMOTHY 1

We are called to life (v1). Sometimes the enormity and beauty of that is lost on me. Amid the obligations and desires and confessions and consecrations I sometimes lose sight of the fact that this whole thing is about us living. It is about grace, mercy and peace flowing into how we grab our quick breakfasts, how we work through our emails, how we respond to the people who bump into us during the day. That is an exhilarating thought. That is a heck of a promise. We have been saved by Jesus so that we can live the life that is real life. It is a life soaked in the flavour of immortality. It is a life of in-your-face power and love and self-discipline; of the gifts of God being fanned into flame and issued forth. It is a life of suffering for the gospel and finding that that is a deeply joyful place. It is a life of being deserted by many but being wonderfully refreshed by some. It is a life of guarding the great deposit that has been put in us. It is the life of eternity. It is the life of the Kingdom of God lived out in glorious liberation and satisfaction and generosity. It is life to the full. We are called to that kind of life. So what are you doing with that call? Are you even hearing it? Take a moment. Stop everything and breathe in hard. Suck up the invitation to life, nay, the promise of life that is now yours in Jesus Christ. Let it tantalise your thoughts and seep into your feelings. The ancients and the wise tell us that solitude and silence are essential for soaking up grace. An unhurried schedule is a non-negotiable if you want a life that is rich, abounding in blamelessness and love and joy. It doesn't mean doing less. It just means giving space for God to breathe on you as you do your stuff and think your thoughts. I am praying for you right now that you know this grace. I am praying that you awaken yourself to your need to grasp hold of, to fan into flame, to intentionally do (or not do) certain things so that all the immensity of this promise can burn bright in your heart. Jesus has made this rich and joyous life available to you. Through prayer and obedience you can sow that life into your life.

QUESTION FOR REFLECTION

Do you know the joy and peace of an unhurried soul?

📖 2 TIMOTHY 2

I love entrusting people with things. Do you? This passage celebrates the desire to entrust things to others. I like that. The passage provides a few guidelines for how to do it well. It calls us to entrust teaching to people. There are many great and wonderful things God has made, but the teaching of his truth is the one thing Paul encourages Timothy to ensure he passes on. This, of course, is the stuff the writer of the proverbs bangs on about for 31 chapters - we can make others wise, we can equip them with how to make good decisions in the fear of the Lord. The next generation depends on us passing on the legacy of God's laws. And so we entrust people with the bible. We unpack it for them and open it up to them. If you are doing that - with your kids, with your small group, with a friend or colleague - then you are doing a mighty fine thing. Keep on keeping on entrusting the bible's truths into people's lives. And give special attention to those who seem reliable. While God pours grace on all who want it, time and again the New Testament gives special mention to those who are faithful. Those who have been faithful in small things should be the ones who get given big things. We could spend hours and hours and burn gallons of emotional energy fretting over those who aren't showing up, who aren't motivated, who aren't being reliable. But Jesus calls us instead to sow energy into those who are already responding to God's work. We bless what God is doing and work where our Father is working. You can play your part in this sublime strategy of the Saviour. If you choose to become an entruster of the word then you can help turn the world upside down. Why not take a moment right now to ask God to show you someone who is already being faithful in small things, someone you can raise up into bigger things? Why not choose to entrust to them anything good you have garnered from the bible? If you do that, and are willing to entrust the truth of God into people then a dynamic movement will be unleashed. The movement that encircled the Mediterranean could transform your nation as well.

QUESTION FOR REFLECTION

Who around you is being faithful in small things? How could you train them in using the Word?

📖 2 TIMOTHY 3

The closing verses in this chapter are the rhythmic bassline that most evangelical Sunday Schools lay their treble over. All kinds of papier mache projects and puppet pronouncements repeat the proposition that the bible is God-breathed and give us all we need for life. If you think about it, that is quite a claim. And yet, my experience has been that this book meets that claim, and more. It's a breath of God to me. Sometimes it's a breath that smells of last night's kebab and I struggle to take it in, but most of the time it is a breath of exhilarating freedom and resonance with my yearnings. The bible shows us how to meet with God in the midst of sexual ecstasy or the darkest disappointment. It tells us how to plan well and talk well and love well. The bible equips us how to bring transformation to others and how to see transformation come to ourselves. This book of God really does equip us for all of life. But there is something I had not picked up on before about this phrase. Something which the context of the chapter adds; this bassline is struck in a context of hostility. We live in a world aggressively posed against us. Men and women come to decry us, to deceive us and to persecute us. Many will crash rudderless into their conceits. Not only does the bible equip us for life - it equips us for battle. All who follow our Lord will get drawn into the cosmic conflict between Jesus and the power of this Dark Age. But we need not fear. The bible shows us how to thrive in this place. Our fortress is strong, our stance is firm. If we continue in the scriptures then not only do we remain protected from attack but we advance. We press deeper into righteousness, we are thoroughly equipped, we even become like God. These are beautiful words. Like the greatest penknife in the pocket of a jungle guide the Word has a map, it has tools to defend and instructions on what to forage. It helps us know what to build and when to rest. It is the very provision of God not just for us to build a camp but with abundance aspare so we can draw others in. It enables us to furnish them with the skills and tools they need to join the cause and to draw yet others in as well. The scriptures are an incredible provision to us. They are God's provision to you for you to do life really well. You do a wise thing if you read them every day.

QUESTION FOR REFLECTION

What do you love most about the bible?

📖 2 TIMOTHY 4

Jesus is the judge. I don't think about him that way very often, but Paul did. It defined so much about how he lived. These are possibly the last words Paul ever wrote and they reverberate and hum with the judgement of Jesus. Jesus will judge the living and the dead. Every effort will be rewarded. All those long slogs in prayer, all those preparations for house groups, all those difficult conversations with friends. All those will be celebrated by The Judge. All that work of the evangelist, all that preaching the word to the people we meet, all that discharging of the duties given to us by Jesus - He will reward them all. I feel such gratitude that every small effort will be remembered. It makes me want to weep with relief that nothing has been in vain. Because right now not all my labours bear much fruit. Some turn from the faith, some do not long for His appearing, some oppose the message of the gospel, some choose to love this world. And Jesus sees them all too. I don't get pleasure from this but I know they also will be repaid for what they have done. Jesus will judge them and he will give them their dues. The truth of Jesus as judge is like a two faced coin which shimmers on one side and is a bit scary on the other. But the coin is our currency and it does way more than pay the rent. If we learn how to use it, it enriches us in every way. As we think and live in the wake of such huge things we know that the Lord stands at our side. He strengthens us in our weakness and he rescues us from every evil attack. When we think upon such things it causes us to entrust ourselves to Him - not to focus too much on our own actions, but on his action. When we think about such things it gives us grit and grace to fight the good fight of the faith. And so, we would do well - like Paul - to keep the coin of Jesus' judgement in the pocket of our hearts. Not to hit people with it but to grip it when we feel discouraged. To rub it when we are slighted and feel tempted to give up. May the Lord - the Judge - be with your Spirit right now, and may his Grace and goodness keep redefining your life.

QUESTION FOR REFLECTION

Jesus has seen and will reward you for even the tiniest effort you have made for him. What encouragement can you take from that?

📖 TITUS 1

The purpose of this epistle could be summed up with the old Vineyard phrase "people do people stuff". Although Paul's summary of the Cretans is so harsh it makes you weep with joy that he never wrote your school report, he is just stating the bible's opinion on people; their minds and consciences are corrupted. People are mere talkers and deceivers. People ruin whole households by teaching things they ought not to teach. People claim to know God, but by their actions they deny him. But - and this bit is crucial - God loves them and wants to see them saved and changed. So people need pastoring. People need leading to help them stop doing "people stuff" and start doing the "good stuff" of the Kingdom. This is where teaching comes in. A lot of pastoring is about good listening. Even Paul quoting a Cretan poet shows his relentless desire to hear and understand those around him. Become a great listener. But good pastoring must go a lot further than just listening. Too often I come across Small Group leaders who hear people say stupid things and then just smile and bite their tongue. Too often I've done that. Being self-controlled and hospitable are invaluable things but biting tongues does not stop people doing "people stuff". The inconvenient truth is people need rebukes. The corruption in our minds - the deceptiveness of sin - is so strong that sharp rebukes are often needed. These aren't too much fun. But not to use them is like a gardener looking at some brambles and hoping they will just go away. And so, at times, we must rebuke people in a way that they know they are being rebuked. A good rebuke is very clear and focused on a belief or behaviour that is manifestly wrong. A good rebuke lays a very clear path towards purity. And a good rebuke is done in a context of grace and peace. In your life you will have seen hundreds of people do stuff that is not good. If we are called by God to lead, we must be ready to speak up to steer people towards the things that are good.

QUESTION FOR REFLECTION

Why do you think Jesus rebuked people like he did?

📖 TITUS 2

Titus is a book about getting people to do good. And people doing good comes through great teaching. Paul repeats again and again that the purpose of life in this present age is to live in an increasingly good way. Am I doing more good this year than last year? Are you? If we want to grow in goodness then good teaching is what we need. That is why it is so great that you are reading the bible - a daily dose of the scriptures induces your heart to do good. So does sitting under good preaching. Good preaching is hopeful, helpful and humble. Humble in that it actually preaches the word. Helpful in that it addresses the concerns you really have. And hopeful because it focuses on God and his grace, rather than you and your dreams. Sitting under this kind of preaching means that you let it form you rather than you just sit there waiting for bits to "resonate" with what you are already thinking. I fear that we are losing this kind of preaching and this kind of listening in the 'charismatic' church today. Lots of preaching today feels under-prepared, stuffed full of stories and focused on a self-help kind of hope that we have copied from our culture. We tend to judge the preaching by the "way it makes us feel" rather than the "way it makes us live". A battle needs to be fought, and won, for helpful, hopeful and humble preaching that actually causes people to live better lives. We need to keep hold of the creative and engaging things we've learned about how to make people feel good in our preaching. But we also need to put more work into preaching the bible as it actually is. We need to explore what teaching sound doctrines actually looks like in our house groups, on Sundays, in one-on-one conversations and we need to never let it slide away. That is the heart behind this project on the bible. I want us to learn from the book. To be purified by the Book. I want to learn how to engage with scripture in a way that changes my life, that makes me do good. Can I encourage you that by reading this stuff you are doing a great thing? You are playing a key role in the battle of our times. Keep on engaging with this book and wrestling with its truths. Commit yourself again to this great adventure of our faith; to know and teach the truths that help people become good.

QUESTION FOR REFLECTION

Are you listening to the Word in a way that makes you live differently?

📖 TITUS 3

Again we hear it - we were saved so that we would devote ourselves to doing what is good. The ship has sailed, the coach has departed, the train has left the station - the goal and purpose of the Christian faith was defined long ago. When we come to faith we buy into a movement whose purpose is set, we agree to be taken in a certain direction. We devote ourselves to doing what is good. If we want to debate that then Paul will listen twice but on the third time he will just throw us overboard. There comes a time when we just need to submit, we just need to yield ourselves to God's purpose for Christianity. So I ask myself whether I actually do good? And how much effort have I put into doing more good? What does that mean anyway? A growing sense in the evangelical church is that we've prioritised racing pulses, large gatherings, quick fixes and pragmatic solutions to the reformation of our souls. We've wanted results rather than renovated hearts. We've lost the vision of what it really is to be a Christian - we've publicised busy buildings instead of people who do good all through the week. How could we rebuild a vision of a truly good life, lived in joy before God? Well, Paul says at the start of this chapter that doing good is to slander no-one, it is to be peaceable and considerate and to show true humility towards all men. Doing good is played out in relationships more than in activities. Doing good is about what attitude I have to the people who are already in my life. The vision of the good life is a life of good relationships, of genuine cleanness in how we relate to others. We earn money to keep our family fed and well and we give them attention and honour, celebrating what they do well. Doing good is to be someone who serves sacrificially at church and also speaks well of the atheists and the backsliders and the bozos who vote for "the other party". Doing good, refuses to be divided over politics or to be quick to pass judgement on someone who has done something wrong. It doesn't get easily stressed, it isn't often too busy for people, it rarely snaps back with an answer that it regrets. Ultimately doing good comes down to seeing the image of God in people, to interrupt our preoccupation with ourselves to attend to others. And this is the gospel - you can become that kind of person. Through Jesus the Holy Spirit has been generously poured out. He will enable you to become good if you allow the Spirit to reform your heart. That is what it means for grace to be with you.

QUESTION FOR REFLECTION

How beautiful would it be to have a truly good heart?

📖 PHILEMON

Paul expected the gospel to produce dramatic life change. The punishments for runaway bondservants were severe, often resulting in death. If a runaway was brought back they would most likely be given the lowest levels of service in a household; minimal trust and maximum labour were the norm. And so, the request of Paul regarding Onesimus probably made Philemon fall off his chair. I suspect he strutted around his room for half a day, hitting tables and ranting about the cheek of the apostle. But then - once his emotions had cooled - Philemon would have grasped the appropriateness of the request in the light of the gospel. This is the gospel that has made Philemon a refreshing guy to be around. This is the gospel that has oozed goodness into Philemon. So if the gospel says forgiveness and restoration is the "right thing to do" it will also make it achievable and an enjoyable thing to do. It will be a win-win. In the same way that Philemon has not been condemned, has been embraced as a brother, has been offered inheritance and hope; he can break condemnation over Onesimus, he can embrace Onesimus, he can offer Onesimus a share in the farm. And - history suggests he did do just that; an Onesimus in Byzantium was known to have moved from slave to brother to a bishop over the church. Paul expected lives to be dramatically changed by the gospel. He saw it happen. It wasn't automatic - it required the collaboration of ordinary people like Philemon. But Paul saw that happen again and again. And so can we. If we digest the grace we are offered, and we choose to treat others like we have been treated by Jesus, then their destinies can be unlocked and their lives turned around. So much stuff today pushes us into complex and condemning crazes to create change. And so little really does change people's lives. We can become cynical about claims of changed lives. But the refreshing truth is that in Jesus life change is easy and change is fun. All we need to do is listen to the appeal of Jesus, to see what he's done to us, and to do the same to the world.

QUESTION FOR REFLECTION

What has Jesus done to you?

📖 MARK 1

The short, sharp anecdotes create a relentless feel to Jesus' ministry. Jesus seems to be one of those reactive care-givers always rushing from one thing to the next, bringing compassion to all the needy people he can find. You know the type - often late but a great listener, often tired but always doing something for someone else. And yet Jesus is also shown to be utterly in charge of his own agenda, there is no doubt that he is the one calling the shots, the One with authority making bold declarations and leaving people staggered at what he does. You also know that type... And so we see Jesus embodying two extremes that the church has ever since struggled to hold together; extreme compassion and extreme authority. Oh that we could draw these divergent twins back to our table. This is how it happens; by living Kingdom come near (v15). When we live like the Kingdom has come near we know we carry authority and compassion that are not our own. Any authority we have is actually Jesus' authority intended to show everyone that Jesus is reclaiming his earth. Any compassion we have is actually Jesus' compassion, alerting us to the people Jesus wants to bring under his rule. Showcasing Jesus' authority and showcasing Jesus' compassion; that is the kingdom way. We must pray hard into both. We must push hard into both. This is why healings and exorcisms need to be at the core of our gospel. These miracles are where authority and compassion come together and kiss. And that is why I pray for them every single time I can. They aren't everything about the Kingdom - submission to Jesus is the Kingdom - repentance and obedience to Jesus is the Kingdom - but they are the signs of the Kingdom, they are the showcasing of the Kingdom. So, as we start this gospel can I encourage you to lean hard into who Jesus really was - to let these short, sharp anecdotes relentlessly refine your regard of your Redeemer? Let his extreme compassion beguile you. Let his extreme authority humble you. And then pray to become like him. Ask Jesus to help you embody more of his authority and more of his compassion. And, then take every chance you get to show Jesus' authority-filled compassion for the sick, and Jesus' compassion-filled authority over the demonic.

QUESTION FOR REFLECTION

Which surprises you more - Jesus' extreme compassion or Jesus' extreme authority?

📖 MARK 2

In the opener of his gospel (1:2-3) Mark shows Jesus to be a super-healer, coming to make straight any crooked path. He now gets onto the question of who gave Jesus his medical licence; whose authority was he practising under. The natural assumption would have been that Jesus had come as a Jewish healer-prophet... but he didn't seem to be wearing their uniform correctly and he wasn't following their standard working practices. So Jesus was challenged about his source of authority. Jesus' response is incredible. He not only says that he has given himself his authority but also that he is now redefining the whole Jewish healer-prophet movement. This seems to be equivalent to a British Airways employee showing up to work one day wearing a different uniform, treating customers in a different way and claiming that they were now the boss of the company. I suspect that neither the shareholders, nor the BA CEO would not stand for such activity for long, especially if it made headline news. So it is not surprising that the Pharisees and the Herodians plotted both to kill Jesus and to smear him as an agent of Beelzebub. What is surprising is that Jesus neither completely ignored nor pre-occupied himself with winning this ideological battle. Rather, he got on with the job in hand; healing diseases, exorcising evil spirits, appointing apostles and teaching about the authority of his kingdom. Mark shows that Jesus was about so much more than just proving the authorities wrong; he was about tying up Satan and robbing him of all of his people, be they the sick, the possessed or the ideologically-misguided. And, as we read this, we realise with trepidation and joy that Jesus has added us to his medical licence. We realise with shock and excitement that the job of a Christian is neither winning ideological battles nor keeping everyone happy - the job at hand is inviting person after person to come follow Jesus and to apprentice themselves to his new way of doing life.

QUESTION FOR REFLECTION

What is most attractive about the new way of doing life that Jesus invites you to?

📖 MARK 3

Like trying to fit a post-Christmas stomach into a mid-November pair of trousers, I just can't seem to cram Mark's enormous vision of Jesus into my inherited understanding of faith. Jesus keeps on popping the button open… if you get what I mean. And, of everything that breaks my heart about my faith up to this point, my shrunken vision of Jesus is the thing that hurts the most. In Mark 3, crowds flock to Jesus, conspirators plots around him, dozens abandon all just to be with him and his family think he has gone stark raving mad. He was big news. He was The Divisive, Irritating, Astonishing, Big Thing. What is the Big Thing in my faith today? Whether we are recycling the coffee cups? How many people came this week? Whether the sermon was any good? Please God would we give Jesus his church back? Jesus will embarrass us - he will make us expose our withered parts in public. Jesus will give us strict orders about some things and will make others cry out in exasperation. Jesus will lay claim to things we want him to leave alone and will give highly inappropriate levels of authority to the wrong people. Jesus will expose a spiritual world that we just don't know what to think about and will ride roughshod over some of our closest affiliations. In short, if we give Jesus his church back then he will do what he wants without consulting us and it will be totally wonderful and totally baffling all at the same time. But I want that. I so much want that. Don't you? Giving Jesus his church back starts with every one of us - will we simply do what God says he wants? Will we choose not to moan or be insecure or to leave it to others but simply to do what Jesus wants. Will we choose for our conversations to be about Jesus, our questions to be about Jesus, our obsession to be Jesus? Will Jesus become our Big Thing no matter how uncomfortable it gets?

QUESTION FOR REFLECTION

Do you have a shrunken vision of Jesus?

📖 MARK 4

When I was studying theology there was a lot of talk about this cushion that Jesus was sleeping on (4:38). The common theory among theologians is that Mark is the first gospel written and that Matthew and Luke then copied Mark, cutting out some of his eye-witness observational points (such as that he was sleeping on a cushion), instead adding their own theological slants. The theory raises some interesting points and can lead us into some valuable thinking about who the gospel writers were and what intentions they had for their works. But, what seems to me more than a little perverse is that we have here a story about a man rebuking a lake - and it listening! - and the main topic of theological conversation is what the man had under his head when he was sleeping. Surely this is a catastrophic distraction from the mind-funking revelation of the power that surged forth from that boat. Surely this is the plight and the rebellion of mankind summed up in one neat anecdote? As people we just seem to have an innate inability to focus on the glory and power of God. We seem to set ourselves up to discuss and analyse from a distance rather than introduce ourselves to the truth and eyeball it out. It's like we are forever seeing but never perceiving, like we are forever hearing but never understanding. I'm determined, in the power of the Spirit, to buck this trend and to fixate myself on Him. I know this is the same point as I made in chapter 3 but its magnitude seems to warrant the repetition. Will we look at him, revolve ourselves around him and be willing to be flummoxed and re-formed by him? Will we actually consider and try to comprehend these things that he did? Will we thrust our gaze continually back to the Messiah and his deeds as recorded by those who knew him best? If we do, the omens are good - Jesus is the one who said to the wind "quiet, be still" and even the chaotic sea became completely calm. Perhaps our attention to the Son could release peace into our plight; could it even bring order to our so-easily-distractible minds?

QUESTION FOR REFLECTION

What about Jesus feels new and fresh and mysterious to you right now?

📖 MARK 5

Shame. It's an ugly word that gnaws at your innards. And yet it hangs around Jesus like an unshakable fug. Some people, like the synagogue ruler, have to put themselves through it for the sake of their loved ones; it can't have been easy to wriggle and squirm around on the floor in front of the people you were meant to be leading. And others, like the bleeding woman, are put through it by Jesus for the sake of their healing. But, they were the lucky ones. Through letting Jesus expose their shame they actually saw him euthanise it. Through showing their shame to Jesus they saw him grab it, conquer it and ultimately kill it in his atonement. The ones who really suffered from shame were those who were not willing to shame themselves before Jesus. The grieving relatives just thought they knew better than Jesus and broke from their mourning to make sure everyone knew it. The inhabitants of his home town chose to turn their feelings of shame into a finger-pointing rejection. The tragedy is that all these carriers of shame had a chance to see their crushing burdens lifted but they preferred a moment of saving face to a life-time of walking free. We all have some inner monologue that recoils at the prospect of tongues being tutted at us or heads being shaken at us. This monologue is the death of us. Through clinging to our own shame-management techniques we strengthen the strangle that shame exerts on our lives. So next time you have the chance to confess sin, or to expose weakness, or to ask for prayer - take it. Stretch out your withered hand, squirm on the floor and let your darkness come to light - that's the way Jesus, the shame killer, will take all of your shame and cast it into the sea.

QUESTION FOR REFLECTION

What do you do with your shame?

📖 MARK 6

Again we see the curious intermingling of compassion and authority played out across the Judean landscape. Jesus gives the disciples authority to cast out evil spirits. Jesus tells the disciples to go out to build dependent and lasting relationships with those who will receive them. Curiouser and curiouser. Authority and Compassion, arm in arm, expressed in words and deeds, in shaking off dust, in feeding the masses, in rebuking the king, in burying a friend. And miracle after miracle flows from these unexpected bedfellows; the beautiful offspring of power and mercy. If we can get this right - to harness both the spiritual authority that gives no truck to evil and the gentle compassion that cares for the needy - then we will see complete amazement restored to the church. More and more I'm convinced that the "date night" of authority and compassion is the call to repent. The place where, more than anywhere, we draw together authority and compassion is in the deliberate decision to repent. And to offer that option to others. This call to repent must be protected if the marriage of power and mercy is going to last in our lives. We need to rhythm repentance into our routine. So what really is repentance? It's choosing to turn from self-reliance and to trust God that He will provide for us. Sometimes that means deliberately leaving behind your bread and your bag. It's valuing God enough such that we know friendship with Him is greater than any other relationship. Sometimes that means leaving other friendships behind and shaking off the dust. It's choosing to place ourselves under the leadership of Jesus. Sometimes that means serving too little food to too many people when you are too tired to bother. So, if I may be so bold, which of these tangible acts of repentance have you recently performed? If your life was written in a book, would it remotely look like Mark chapter 6? The invitation is there, the door is open to you. Will you walk on in or will you walk on by?

QUESTION FOR REFLECTION

Which of these stories about Jesus captures your attention the most? Why?

📖 MARK 7

Mark's gospel is probably a record of the teachings Peter gave to the early churches across the Mediterranean. As such, it gives a great vision of what Jesus' own disciples focused on when it came to making disciples. Until now the gospel has been about getting us to follow Jesus and to live as compassionate, authorised missionaries. But here we see a Very Interesting Thing: Peter wants to make sure Jewish Christians would embrace Gentile Christians as co-equal members of the Jesus community. This - for Peter - was a major part of discipleship. Hmm. What Peter taught the early Christians was that Jesus' global vision for his Kingdom (every tribe and tongue gathered around the throne) needed to be something that they actively embraced in their day to day life. The followers of Jesus needed to be in the habit of stretching out their hand and touching people from different cultures, eating with them, praying for them, treating them as brothers and sisters in their church. Peter knew how challenging this would be for ordinary believers to accept - he has to really spell it out in brackets so people can't ignore what Jesus meant (v3,4,19). And yet, for most of my faith I fear I have ignored it. Like a deaf and mute man I thought I could follow Jesus on my own, or at least just do discipleship with people who were most like me. Ephphatha! Real life comes into our faith when we do Kingdom stuff with people we previously avoided. Be Opened! Real "loosening" of our faith comes when we stop being so dull, when we abandon our man-made traditions and deliberately, intentionally follow Jesus with people from different cultures. So, who do you pray with? Who do you invite round for food? Who is in your small group? Do they have a different skin colour, a different accent? Do they make you feel uncomfortable at times? It is when we push into cross-cultural discipleship that we often hear the true beauty of Jesus, when our ears are opened to draw in the true teachings of God, and not just the traditions of men.

QUESTION FOR REFLECTION

Jesus was a Jew from what we call the Middle-East. What would he make of our modern, Western church?

📖 MARK 8

Peter's confession of Jesus as Christ is often referred to as the turning point of the gospel. But is this correct? What was Peter confessing? Peter was expressing faith that Jesus was the divinely-appointed king of Israel who was going to bring about the end of Israel's exile and the re-establishment of David's Kingdom. Peter is seeing something, but it looks like a tree walking around. Peter was still misunderstanding Jesus in two crucial ways. Those misunderstandings persist in many churches today. Jesus was bringing two fundamental twists to the prevailing understanding of "Messiah". Firstly, Jesus' rule wasn't going to be quite like David's rule. David crushed the head of Goliath and Jesus would indeed crush the head of Satan but the glorious enthronement of David would not be for Jesus... yet. Instead, Jesus' Christ-ship at this age in history was to be defined by suffering and rejection and death. Jesus would bring in his Kingdom not through human victory but through human failure. Which is a bit weird. Secondly, Jesus was not just divinely-appointed but was actually God himself. Which is even weirder. Jesus wasn't just bringing in Israel's Kingdom but he was re-defining it around himself. Jesus would fill the kingdom with whoever he chose, no matter what their bloodline or geographical location and he would push away many who thought they were most entitled to positions of power. This must have blown the disciples' minds. So where does that leave us? I guess it leaves us concluding that confession of Jesus as Saviour is great, but not enough. Jesus demands more than just reverence and allegiance - Apple Computers can have that. Even Christiano Ronaldo can have that. Jesus demands that we let him reshape even our view of salvation - that he would re-work even what our view of hope and heaven and fruitfulness and faithfulness are like. That is not something that we achieve on our own - it is entirely dependent on His Spirit taking His Word and making it renew our minds. Our confession of Jesus as Lord is only the beginning - we have a life-time of discovering and rediscovering who he really is and what he really wants to do.

QUESTION FOR REFLECTION

How has your vision of "a good life" changed since you first came to faith?

📖 MARK 9

I know only too well the volcano of awkwardness that would have spewed up inside each of the disciples when Jesus asked them what they were talking about on the road. It's that moment when you realise what a dufus you are for thinking that this stuff is about you and your reputation. Jesus turns all that posturing on its head and reinstates the Father at the top of the pyramid. I think the problem is that the disciples haven't yet realised how important Jesus is. Peter thinks Jesus is just about on a par with Moses and Elijah, a present day super holy prophet of God. But Jesus is several levels above that. That bomb of revelation still needs to go off in Peter's brain. Does it need to go off in yours? If you are still groping around for human reputation then it probably does. Quieten yourself down and listen to Him. The disciples also haven't grasped the immensity of the resources that Jesus has given them. They know they can cast out a few demons but when a tricky case presents itself they begin to wonder whether they have met their match. They haven't let it sink into their soul that nothing is impossible with God, that through prayer all the unrivalled power of the Kingdom can be accessed and dispensed by them. It's the same problem manifesting itself in a different way. When we make this stuff about us we worry what we can manage, we keep on pitting ourselves against others - whether they be friends or demons. But when we fix our eyes on Jesus and realise the enormity of his power we realise everything is possible. And when we perceive the pre-eminence of his position no-one else's power (ours included) seems to matter a penny. So let's embrace our position as servants of the Son. I am just a servant of Jesus. I'm just spare change in his pocket for him to spend however he wants. If we can say that - and say it with joy - we become like salty salt. Whatever we do, however big or however small - all of it honours Him, pleases Him and will be rewarded by Him when he returns with his angels.

QUESTION FOR REFLECTION

The attention you give the Son determines who you become. How is your vision of Jesus changing you?

📖 MARK 10

Mark's thrust seems to be that if you aren't willing to be considered scum then you need to step off the Jesus-train. There is nothing glorious about being last, about being dirt poor or about being like a little child. As Job found out, even a holy person in such a position will be patronised, despised and disrespected. The bitter truth is that people who are last have next to no status; they are assumed to have not worked hard enough or to have messed up personally or to be just plain ignorant. People generally don't listen to the poor just as they don't listen to children; they are there to be looked after by us, not the other way around. So Jesus' call to become 'the last' is really very hard. And so I'm struck by the amazing privilege I've had to be part of churches where so many have been so prepared to knuckle down and divest themselves of status. I've seen qualified professionals pick up litter for Jesus, or try their best to soothe a sorrowful stranger, or to bite their lip when someone else in small group cuts them off. I've also seen some of the poorest among us lead the way in serving on kids teams, or making meals for their neighbours or in grovelling on the floor in thanksgiving before their God. These people are utterly inspiring. They divest themselves of status for the sake of their God. They help me stay on the Jesus-train. And the attractiveness of serving others isn't just because humility is beautiful. Jesus also says he is preparing for us a hundred times more than we have ever left or given away. While serving others may cause us to be disrespected or patronised or persecuted by those around us right now, Jesus will, one day, bring a Great Reversal when all things are put right. That will be a great day for us. Oh what a day. The destination of this train is going to be everlasting and glorious. Jesus has already been there and he popped back to show us what it is like. The more we look at that day the more we can be like little children right now. Our adulthood is ahead of us, all we need to do now is hang out with our Father and humbly do every humble thing that he wants us to do. Because that is beautiful. And because it will bring us very great reward.

QUESTION FOR REFLECTION

Today, how could you humble yourself like Jesus?

📖 MARK 11

Peppered all across the gospels are little quotes from the Old Testament. Often they are laid out differently from the rest of the narrative and have little letters next to them which, if you look up, show you the specific passage being quoted. A great way to enrich your understanding of a passage is to follow the trail back to the passage and see the context the quote has been taken from. If you do that here with the "den of robbers" quote it is pretty EXPLOSIVE. Jesus was not messing about. The "den of robbers" quote is from Jeremiah's most visceral lambasting of the worthless religion of old Jerusalem. You know; the old Jerusalem that God poured out his wrath upon, plundered, destroyed and left empty for many generations. By hitting the temple rulers with the stick of Jeremiah, Jesus is saying "you have learnt nothing; you are as despicable before God as the old leaders of Israel." And it wasn't because they were charging a bit much for a pigeon. The Jeremiah passage shows the real sin of old Jerusalem was preferring their own words to God's words. "I spoke to you again and again, but you did not listen" says Jeremiah. "You are trusting in deceptive words that are worthless" he wails. That is the rebuke of Jesus to the temple leaders. When people prefer their own words to Jesus' words God tends to come and tip things over a bit - just to make a point. This is why we are going to make so much effort to read the New Testament in a year. This is why I'm labouring hard to write these commentaries. This is why we advocate for preaching the bible and not just giving christian pep-talks; God wants to be listened to. God wants to be listened to by you. Our christian culture enjoys re-posting soundbites and sharing glamorous preaching / worship / testimony videos. They are easier to watch and quicker to "get done" than finding a little letter next to a quote, looking up the reference and then reading its passage in the Old Testament. But the latter gets you right into God's voice. The former… well, it might not.

QUESTION FOR REFLECTION

Are you listening to God's actual voice, or are you preferring an echo?

📖 MARK 12

We all know a guy who loves to go swimming in his speedos. All you have to do is glance at them and everything is revealed. Much to our frustration Jesus isn't like that. Time after time I've met people who want the speedo Jesus - revealing everything to anyone at just the slightest glance. But Jesus isn't like that. Like a riddler or a coquettish friend, Jesus uses questions and answers to hint, to suggest, to spark curiosity, to arouse desire. Jesus is so committed to questions that when no-one dared ask him any more questions (v34) he simply starts asking some of his own (v34, 37 etc). That says a lot about our God, that does. Even when Jesus comes out and actually answers a question - about the greatest commandment - it provokes more questions than answers; "why have you said two commands rather than one?!"; "what does it mean to love God with all my understanding?!"; "how can I love all my neighbours like I love myself and still get everything done?!". At once baffling and intoxicating the gospels assure us that mystery and discovery are at the core of our faith. If you are looking for a Spiritual Maturity that looks like clarity, certainty and revelation on tap then you've got the wrong faith. (Or at least you are "a bit early" - that stuff will come post-Jesus' return). No. Our "modus operandi" is not so much "instant revelation" as "loving discovery". The inclination of the spiritually mature is towards inquisitive, insistent relationship with Jesus and towards committed curious affection for our neighbours (and spouses) especially when we haven't got a clue what is going on in their brain. And so we must love questions. But what kind of questions? Some questions (like those of the pharisees) are intended to close down discovery, to catch others out, to build a wall around our knowledge that others cannot cross. People who ask these kind of questions eventually give up (v34). Jesus is too smart to ever be caught out. Other questions - Jesus-type questions - want to know what others are actually thinking. They aren't happy just to assume or not to care; instead they put in the effort to enquire, they dare to find things out, to take the risk that the one we are asking may not fit neatly or easily into the box we have made for them. These are harder questions but better questions. These are the kind of questions that lead to discovery, to amazement and to genuine growth in faith.

QUESTION FOR REFLECTION

How many good questions will you ask today?

📖 MARK 13

Another great example of the footnotes being our friends. Verses 24 and 25 sound like the explosion of the universe. Too often these kinds of verses (which are extremely common in the book of Revelation) are ripped out of their context and used to conjure concern about a coming cosmic calamity. When this happens a few Christians jump in with two feet and constantly talk about "the rapture" and the "mark of the beast" but most back away slowly, thinking the "end of the world" is about as welcome as an endless dinner trapped talking to their "awkward work colleague". So the footnotes are our friends because they liberate us from a very superficial reading of the verses. They expose the inadequacy of much that is preached on them. They show us that Jesus is quoting from two "judgement" chapters in Isaiah. One chapter (Isaiah 13) is the condemnation of Babylon for its pride and the second (Isaiah 34) is the rebuke of all nations for how they have mistreated him. Neither predict the sky falling in. Rather the specific images of stuff happening to the sun, moon and stars are intended to emphasise the totality and expansiveness of God's judgement. No one can side-step God's decisive action to bring evil to an end. So - in a classic Jesus twist - the Big Fear in these verses is not that one day the world will explode. Instead it is that Jerusalem has become Babylon and will receive the devastating consequences. The epicentre of God's project is now under God's judgement because they failed to "keep watch". They fell asleep to God. So don't back away from these passages. And don't get a telescope to anxiously look up. Instead, use the verses to refine your alertness to Jesus. Follow them to greater responsiveness and obedience to the Global God. Jerusalem lost that and it ended up being sacked. Much of God's church is in danger of going the same way. Please don't get dragged along with them; switch on your brain, make friends with the book and understand what it really says.

QUESTION FOR REFLECTION

Why do you think Jesus used so much poetic language?

📖 MARK 14

Jesus knew where the donkey would be, where the man with the jar would be, that one of his disciples would betray him, that Peter would disown him (and how many times, and before when). And he knew he would be crucified. While the crisis unfolded around him and enveloped him in its murderous wake, Jesus suffered no crisis of faith. He knew what he was doing. He was the master of his ship. Compare that to everyone else in this story. No-one else holds it together. Not even those who are bringing their wrath down upon him. One by one their composure slips from them like the linen garment from the unnamed man. The disciples scatter, the false witnesses can't agree, the temple leaders lose grip of their fury, and even Pilate doesn't know what to do with the Christ. Here we see the de-creating power of suffering. Suffering unpicks plans, fractures faith and wrecks relationships. Suffering de-creates everything… except for God. Suffering may feel it has kidnapped the Christ but Jesus has willingly complied and he will wriggle free on the dawn of the third day. This is the glorious triumph of these closing chapters of Mark. We see that our King can not only resurrect but can remain righteous in the de-creating riot of pain. Nowhere is this "stability" needed more than in our godless 21st century society. We may be richer than ever, but we have no grid for suffering and it is spitting on our spirits and mangling our mental health. Believers and non-believers alike seem to morph into different, confused people when suffering comes calling. Anxiety and anger have become the amniotic fluid of those pregnant with pain. But not so with Christ. And, therefore, it need not be with us. If we follow Jesus towards intimate prayer and trusting obedience to the Father then we too can become people who suffer well. In Christ you can remain yourself even in the darkest trial. The way to do it is consistent drinking from the cup of the Supper and committed drinking from the cup of Submission. Put these habits in your life, and you will be able to suffer well.

QUESTION FOR REFLECTION

Do you suffer well?

📖 MARK 15

Jesus died. That idea had become so familiar to me I almost treated it with contempt. If I'm honest Easter felt like a more boring version of normal church, until we sang the happy clappy songs about the resurrection and ate some chocolate eggs. I liked that bit. The death of the Christ was - in my mind - a transaction that highlighted my guilt. Most of the time my practical reality held the cross to be an irrelevance. Then one thing changed; I became real friends with Jesus. Now, when I read this passage it seems throat-chokingly sad. When I meditate on this narrative today it isn't a crucifix I'm picturing - it is my friend. In pain. And then dead. I remember seeing my grandfather's dead body being carried out in a coffin and that scarred my heart. I loved that man. The thought of my Jesus' body wrapped in cloth, being carried away and put in a cave is almost completely overwhelming. I know it had to happen and I know that unbelievable amounts of goodness came out of it but so much of my maturing in faith has come when I've stopped looking at what came out of the cross and started looking at the cross itself. Mark (and hence Peter) obviously agreed. Mark's gospel has been described as a death narrative with an introduction. The gospel gives almost no explanation of the theological outcomes of the cross. The thrust of the narrative is on the events themselves, every damned detail of Jesus' dereliction and death. I know it's not trendy, but can I ask if you are making time to dwell on Jesus' death? Maybe this week you can give yourself 20 minutes just to sit and think of Jesus and his cross? Don't make it a time of feeling guilty, nor even really about worship or theology - just choose to sit and imagine Jesus hung on the tree for hours. There is a deep deep power in finding intimacy with Jesus on the cross. It's the kind of power that will change your life and never let you live the same way again. It's a power I long for you to find.

QUESTION FOR REFLECTION

Why did Jesus have to die such a shameful and painful death?

📖 MARK 16

I love the idea that Mark's gospel originally ended at verse 8. The descriptions of Jesus' followers in the run up to this finale are "alarmed", "trembling and bewildered" and "afraid". Isn't that how we should feel when we realise what really happened in that tomb? Jesus' resurrection confounds everything that we know about this world. Of all things that are true and certain, dead things staying dead is at the top of the list. And so a man who has come back from death should alarm us. Remember, this isn't a guy who was in a coma or who had someone else pray over him. This was a man, long dead and mourned and buried who - through his own inherent power - restored breath and brain function to his rigor mortis corpse. Fear and trembling must be found in any person who has honestly grappled with the impossible reality of that. This fear is not anxiety. Instead it is reverence that I am touching God's Spirit who could scatter me to the ends of the earth and then re-form me again. The trembling is not worry. The trembling is overwhelming wonder that I get to be involved with this "other-worldly" thing that will make all things new. I've got to get more fear and trembling in my faith. Verses 9-20 may have been added later, and they slightly change the feel of the ending, but I love them all the same. They have more triumph in them, more of a guide as to what the empowered church is meant to be doing and what the result of their activity will be. I love the idea of ordinary people doing this extraordinary stuff. And so as we finish this gospel we could say that our call is to hold both of these "endings" in tension. We must always be focused on mission, on empowered speaking and dynamic praying, but at the same time we must cling to trembling reverence and fearful focus on Jesus. He is the one who reassures us. He is the one who soothes us and comforts us. He is the one who counters poison, heals the sick and drives out demons. This gospel is Jesus' gospel, this Kingdom is Jesus' domain. When all is said and done am I a Jesus-man? Is this spectacular, baffling, suffering and resurrected Jesus my first and my last, my heart, my mind and my soul? If he is, then the gospel has done its job. If not, I need to read it again. Or read Luke and then John and then the rest of His word.

QUESTION FOR REFLECTION

What about Jesus makes you tremble?

📖 ROMANS 1

Senseless, faithless, heartless and ruthless. In this letter Paul is making a bid for all people - Greeks and non-Greeks, Jews and Gentiles - to admit their human life has been defined by those damning descriptors. And in this letter Paul is making a bid for all people, through Jesus and the Spirit, to let themselves be redefined as a new humanity full of sense, full of faith, full of heart and… full of ruth. Ah. So, that word play doesn't really work for the ruthless bit... but I can claim it does in the Greek! The motive of this life-changing letter is to make a diverse church strong and ready to support a wider stretch in their mission; even sending Paul to Spain. And you need to keep that motive in mind as you read through Romans in these next few weeks. This is a dense and tricky letter but God wants you to read it in order to make you strong. This letter - if you read it right - will wreck you and rewrite you as someone you never dared believe you could be. This letter will expose to you how utterly senseless it is to ever depend on yourself. It will pull no punches when drawing attention to the despicable depth of your depravity. This letter will call you to total and utter faith in Jesus; a faith that requires a total reimagining of everything you were, are and will be. It will be an extreme makeover beyond anything you thought necessary. And then - maybe for the first time in your life - it will put real heart into you; it will display vast vistas of Holy Spirit's availability to you and mentoring of you that should leave you gobsmacked for days. Finally it will comfort you and cajole you into playing your part in a compassion-filled community that overflows with real kindness even in the midst of diversity and challenge. When this letter is done with you, you'll be a glorious manifestation of the Spirit's new humanity; you will be established in love. Oh this letter. I love this letter. I'm so indebted to this letter. It has changed my life in countless ways already and I've barely even scratched its surface. Please choose to read this letter and to let it re-define everything you've ever known to be true.

QUESTION FOR REFLECTION
What do you make of Paul's description of the effects of sin on humans?

📖 ROMANS 2

There will be wrath. The bible is very honest in acknowledging a soul-crushing flaw in creation; Ecclesiastes and Job put a magnifying glass up to the agony of injustice in this life. Bad people often do better. Even good people - like Abraham or David - can do Very Bad Things. Being human is more than annoying. The Old Testament prophets saw no easy solution to this, but they promised a fix would one day come from God's own hand. They named this fix "the wrath of God". This wrath would release God's decisive "no" to all injustice. This wrath would compensate all who had suffered from injustice, it would hold to account those who had caused the injustice and it would remove every potential source of future injustice in the world. Or in more poetic language; Justice would roll like a river across the land, even seeping into every long-forgotten loss of the dead, carrying rebuke and restitution along in its flow. Paul wholeheartedly affirms this doctrine. But then he takes this truth to its terrifying conclusion; if every potential source of future injustice needs to be removed then God's Wrath needs not only to tackle big and obvious wrongs but also every secret instance of stubbornness or sin. The unnoticed lie of a parent does injustice to the child deprived of the truth and can yield painful fruit for generations to come. The stealing of stationery by an employee subtly subverts trust as essential to human relationship. Lustful looks at a lady may not be spotted but they have already turned her from a creature of God into a commodity for my glee. So the wrath must come. It's like trying to remove an infection from a fish tank; not only must the very visible causes of the problem be dealt with but - to safeguard the lives of the fish - every slightest hint of future infection must be thoroughly cleaned up and removed. And so Paul wants you to be honest with yourself. He wants you to look in the mirror and - even though you've done many beautiful and wonderful things - he wants you to admit that, for the future of the world, the wrath of God needs to do its work on you. This is tough food. But there are miracles in store, if you can swallow it into your soul.

QUESTION FOR REFLECTION

What does the wrath of God need to do in you?

📖 ROMANS 3

"All have sinned and fall short of the glory of God." So much of our culture is built around trying to tell us we are OK. Much "christian" teaching tries to build up your self-esteem. Do not believe that lie. Do not try to feel good about yourself. In the sight of God we all come up short. Freedom is found in acknowledging that. In fact the fullness of kingdom life cannot be enjoyed unless you acknowledge that. Find esteem not in yourself but in the atoning work of Jesus. Atonement is not a drab "don't worry about it" mumbled by God. Atonement is a very targeted piece of work that the Law of the Old Testament trained people to understand. The process of atonement was to become conscious of sin - it confesses abject failure and submits no excuse. My sins are awful acts that must be punished; they have contributed to the swamp of spiritual pollution festering on the earth. Atonement then provides a deliciously grace-filled administration of that punishment; the death of a representative standing in your place. A spotless lamb for the wretched sinner. And finally, once the sacrifice has been made, atonement joyously, gloriously declares those sins dealt with. In a startling, destiny-shifting statement the sinner is declared clean, spotless like the lamb who has been slain. Jesus was your atoning sacrifice. Don't let familiarity breed contempt. You brought sin to the party and Jesus took it from you. Then Jesus told everyone you brought a perfect gift; celebrating your arrival like a guest of honour. Paul drills into atonement so relentlessly because Kingdom life cannot be enjoyed unless you fully embrace the implications of its grace. We should all walk away from this atonement in bewilderment, utterly undone by the reckless grace we have received. When we understand atonement we can carry no pride or sense of privilege into the kingdom. We come in empty. Atonement strips us bare, reclothing us - and all others who are atoned - with royal robes we don't deserve. We look at our redeemed selves with wonder; "if this is how it begins, what unspeakable delights might be next?".

QUESTION FOR REFLECTION
Why did God show you grace?

📖 ROMANS 4

"Blessed is the one whose sin the Lord will never count against him." "Blessed" feels too small a word to carry the freight of the fullness of God's favour. But that is what it means. The atonement of Jesus grabs you by the neck and shoves you under the shower of boundless generosity that God had poured out on Abraham. Verse 13 in particular is mind-blowing; Abraham would be heir of the world. Stop a second and dwell on that. If you have gone through the process of atonement you now hold the righteousness that comes by faith. You now stand with Abraham's arm around your shoulder; his beard tickling your neck. He waves his arm towards the hills and assures you that you now are a co-heir with him of all the nations of all the earth. A chapter ago you were storing up wrath for yourself and had run out of options. Now you are a prince and a co-ruler of 195 countries and 5000+ tribes. The staggering shift in your fortunes deserves a long hard consideration. The assurance of our exalted future is something most of us never really make our own. The next 4 chapters will help us mull over that magnificence. But the focus of Paul's chapter here is the collaborative nature of this promise. If you pan out just slightly you see Abraham has a crowd of arms around his shoulders. His beard is tickling the necks of billions. And many of them are black, or bald, or Chinese, or Jewish. They will co-rule their tribe and your tribe with you. The twin challenge of grace is to comprehend the super-abundant generosity that God has lavished on you and also to grasp that your privilege is one shared equally with others; many of whom were utterly different to who you were. So no one can boast. No one can really act or talk or think of themself as an individual saved by Jesus; all of us have been drafted into a whole new collaborative family of faith. We - the redeemed - all stand together as partners and co-heirs. The shower of God's crazy kindness to Abraham has become communal. We stand under the blessing together; rejoicing in its refreshment, bewildered by its beauty, soaking in its promise.

QUESTION FOR REFLECTION

What will it be like to co-rule all of creation?

📖 ROMANS 5

It is a glorious present experience. It has a robust expectation for increase. It is the Now and Not Yet of the kingdom. To reap this glorious experience and to be utterly confident in its robust hope we need to grasp that Christians differ from other humans. We are a whole new race. Do you think of yourself that way? In the same way that normal human experience follows the pattern of their forefather (Adam), Christian experience will follow the pattern of our forefather (Jesus). The same shalom that shimmered on Jesus should shimmer on you and me. An unshakable conviction that we are deeply beloved should overflow and nourish our lives. Paul describes this present experience as super-abundant grace or "reigning in life". This language nods back to the promise to Abraham that we saw in chapter 4. Our new race stands as people already inheriting all the blessings God promised to his people. And yet Paul constantly heralds a coming day when the Jesus race will come into its inheritance. Even greater abundance, even more soul exploding beauty and goodness will come to us on that day. We are overcome with joy right now but our joy will increase even more when the Life of Eternity dawns and the whole of creation comes of age. And so two things are our friends right now. The first is Holy Spirit who has already been given to us. We access our glorious experience through fellowship with a present friend. Let's increasingly engage with the one who has already engaged with us. Our second friend is suffering, which is probably a bit of a surprise. Suffering strengthens our hope. Next time you suffer, remember this; every piece of present pain points to your future. Pain is your body's alarm system to alert you to things Not Yet being as they will be. And it is an alarm that Jesus has answered. Jesus went to the cross to answer our pain. Jesus' atonement won God's victory over everything that has caused us pain or could cause us pain. We can enjoy the glory of that victory right now by befriending Holy Spirit. All the while having a robust expectation of even better things yet to come.

QUESTION FOR REFLECTION

What does it mean to be the child of Jesus rather than of the race of Adam?

📖 ROMANS 6

The robustness of our hope is so extreme that some could see it as a licence to sin. If the atonement really did birth us into a new race then we can't be un-birthed. If a glorious increase is guaranteed then why bother putting in the hard work to be a good boy? It's the classic risk of a trust-fund kid becoming a profligate playboy. The fact that Paul has to spend significant time addressing this question shows how mind-bendingly awesome an assurance he asserted. In no way does Paul downplay the reach or resilience of God's favour on our lives; that is guaranteed. Instead he takes us back to the maternity ward to show us the plan behind our rebirth. He assures us that our new parents are liberators. Father, Son and Spirit are pioneer philanthropists setting new standards of glorious generosity. If you realise that, you are a numbskull if you don't then entrust yourself to their care. Everything they do is kind and good. But Paul does not just leave it there. He reminds us that storing up future wrath was only part of the tragedy of sin. Sin was also bad because it enslaved us and ashamed us and rotted us from the inside. Sin tormented us and abused us and pushed us ever closer to death. God's generous plan in making us a brand new race was to free us from that toxic slavery. New birth would enable us to live a new life, a liberated life imbued with delicious holiness. Perhaps it is Paul's understanding of holiness that packs the biggest punch in this passage. I used to think of holiness as hard work or inhibiting. But Paul presents holiness as delight. Holiness is a short-hand description for the joy-filled, love-consumed, peace-exuding presence of God. Holiness is a badge of honour. Wanting to be holy is to desire the family likeness, it is the flourishing of freedom and the fragrance of eternal life. It is becoming like a pioneer philanthropist all across your life. And - get this - holiness is within our grasp. Holiness is already being nurtured in us by our new parents. All we need to do is count ourselves dead to our old life and then to cooperate fully with the Father, Son and Spirit who have adopted us as his own.

QUESTION FOR REFLECTION

In your mind, how attractive and beautiful is holiness?

📖 ROMANS 7

We've seen how atonement dealt with wrath. It ushered us under the shower of God's bountiful blessing (ch 2-4). We've seen how rebirth into the Christian race set us free from slavery to sin. It placed delightful holiness within our grasp (ch 5-6). This chapter (7) looks at the same process using marriage imagery. Previously we were married to a noble and good husband called The Law. But The Law had a brother who came with the package. They call him Sin. He lived in our house and travelled everywhere we went. Sin secretly hated his brother and now hated us as well. Even though our husband warned us not to listen to his brother, the constant sarcasm, the bitter comments got into our heads and messed with our minds. We became so conflicted that we began to do what Sin was telling us even though we knew it was wrong. We fell under his spell and wretchedness reigned. But then - alleluia - our husband died. Quite quickly (some might say) we remarried; a noble and good husband brought us into his house. His name is Holy Spirit. Holy Spirit has no brother who carries evil intent, in fact all his family are generous and true. And so - Paul tells the Romans - while it is appropriate to feel sadness over the loss of our old husband, don't go back to that house. And definitely don't hook up with your ex brother-in-law who still has your number and messages you now and then. That would be hugely destructive for you and totally dishonouring to your wonderful new spouse. I know many believers have found comfort in verses 15-20, feeling affirmed by what they say about conflictedness. But we need to realise that they describe life under our old marriage, not new life in the Spirit. It is listening to Sin that sows conflictedness into our lives. Our answer to such feelings is not a mis-reading of Romans 7 but a deliberate shunning of the whispers of Sin. Block his calls and don't invite him into your house. Instead choose delight. Choose a joy-filled life. Learn to enjoy the embrace of the new husband in your life; His name is Holy Spirit and he is right by your side.

QUESTION FOR REFLECTION

What does Sin whisper in your ear? What different words does the Spirit speak to you?

📖 ROMANS 8

If I had a Desert Island Bible Passage, this chapter would be it. We won't be condemned. Ever. We can't be condemned. Oh the liberty of that thought. I want to hold it by the cheeks and give it a kiss on the lips. Any accusation I face I can shrug off as a lie from hell. My destiny is secure, my abundant inheritance guaranteed. But there's more. We walk each day in Holy Spirit's embrace. God himself breathes life into our bodies, he serenades us of our sonship, he lulls us to sleep in his love. Oh the beauty of that song. It isn't just a soft thing. It isn't just a star-crossed lover blind to who I really am. No. The Spirit lives in me. He knows me. He knows the misdeeds that my body kind of likes. And yet he sings to me anyway, he stands loyally by me anyway, helping me put to death the things that kill me, helping me become a better man. But there's more. The Spirit makes me a conqueror. More than a conqueror. What the heck? The Spirit helps me set my life in the context of God's redeeming work in history. When I hurt he shows me that the whole world hurts with me. When I cry he shows me that the trees are crying along as well, as all of us are groaning for Everything to Be Made New. That solidarity with all substance makes my suffering seem less severe. Especially when I see that this experience is just fleeting; that endless, glorified epiphany and ecstasy are predestined and purchased by the Creator and his Christ. If I actually step back to see this story - and let it soak in - it really strengthens me in my soul. But there's more. Even when that story fades from our view and the song of God seems silent and a sense of condemnation has somehow crept back in; even then nothing can separate us from God's astonishing work on our behalf. Because then the Spirit earnestly intercedes for us and holds us fast in God's plans. Nothing - not a single thing you could imagine - can threaten this incredible work of grace that God is pouring all over your life. And, finally, there's more. Even if a plan of the enemy does make its mark on you. Even if some of the horrors of this age steal your strength or blight your body - even then this beautiful, faithful Saviour will not give up on you; he will work that bitter "loss" into another avenue for your good. This chapter is so amazing. Please get its truth into your life.

QUESTION FOR REFLECTION

Have you even scratched the surface of what the Spirit wants to do for you?

📖 ROMANS 9

These three chapters (9-11) are often skipped by churches today but they actually present the climax of Paul's arguments so far. We walked away from chapter 8 spellbound by its goodness. Or we should have done; a repeated strategy of "the powers" is to cause distrust of Paul's message. All across the Mediterranean Paul won people to the staggering truths of chapters 1-8 but then saw his churches ravaged by allegations against him. These allegations majored on the idea that Paul had abandoned the Old Testament. So - the logic went - His words could not be the very words of God. We hear those exact allegations today. People say Paul is just one voice among many, one of many preachers pushing his own views. With this allegation in our minds we struggle to receive Romans as the Unchanging and True Words of God. That then leads to the growth of an opt-in / opt-out approach. And before long whole churches are weakened through division or complacency. Paul speaks into this directly here with an emotional reflection on the hope of the Old Testament. Paul knew he was one voice among many; everywhere he went people preached alternative truths. Paul stresses how much he has agonised over that very fact. Then he fights to show his message is the message of God. Paul shows how his every word is directly in line with the promises of the Old Testament. Paul's gospel is exactly what the Unchanging God always said he would do even if He did it in a way that was slightly unexpected. Think about the gravity of this truth. Let it obliterate any opt-in / opt-out approach in your heart. We are not believers in a new doctrine that happened to win the Roman empire; these aren't just Paul's words. The magnitude and urgency of Paul's words should arrest us and redefine us. If they don't we need to beg Holy Spirit to to convict us and make it so. Please don't diminish the awesome power of the words of Paul. Let them seep into you and change you as God's Unchanging Truth in this ever-changing world.

QUESTION FOR REFLECTION

Do you opt-in/opt-out of accepting the truths of the bible?

📖 ROMANS 10

People's strongest objections tend to flow from emotional responses. One of the biggest stumbling blocks in the first century was a feeling that Paul's God had abandoned the Jews. It didn't seem right that the zealous nation would be passed over and idolatrous sinners be favoured instead. If Paul's God acts like that, can I trust him with my life? The inevitable end-point of those "feelings" was churches separating into factions, with each faction worshipping the God who felt best to them. All Paul has said so far in Romans would fall on rocky soil if saints started self-selecting emotionally easy views of God. So Paul lovingly addresses this. Paul was a brilliant theologian and philosopher but when he addressed this emotionally-driven issue he chose to wear a pastor's clothes. Paul twice quotes from Isaiah 28; "the one who trusts in him will never be put to shame". This is a verse of reassurance. It speaks to emotions. It soothes anxieties. Paul acknowledges the emotional challenge of what has happened to Israel. He exposes the depths of his soul in how he has grappled with his God. But he makes clear that those emotions need to be brought to scripture, to be yielded to his God rather than expect God to yield to them. In a genius twist Paul shows that Israel's awful plight has been caused by this mistake; they have been so devoted to their emotion of zeal that they refused to yield it to the knowledge given by their God. They heard the message but their unsubmitted emotions pushed their God away. So, as we read this passage, we need to look into our hearts. Are we submitting our emotions to scripture and to God? Are we letting God speak into our fear of shame, our passion, our zeal? And when he speaks, do we let him win or do we hold on to our emotions and expect God to yield to them? Emotions are incredibly powerful. They can drive the greatest evils and the greatest good. So learn to yield your emotions to God. Let him meet you in your emotions and to re-shape them with his words. That is what Paul has done. That is part of what it means to be richly blessed by God.

QUESTION FOR REFLECTION

What are your strongest emotions? How might God want to use them for his glory?

📖 ROMANS 11

The doxology of v33-36 is one of my most favourite passages in all of scripture. What has got Paul so excited? Unexpectedly it is the fate of Israel. Paul has already confessed to agonising over that. How can it now evoke such praise? When we place this passage in context we realise chapters 9-11 have been Paul advocating for the absolute embodiment of his gospel in the church. Our glorious current experience and robust hope must be demonstrated in fullness in the church. Saints need to accept Paul's words as the Everlasting Words of God. Saints need to yield their emotions to the wisdom of God. And now - here - we see that saints must devote themselves to collaborative bodies of mercy. And to do so without a hint of conceit. When Paul looks at churches he sees they are made up of the most unlikely people; devoted Jews are now like family with the gentiles. Only the unsearchable mercy of God could make something so beautiful out of such an assortment of… sinners. And that is the key pastoral message of this chapter. We are sinners saved by grace. Our journey through the process of atonement, our re-birth into a new race in Jesus, our staggering hope of co-ruling all the nations - when we look at those things and look at ourselves we should shake our heads in bewilderment. That should lead us to ask "How can I be part of this?!" and then to embody humble devotion to Jesus' church. Paul - to his horror - found that some of the Gentiles were parading around like they deserved to be in church, treating the Jews like they should not be there. Such behaviour is totally anathema to a true understanding of the gospel of Paul. This passage doesn't promise that millions of Jewish believers will pour into the Kingdom in the last days. But it does urge Gentile believers to have that desire. And to manifest that desire in how they respond to all believers of any nation today. Grateful devotion to a body of believers (with all their quirks) is what it means to live without conceit. When you humbly love the church it is like you are joining Paul in a doxology of devotion to the wisdom of God.

QUESTION FOR REFLECTION

Does your treatment of others mirror the mercy God has shown to you?

📖 ROMANS 12

When you humbly love the church you are joining Paul in a doxology of devotion to the wisdom of God. That was the conclusion of Romans 11. Paul rams that home in this stupendous section. He tells us what it looks like to love the church. In our individualistic West we have suggested being a "living sacrifice" is all about personal holiness; we are told not to swear or be naughty in bed. That saddens me because in this chapter Paul's only application of being a "living sacrifice" is to devote yourself to others in the church. Devoting ourselves to one another includes our words and our sex lives but it is so much more than that. It involves deliberate effort to bring gifts into the church. As Vineyard churches we do all we can to celebrate "everyone gets to play"; every person is precious and necessary for a healthy body of Christ. So, do you play? Do you gather with other believers to serve them with your gifts? Secondly, living sacrifices show hospitality to the church, especially to people of lower station than ourselves. This hospitality isn't just about having people into your house; it is about an attitude of sharing. Share rejoicing with people who are rejoicing. Share mourning with people who are mourning. Sharing stuff with people when they are in need. Do you do this? Have you learned to read people and adjust your behaviour to create harmony with them? Every such hymn of harmony is heard by Holy Spirit and warmly celebrated by him. So we bring our gifts, we show hospitality and then we devote ourselves to people even when they are really annoying. Even in church people will do evil to you. It will hurt a lot and you will be tempted to get them back. Or to step back. Paul calls, instead, us to lean back in trust on the justice of God. Chapter 2 told us about the wrath of God rolling like a river, bringing in its flow restitution and rebuke. Wait for that. Trust in that. God sees you. He will one day make it good. And while you wait for that time, do good to the church. Choose to be a living sacrifice by devoting yourself to the church. It is an act of worship that's deeply pleasing to God.

QUESTION FOR REFLECTION

How could you devote yourself more sacrificially to Jesus' church?

📖 ROMANS 13

Anyone who yearns for social transformation should sit long in this chapter. Should we try to overthrow evil regimes? Should we lobby for Kingdom values to be embodied in all of society? In this chapter Paul sets out a staggering vision for how the church engages with that question; clothe ourselves with the Lord Jesus Christ. The Roman government had arrested Paul and killed his friends. The Roman government epitomised the depraved minds Paul highlighted in chapter 1. And, even though Paul has just told the Roman church that they are more than conquerors, that they will co-inherit all the earth, Paul then tells the church to submit to these senseless and ruthless authorities. How does that make sense? Well, Paul really meant it when he said we should clothe ourselves with Jesus as Lord. Jesus said we defeat evil by turning the other cheek. Jesus said we lead people into new places by washing their feet. Don't get him wrong- it wasn't that Jesus didn't care about social injustice, nor that he just withdrew from society and passively let it happen. No, Jesus went to war with the world... but he did it with love. Fighting against injustice with love is what Paul urges the church to do. This is so at odds with our cultures view of how to achieve justice. In a culture that doesn't believe in God, of course we humans have to be the agents of social transformation. We rise up and use all our power to overthrow abuses of power. (Intersectionality and Critical Race Theory are based on this idea). But we are a counter-culture convinced that God used the Cross of Christ to conquer all evil. Counter-intuitively our conclusion must be that evil is defeated by loving those who practice it. Tyrants are overthrown by God when God's people humbly submit to them. We hate racism so we deliberately love racists... trusting that as we lovingly serve them God will bring justice in the end. This is a huge topic, far beyond this quick paragraph. And - let's admit - even what we've said so far is actually quite hard. But just because it is complex and hard doesn't mean we should just skip on past it. No. This is what "love" is, isn't it? If love were easy or simple then everyone would do it. Love is a choice that we make out of trust in our Father and in apprenticeship to our Lord. We know love fulfils all the law, even how to thrive in an evil age.

QUESTION FOR REFLECTION

Who is a "ruthless, senseless, faithless" person that you could lovingly serve?

📖 ROMANS 14

Evidently there was a major flare up about the appropriateness of eating some foods, probably because all meat in Rome would have been devoted to idols in the process of production. The fault lines in this flare up seem to have fallen between the culturally Jewish believers (who would have been worshipfully anal in watching what they eat) and the culturally gentile believers (who would have wolfed down anything that tickled their taste buds). Paul is remarkably relaxed about it. For an ex-pharisee it is shocking how astronomically accepting he is of all kinds of people. But of course, that is because he had such a strong view of the atonement, of the reality of a new Jesus-race being formed by the resurrection and of the blessings of Abraham now being expanded to all the nations. If Jesus accepts you, who am I to be fussy? In modern Western churches we love this. We have embodied a relaxed "come as you are" culture in most of our gatherings. But we also need to notice that Paul is far from relaxed about any behaviour that breaks the bond of the brotherhood. Our idol of individualism means we gladly give you loads of space to be yourself, but we aren't so strong on serving you as a sister. What we are called to here is a "both-and" approach. We should both view other believers as people who belong to the Lord (so we shouldn't demand things of them that aren't the clear calls of Jesus) and we should also see them as people who will stand before the judgement seat of Christ (so we help them be ready to give a good account on that Day). As Paul says, this means our focus isn't on what we or they eat or drink but on helping people push into righteousness. We adjust our behaviour and change our calenders to help people grow in the delight of holiness, to rest in the peace of God's presence and to be ravished by the joy of being wedded to the Spirit. That's the kind of Kingdom Culture God wants in his church. Let's ask him to show us how we can push into that today.

QUESTION FOR REFLECTION

Who in the church do you radically disagree with? How could you serve them?

📖 ROMANS 15

Endurance and encouragement are essentials for the ongoing enjoyment of our inheritance. I've seen so many friends lose their joy and their peace because their endurance faded away. Paul has laid out such a glorious expectation for us, not only of future increase but also of a life abounding in God's goodness right now. But Paul hasn't sold us a lemon. He has also flagged up the very real threats to our joy; nuisance calls from our ex-brother-in-law (Sin), pressure from 'the powers', clashes in the church and the daily difficulties of our body of decay. He has painted for us a grubby orange experience; glorious gold in the midst of a dark red world. And so endurance and encouragement are essentials for our joy and peace to remain. Paul seems to point to three sources of endurance and encouragement. We would do well to latch ourselves onto these sources, like hungry leeches on a blood-filled foot. The first is scripture (v4). The stories of the Old Testament teach us endurance and give us encouragement. The New Testament woos us and wafts us in the direction of grace. Keep on pursuing the presence of God in your bible. Keep on grappling with it and asking questions of it. Make it your companion in life. Endurance and encouragement will flow as a result. The second source of endurance and encouragement is God himself (v5). Build a habit of going to God to get endurance. Ask God to strengthen you and to fill you with all joy. Do this on the easy days and you will be able to do it on the hard days as well. Make it a habit you can't live without. And then, thirdly, ask people to pray for you (v30). Paul, the great teacher and apostle was astonishingly dependent on the prayers of ordinary people. In every single letter he seems to envy people's prayers as if he doubts his survival if they will not pray for him. I'm not sure I do that enough. I think I'm still too prone to self-sufficiency. I want to get much better at asking people to pray for me. I want to encourage you to do the same. Let's just ask people to pray for us a bit more. In fact, why don't we just stop and pray for each other right now?

QUESTION FOR REFLECTION

How often do you ask people to pray for you? What do you expect to happen when they do so?

📖 ROMANS 16

It is finished. The mighty epistle has ravaged me and brought me to my knees once again. I've found myself weeping or sitting in stunned silence or perplexed and then slowly starting to see. Oh the strength of Jesus so mysteriously disclosed. Oh the abundant mercy of Jesus which can keep us secure until Satan is crushed beneath our very feeble feet. The vistas of God's grace displayed in this book are still far more magnificent than I have grasped. The robustness of our hope still feels a little elusive to me. But I think that is part of the point; Paul's closing prayers and greetings once again remind us that we are living in a story. We are passing through this grubby orange age. The only wise God has disclosed enough of himself in Jesus to make us strong in him right now. But we ain't seen nothing yet. Our glorious current experience; our lavishing with the love of God, our adoption into the family of pioneer philanthropists, our re-birth by the Spirit into a brand new Jesus race, our freedom from wrath and shame and condemnation and fear; all of it compares quite dimly with the full extent of what is to come. And so while we enjoy the now and while we celebrate the sacrifices and the hard work of the Priscilla and Aquillas, the Rufuses and the Junias, our greatest desire is to help those beloved saints endure until The Day. And they will need our help and our prayers and our enduring devotion. "The powers" will pressure them and make them risk their necks. Clashes in the church could divide them and see them fading in their faith. Their ex-brother-in-law (Sin) will seek to seduce them. A whole host of things will cause obstacles for them. And, even when all of those things are held back, they will still be living in a body and a creation that is groaning and in decay. But if we help them, if we bring our spiritual gifts to serve them and show hospitality to them and bear with them when they are wrong, then not only will they endure. Then they and we together will manifest the presence of our Saviour - the beautiful delight of holiness - and we will refresh the hearts of many in many nations across the earth.

QUESTION FOR REFLECTION

Which part of this incredible letter struck you the most?

📖 1 CORINTHIANS 1

After being re-founded by Julius Caesar 100 years before Paul visited, Corinth had bustled and flourished into the preeminent city in all of Greece. It was "where it's at, man". And the church - like most churches - mirrored both the good and the bad of the culture in which it was planted. It was growing through baptisms, was bustling with experiences of the Spirit and was rich in speech and knowledge. But it was also proud, selfish and had lost sight of the big story. The church thought they were "where it's at, man". And that's a big problem. So Paul, through gritted teeth (I'm not angry... I'm just disappointed), pens this letter to show them the most excellent way. Right from the start we see his correction coming into sight. He mentions God or Lord 15 times in the first 9 verses. And then he riffs hard on the foolishness and weakness of him and his mates. In doing so Paul sets up a comparison between the calling, empowering, wise and strong God and... everyone else. Even a self-obsessed Corinthian couldn't fail to get that point. It is not about us. We may be smarter and slicker than the church down the street. We might be more righteous than the unsaved sinners around us. But all of us are dumb and weak and grubby compared to the God who called us. I wonder if we really do believe that? I feel that my vision of God is still so woefully small. If even the most impressive saint compared to God is like a candle compared to the sun then why am I so obsessed with the candle? Why am I (to my shame) still so prone to competing with or copying other Christians? Why don't I compare myself to God more, copy him more, even "compete" with him more? I have no real explanation... except for my pride; I must still think we are "where it's at, man". In this letter Paul will lead us and the Corinthians to the pattern of life that Jesus lived. Paul has already described Jesus as the one we are called into fellowship with. On this ship of faith the central "fellow" is Jesus. And, as we wait for his revealing, we look to him, boast about him, serve like him and love like him. We copy the pattern of the cross. We become happy to be thought of as scum if it enables others to know God's power. We become happy to be thought of as foolish if it shows the love of God. O Jesus, become bigger in our eyes in this book.

QUESTION FOR REFLECTION

How could you think about God more, and yourself less?

📖 1 CORINTHIANS 2

The ruthlessly counter-cultural nature of the cross turns our vision of maturity upside down. The contents of the mind of Christ have been made known to us... but they are not neat things to tweet. Instead they are weak things to live. How can that make sense? We often think a more mature "us" would be faster, stronger and smarter. We work and pray towards that vision of ourselves. But that vision is wrong. A more mature version of us is one that is more like Jesus. To be really spiritually mature is to embody the wisdom that took Jesus to the cross. If Jesus was in our shoes would he vy for attention? Would he jostle others out of the way, or prance past those who won't be useful to him in his pursuit of his vision? The wisdom of God is to stand before a bustling, jostling world and to show God's love in our weakness, God's power in our trembling. That was what Jesus did, so why on earth would we think a mature church should do anything different? Our demonstration of weakness is not because we are intimidated by "strength". Too often I've met Christians (and been a Christian) who have lived out of insecurity and cowardice and called it weakness. No. Weakness isn't a lack of courage. Trembling isn't fear. The trembling is the trembling of one doing something different from everyone else, which many others despise, and yet bubbling up with the belief that the power of Jesus's resurrection is just around the corner; is waiting and ready to rush into a cross-shaped life. "I know nothing except Jesus the King who was crucified for me." Paul's vision of maturity was to become weaker and less impressive in himself, to make everything about Jesus; to make space for the King who was killed to release the power of his resurrection. I wonder what it would look like for us to pursue that vision in our workplaces? For us to be people who don't pretend, who don't put on a front, who don't jostle for position but who freely admit where we have failed, what we don't know, what we can't do. And, then to look with trembling lips and hands for an outpouring of power and favour like the empty tomb that followed the cross of Christ.

QUESTION FOR REFLECTION

What would it look like for you to embrace weakness today?

📖 1 CORINTHIANS 3

For a weak and trembling man Paul kicks pretty hard. His rebukes of the church - "you are still worldly" (v3) and "do not deceive yourselves..." (v18) - are robust to say the least. To understand how such robustness can be in bed with such trembling we must distinguish between the message and the messenger. We've seen Paul all the way through Acts and we know that he is uncompromising about his message. God is the immovable object in Paul's life. God has revealed himself to Paul and has sent Paul to testify to who He is. You never catch Paul adding 'maybes' or 'from my perspective' to his statements about the character or work of God. "You are God's field". "You are God's temple". "If anyone destroys God's temple, God will destroy him." Instead, Paul trembles about himself. Paul trembles over the meagreness of himself and Apollos and the saints of Corinth. He is fearful that they - or their leaders - will become the focus instead of Jesus. We are nothing, he says. The only one who counts is God, he says. Paul sounds like an accident-prone delivery man realising he is carrying a ming vase. The more conscious he is of the value of the vase, the more alert he is to the risk of him wrecking it. This sounds so far removed from most of my "ministry" up until this point. Far too often I've bent over backwards to allow different perspectives on the character of God as long as people have stayed in my group. I've added way too much wiggle room into my presentations of who we are in Christ in order that people will continue to want to hang around with me. What have I been thinking?! I've been acting like a mere man, I have been building with straw. I have been anxious over conversations not because someone believes something wrong but because they believe I am wrong! In this I have been worldly and I can deceive myself no longer. I ask Holy Spirit to lead me in a better way. It is God who makes things grow. If they follow me but are not following God then I'm like the delivery man ringing their bell, puffing out my chest and then giving them a broken box. Maturity in Jesus is to present Jesus to his people in his pure unadulterated form and then to get out of the way.

QUESTION FOR REFLECTION

How does "all things being yours" (v22) affect your desire to be well thought of now?

📖 1 CORINTHIANS 4

Paul continues the same argument. We are back with the delivery man and the ming vase. We are just servants. We have been entrusted with deeply precious things, even secret things. These precious and secret things have unrivalled power. They have the only power that can really change things and so it's imperative that we simply serve them up, that we deliver them intact. And - this is the crucial thing - because we live in a hostile and foolish world, doing that exacts a heavy toll on us. To minister pure unadulterated Kingdom into people brings us into disrepute. We become dishonoured. We are slandered. We get treated like scum. The huge temptation when being treated like this is to talk ourselves up, to turn our mission into sounding clever or looking good. The huge temptation is to hype. But true servants of the Kingdom come out in a rash when they smell a whiff of hype. Now I know how controversial that is when church culture has become obsessed with creating a "worshipful atmosphere", of "winning others", of "raising the faith" of the flock. None of those things are problems as long as they sit in their proper place, but our obsession with them has become like idolatry. We shun the slightest suspicion of having to suffer or feel dumb. You can experience the power of God among smoke machines and flashing lights, we all know that. But they do sometimes get in the way. More normal is to experience the power of God while feeling stupid on the streets or paying a heavy price to minister Jesus to some friends. We need to rewrite the narrative, recast the vision of what it looks like to be mature in Christ. The "way of life" of a mature believer isn't prancing from one "supernatural" experience to another but it is rolling from one grubby moment to another, doing your best to get out of the way, serve up Jesus, and praying for God's extraordinary power to break in. I wonder if you really believe this? When a chance comes to pray for someone, what do we do… what do we instinctively think? Do we lean on our own understanding, do we think what happens will depend on us? Or do we act simply as a delivery man, delivering Jesus to the person and trusting his power to do the job? The latter leaves us open to looking foolish if "nothing happens" but it also gives the space for "the mysteries of God" to be revealed by Jesus with astonishing kingdom power.

QUESTION FOR REFLECTION

What would it look like for you to adopt the way of life of weakness (v17) that Paul is talking about

📖 1 CORINTHIANS 5

Paul expected immorality to constantly define the people of the world. He refused to judge them for it. Instead he looked past any lewdness, sold them some tents and kept on witnessing. His focus was on getting holiness into the house of God. Some of you recoil against this idea. It seems far too insular. Surely God wants us to fight systemic racism and work for the good of our world? Yes, of course. God made the earth, in the end we will inherit it (3:22) and we practise now our stewardship of it. But, Paul never aspired to be Rome's moral policeman. He did not engage in culture wars. Instead he let the world get on with it and turn his attention to the church. And he urgently demanded utter sexual purity in the church. Do you hear that? In our age many Christians are saying the church needs to relax traditional views on Christian sexual ethics. In our day it is normal for christians to sleep together, live together, express their sexual desires in whatever context seems best to them. Paul very strongly speaks against that. Paul even says it would be better for all if people who deliberately persist in sexual impurity to be asked to leave the church. This is the man who gave up all he had to see some come to faith. This is the man who was compelled by the love of Christ and who regarded himself as the worst of all sinners. This can't just be written off as bigotry on Paul's part. We must ask why Paul would even suggest such a thing. Could it be that Paul's compassion led him to demand a certain way of living; sacrificial, painful at times, but riven with holiness? Could it be that Paul saw greater benefit for every person if they prioritised holiness over happiness? I wonder how you respond to this? You might be deeply conscious of your sexual sin. Do not fear; repentance is real and God loves to cleanse you of every sense of shame. Or you might - like the Corinthians - be angry. I get that. Paul makes me angry sometimes too. In these moments we need to really hear Jesus and not let memories of other voices swamp what he really says. But we also need to be honest about the choice we have - when we actually hear Jesus will we let his Word form us? Do we want to be people who worship Jesus when he says stuff we like but reject him when he says stuff we don't? For Paul, it was "everything Jesus said" or it wasn't worth showing up. That was what it meant to live in weakness. That was what it meant to live in fear and trembling, and to see the foolishness of God as wiser than the wisdom of the world.

QUESTION FOR REFLECTION

Are you allowing Jesus to rule your sex life?

📖 1 CORINTHIANS 6

Like water from a tap, your behaviour flows from your story. If you want to live differently, start believing a different story. One story looks back; it focuses on who I was or what has happened to me; I was wronged by this person, I've always been controlled by my sexual desires, I was a drunkard and swindler and on and on. A story that looks back assumes you are defined by your past and, due to the limitations and struggles you have had in your past, you end up living like you did. You turn on the old rusty tap and hope that a cold, cloudy bath will be "permissible". Paul sings about a different story and a different tap. This story looks forward, not back. In the future you will co-rule the world. After the return of Jesus the saints will co-rule with Jesus as judges on the earth. Doesn't that change everything? Doesn't it bestow dignity and gratitude upon you? Doesn't it stagger you with a sense of privilege and make you want to live up to the honour that has been poured onto your life? Also this story tells us that any wrong done to us now will be repaid on "That Day". I can cope with being cheated because in the future I will be repaid. Any loss now will be noted by God and more than compensated from his bountiful purse. Doesn't that change the equation of every interaction in your day? If we really believe that anything anyone takes from us will be repaid seven times over then we can be much more generous when being treated with disdain. And the third delicious truth about this future story is that we will inherit the Kingdom - the full magnificent abundance of the Kingdom - as long as we remain connected to Christ. He has already spoken over us the "elevation" that will be given on "that day" and that statement will hold as long as we don't recant our salvation through persistent denials or pervasive misdeeds. And doesn't that change how we think of our desires? So many fleeting attractions - like an illicit sexual moment - are so small and grubby compared to what is to come. When we listen to the forward-looking story we can, like a weary worker coming in from the fields, know that there is a bath waiting for us that is delightfully warm. So we walk towards the house with a spring in our step; grateful to the one who has run it for us, and refusing to be distracted by the cold and cloudy puddles on the floor.

QUESTION FOR REFLECTION

When you co-rule creation, what particular project would you love to do for the glory of Jesus?

📖 1 CORINTHIANS 7

This ruffles a few feathers. The verses about slaves remaining in the situation they are in have been grossly abused. The stuff on marriage and divorce is increasingly ignored. The problem comes from our feeble view of salvation. The gospel that Paul preached included forgiveness of past sin and receipt of the Holy Spirit. But - I feel utterly foolish for saying this - that is a feeble view of the immensity of Jesus' work. For Paul the biggest achievement of the cross was not to enable forgiveness for individuals. Jesus' death and resurrection gave undeniable confirmation that God's great day of justice is coming. When Jesus was raised it proved God will bring "an end" to this present age and will bring in a glorious golden age. And it also showed the church what to do while they are eagerly waiting for that day; don't lack any gift of the Spirit… stay strong… walk in the way of Jesus. 1:4-9 is the foundation stone for all the ethical imperatives we see in chapter 7. And so slaves shouldn't seek to change the situation they are in because Jesus submitted himself to cruel men, showing a self-sacrificing love to win some for God. This in no way validates enslaving people - it is a command to those already enslaved in how to subversively sow the Kingdom into their situation. The only instructions we see Paul giving to slave-owners is to similarly sow the Kingdom into their situation by treating their slave as a brother (Philemon). Equally marriage should be seen not as the pinnacle of pilgrimage and pleasure but as a fleeting opportunity to sow kingdom love and hope into a human relationship. The pinnacle of pilgrimage and pleasure is the Coming Kingdom. We wait in hope for that day. And now we walk in the way of Jesus through faithful love, through self-giving kindness. This might mean remaining single, it might mean a Jesus-shaped marriage, it might even mean allowing an unbelieving spouse to walk away if that is the path to greatest peace. The details are worked out in a pragmatic way in the shadow of the coming age. This is so rare today. We've got so used to comfort in this age that the Coming Age barely seems to feature in our decision making. I yearn to embody something different. I want to do all God wants from me now, knowing God will give me all I want from him then. I want to live like Jesus.

QUESTION FOR REFLECTION

Are you at risk of "idolising" a certain way of life now (being rich, married, having kids, retired, living in a new home)? What would it look like for you to put that hope down and to live as a believer in the situation you are in right now?

📖 1 CORINTHIANS 8

Paul has graffitied on the prized plinth of the patriarchs. The Shema of Deuteronomy 6 was the pinnacle of Jewish monotheism. "Hear O Israel, the Lord our God, the Lord is one." If you desecrated that, you were dead to the Jews. In fact you were probably dead. By stoning. But Paul graffities Jesus' name right into the great prayer of Judaism (v6). He has a new schema for the Shema. It is staggering. The fact that Paul can speak this way shows how robustly he has integrated Jesus into his understanding of God. Paul has integrated Jesus into the Old Testament picture of God and this has given him a shatter-proof understanding of all creation. Paul can approach all questions about life from the perspective of his creator God who he understands so well. The particular issue at hand in this chapter is about food sacrificed to idols. We don't think about idols much today. Except for Father Christmas. He's an idol we roll out every December. Or is it September? Anyway, in Corinth idols had been fused into the fabric of society. And division sprung up in the church between those believers who, at great difficulty, avoided the food from these idols and those who didn't bat an eyelid about them. Paul approaches the topic by remembering who God is. God is creator of all things. We live through God. You can't get a more Old Testament idea than that. And therefore any food we receive is a gift from God. Any claim that the food belongs to an idol or fuses you to the idol is ridiculous to Paul. It's like saying your house is mine because I put a post-it note on it. The meat is God's. We are God's. So crack on. But the caveat from this monotheistic preacher is that one God means one church. And one church means we all belong to one Lord. And if we all belong to one Lord then if we do anything to separate a brother from his Lord then it is also separating them from our Lord. And our Lord doesn't like that. So crack on… but only in a way that builds up the one body. The conclusion of this argument may not be hugely interesting for us today. But the process by which Paul gets there should inspire us. Could we get to know God that well? Could we get to know God so well that every decision we make flows from a deeply integrated understanding of his generous and unchanging character as the creator of all things?

QUESTION FOR REFLECTION

Is there anything God made that you actually look at negatively? What would it look like for you to embrace all creation as a generous gift from God?

📖 1 CORINTHIANS 9

Does your bible have subheadings at certain places? Mine has one over this chapter saying "the rights of an Apostle". These aren't original to the text but are added by each publisher to try to help us understand the text. I think they got this one wrong. What Paul is doing here is continuing the train of thought he was on in chapter 8. In fact, he is still continuing along the tracks he laid out in chapter 1; that on the ship of faith our central fellow should be Jesus. Jesus should form our approach to everything. Paul had fully integrated Jesus into his understanding of the Old Testament God and then used that rich and robust knowledge to make every decision. We see here how that led Paul into a pattern of life that echoed Jesus' incarnation. Just like Jesus, Paul was sent by the Father. Just like Jesus, Paul didn't see this as a licence to lord it over people. Just like Jesus, Paul gave up his rights so that he might discharge his duty more effectively. And just like Jesus, Paul showed people an exact picture of what it would be like for them to be mature in God. I think that is amazing. Previously when I read "to a Jew I became like a Jew, to win the Jews" I thought it meant quite a superficial and temporary effort to speak in the language and ideas of his audience. Like wearing a hoodie for youth work, innit. But now I am grasping the deeply embodied nature of the mission that Paul took on. He strained every sinew to understand the fears, ambitions and struggles of the people around him so that he could show them what they will look like when they are mature in Jesus. This wasn't shadow boxing; it was getting in the ring in Corinth to live as a Corinthian completely given over to Christ. It was real selfless love. I believe the variance in language and ideas in Paul's letters (which cause some theologians to say different people wrote them) are actually a bi-product of how Paul incarnated the gospel slightly differently in different places depending on their culture. And all of this leaves me wondering whether I have ever loved someone as much as Paul loved these Corinthians. I wonder whether I've ever gone into strict training so I can really understand the people around me? I wonder if I would be happy to live a life so much like my neighbour (and yet fully filled with the Spirit) that my neighbour can see in me God's invitation to their shared future. Jesus did that for me. Paul did it for the Corinthians. Holy Spirit, please help me start doing it for others.

QUESTION FOR REFLECTION

In what ways are you beating your body or training your soul so that you might live more like Jesus?

📖 1 CORINTHIANS 10

In the last chapter Paul wrote that selfless love for others is foundational to following Jesus. Having made that point Paul circles back round to the question of idols. He doesn't want immature believers to misunderstand the freedom he asserted in chapter 8. The earth is the Lord's and everything in it. And so any created thing is something we can enjoy with thankfulness. We believers should enjoy stuff. Eating chocolate can be a great form of worship. Hallelujah and Amen. But the abuse of created stuff for our pleasure, or devotion of ourselves to a god other than God, can really arouse the Lord's jealousy. It got many Israelites killed. A neat way to understand this distinction is to say idols are harmless but idolatry brings death. Idols have no negative influence on us. You can admire an artist's design of a Buddah statue or eat halal chicken and it won't do you any spiritual harm at all. But idolatry is toxic for everyone every time. Idolatry opens us up to the demonic and opens the church up to being destroyed. The toxicity of idolatry is that it sows disorder into your life. All of creation was made for God. He sits at the centre of it like the central hub of a spoked wheel. If you start to shift the central hub off to one side you are headed for a bumpy ride and then a horrible crash... probably into someone else in the church. When that starts to happen the one Lord of the one church is aroused with one goal - to reassert himself as the one source and one end of all creation. Only when that is the case can harmony and peace be ensured. And so, while we can admire an artist's sculpture of Buddah and even value some of the Buddah's philosophical claims, if we start to think Buddah is the centre of our wheel then we are headed toward trouble. And of course idolatry isn't just about engagement with the practices of other religions. The most alluring form of idolatry seems to be the pursuit of profit, or influence, or eating delicious food. But these are just warnings about errors; the thrust of what Paul emphasises is the robust confidence we can have in God. God loves us, he has our back, he made all things for our pleasure and, if we just keep God as the central hub of our existence then nothing- not even demons- can take us out of his care.

QUESTION FOR REFLECTION

The pursuit of what idol do you think is most likely to be damaging the church today?

📖 1 CORINTHIANS 11

What are church gatherings all about? Different churches have different flavours and that is part of the rich casserole of the Kingdom… to some extent. What Paul makes clear in these chapters is that not all ingredients in the caserole are equally tasty. The "flavour test" is whether a particular habit creates a culture that honours the magnificent character of the Trinity. Does what we do when we gather show others what God is like and train them to live more like him? Each of us plays a part in this. Just as one small piece of machinery in an aeroplane engine can have huge consequences for the whole flight, Paul asserts that each individual church member's small choices can end up having major impacts on whether or not a community ends up conforming to the Christ. In Paul's day how you dressed was one of those small things. Dress codes said a lot about what you lived as your Way of Life. Pharisees kept their phylacteries broad and their fringes long as physical signs of their 24-7 devotion to Yahweh's word. Worshippers of Dionysus shaved their heads as signs of their ecstatic freedom to do as they like whenever they liked. Temple prostitutes of the Roman gods unveiled their hair as a sign that they would… well, you know. Paul wants attendees at his churches to see themselves not just as "coming as they are" to meet their God but also as small parts in an engine that God is building for his glory. These days long hair and tattoos don't really show much about our Way of Life or which god we worship but the idea that the way we act and speak and even dress at our gatherings affects the whole church is definitely worth considering. If we arrive early or late it communicates something to others that affects the whole body. If we raise our hands in worship or check out to see what our phone notification was then we are either pouring oil or water onto the fire that the Spirit is igniting in the church. If we push others out the way at the Lord's Supper (or coffee queue) or if we use it as a time of reaffirming love for Jesus and his church then that genuinely affects the health of the whole body. And on and on. "Everyone gets to play" is a massive slogan in Vineyard churches. It is one of the smartest summaries of Paul's understanding of the normal church life. So remember, next time you gather with church you are like a footballer stepping onto a pitch, or like an engine part revving up to help the flight. God looks at every small choice you make and uses it to determine the destiny of your church community.

QUESTION FOR REFLECTION

What small choices could you make to play your part in building up your church?

📖 1 CORINTHIANS 12

Church gatherings should manifest the magnificence of the Trinity. That's the point Paul is making in these chapters. Here we discover how magnificently chatty God is. Paul contrasts church gatherings with the Corinthians' previous worship of idols. The idols were mute and powerless so all the work was being done on the human side. Incense was lit, imaginations were used and impartation was sought… but no-one really expected an immediate reply. I guess the hope was that life would go a bit better because of the act of devotion. But the Trinity is a chatty God. Father, Son and Spirit are vocal. They come to church gatherings not just to respond to the requests of the redeemed but to advance their own agenda. They set the pace and they steer the ship. And the way our Triune God loves to do this is through the whole body of people. The One God releases Spirit gifts to the many people so that they will put them together to build up one another. It seems that no individual receives sufficient revelation on their own to know how to advance. All the different revelations must be added together like different paints on a colour-by-number page. And so this brings two questions right to the fore. The first is the main one; do we attend church gatherings knowing that we carry a brush no one else carries? Do we believe only we can paint a colour that is essential to God's design? Our nervousness or shyness can help us come with humility, but if it stops us from contributing at all then it is actually working against God's plans. God's vision for our lives is that he "chats" his truths through us. When we go to a small group do we look to bring something from the Spirit to the group? If we don't we need to ask God to help us begin to try. The second question is the flip side of the first (and the one more relevant to the Corinthians). Do we go to church needing God to speak to us through others? Do we believe we don't have enough on our own and that only through the church can we get what we need to move on? The truth is that no matter how mature we are in faith, God never gives us enough to be independent. We fool ourselves if we think we can stand alone. We need help from one another and church gatherings are the places we receive that help. Our church is the place where we both feed the flock and get fed ourselves.

QUESTION FOR REFLECTION

How could you step away from self-reliance? How can you help others do the same?

📖 1 CORINTHIANS 13

It's the wedding passage! But don't let the distant sound of wedding bells fool you - this is about so much more than marriage. It is one of the most inspiring and most challenging mandates for every church, every small group, every household. The passage is full of poetic beauty and yet it is more down to earth than a long-drop toilet at a French service station. Every single descriptor of love is delicious. Oh to be with someone who is patient. Ah, to never be self-seeking. Eee to have someone who protects you and trusts you and perseveres with you. We read these soaring sentences and life seems better - it seems more excellent and exalted. No wonder we read them at our weddings. But then we walk back down the aisle. Then we leave our quiet time and bump into people who do "people-stuff" to us. Our romantic vision of frolicking in a French field is replaced by a long queue and the unmistakable whiff of continental conveniences. This is because love isn't really poetry - love is a word that rams us into the blokes who are sitting next to us. Love chains us to the moody-looking woman behind us. It was love, not doctrine, that took Jesus to the cross. It was love, not prophecy, that fuelled the resurrection. Love is the mature model of a life lived in God. Love knows that some people have more than us and some people are annoying to us and some people are doing wrong to us but it still stands firm. Love knows that we see in a glass darkly, like viewing a reflection in a muddy puddle on the floor. But it is not phased by that uncertainty. Love never fails. You know that today you will carry scars from evil. You know that today you will be desperate for some protection from others, for some love from others... and that you probably won't get it. But don't let this drive you away from love. Don't let that make you insular and cynical. Instead choose to love. Choose to never grow weary of love. Spend yourself on building others up. Ask God for gifts that will most help other people. Don't make excuses for yourself. Don't think you need to find a new group or that you need to sort yourself out first or that you would in theory but today isn't a great day... Instead, choose to love. Devote yourself to love. Manifest the magnificence of the Trinity. Live the most excellent way, pursue a life defined by the greatest attribute of our faith and you will begin to smell excellent and exalted in everything you do.

QUESTION FOR REFLECTION

Can you imagine yourself abounding in love? What would that look like?

📖 1 CORINTHIANS 14

The bit about women keeping silent feels like a stinking kipper round the chops of our church practice. Should women really never preach? The great theologian Matthew Henry thought so - "Our spirit and conduct should be suitable to our rank. The natural distinctions God has made, we should observe.... For this reason women must be silent in the churches, not set up for teachers". We should commend Henry that he is trying to submit himself to the word rather than have the word submit to him. Far worse is just to dismiss the verses that don't fit with our desires. Much danger that way lies. But there is good reason to question Henry's conclusion. What Matthew Henry seems to have done is give these four verses (32-35) primacy over the many other statements in the book that suggest men and women should both be actively involved in church life. The whole of this section of the letter (chapters 11-14) focuses on how church gatherings are everyone getting to play. Throughout this section Paul has used the Greek word that means "men and women" when talking about people receiving gifts from the Spirit to build others up. This chapter includes men and women in the call to eagerly desire the gift of prophecy and in chapter 11 Paul talked specifically about how women should dress when they were giving prophecies in church. Because Traditional understandings of prophecy included many aspects of preaching we can see that the major thrust of this letter is strongly supportive of women vocally engaging in church life. We also know the wider context of New Testament church practice (which Paul references here) did have people like Priscilla and Junia acting as pastor/teachers in churches. So in our church we do let women preach. More than that; we encourage them to preach and to prophesy so as to comfort, encourage and strengthen the church. Women; we need you and we are deeply grateful for your service to us all. But, with that all said, I must admit these 4 verses still do baffle me. I don't want to just write them off and therefore I am trying to work out exactly what Paul means in them. Why couldn't he have been a bit clearer? Thank the Lord that even the bible itself acknowledges some of Paul's letters are hard to understand (2 Peter 3:16). These stinking kippers aren't easy. But they can wake us up to the mystery of God's Presence. They can increase our longing to see Him face to face.

QUESTION FOR REFLECTION

What do you do with the hard bits of the bible? How do they draw you deeper into God?

📖 1 CORINTHIANS 15

This glorious passage has more fizz than 10,000 soda pops. The source of its tanginess is the explosive idea of Jesus as first-fruits. First-fruits by definition carry a promise. Firstfruits show what is coming. One has been raised from the dead, not as a freak event, but as a sign of what will happen to all who carry His name. We also will be raised. This is the defining hope of our faith. Not just that we are forgiven, not just that we live in relationship with God, but that we will journey right through death into a richer and purer way of being alive. We will do as Jesus did. We taste already some of the delight of the resurrection that is to come. But it is just a taste - the full fizz is a future feast. And so we see all our suffering now as just short days before our Greatest Days. We don't start to stutter when the wild beasts attack. Nor do we get lured to the temporary comforts of sin. No, we know a trumpet will sound and an eye will twinkle and then the full promise of resurrection will be achieved in us. We know that this body may die every day, but on That Day it will be clothed with impregnable immortality. We know that our relatives, and maybe even ourselves, may die a painful death. But we know that we will be brought out of our tombs to live something much stronger, something much purer, something better, that never ends. We know we will live in the new Eden, in a perfect place where the horrific consequences of Adam's sin can no longer be seen. We know that the great and wise God will be all in all in every single way. He will reign everything in his benevolent goodness. We know those things because the firstfruits of Jesus confirmed they must be so. So what do we do now? How should we live? That, ultimately is what Paul is interested in here. Paul wants every believer to understand that there is an unbreakable link between labour in the Lord now and the luscious splendour of life in the Second Man. He wants us to stop our sin and lend ourselves fully to the labour of the Lord. He wants us to work hard and suffer well and not be moved. There are days when our faith feels weaker. On those days we should look at the resurrection. On those days we look at the fact of the firstfruits; the glorious glimpse of what we have in store. For what has happened to Jesus will also happen to us.

QUESTION FOR REFLECTION

Do you have a habit of intentionally thinking about the resurrection?

📖 1 CORINTHIANS 16

Paul has spent this letter casting a vision of a mature community. Mature believers come together to manifest the magnificence of the Trinity. Members don't draw attention to themselves, they don't vie for position or put one another down. Instead a mature church organises herself around the person and practice of Jesus; in purity and humility and - most of all - in that elusive pattern of relationship we call love. When addressing this Paul had to tackle some tricky topics. We still find it hard to talk freely about judging the church, staying in slavery or the silence of women. Indeed this letter has reminded us that the pursuit of real maturity is less like poetry, more like consistently choosing one necessity after another. But don't see this as a negative vision. Glory and delight abound in a maturity that brings us into fellowship with Jesus; we taste and know the honouring of Holy Spirit among us. We get to live like ones already enriched in every way, not lacking any gift. We get to be the New Testament temple. Oh, the joy of a local church when it even gets close to this vision of magnificence. But here in this last chapter Paul zooms out to show that local churches don't stand alone. No church can really be independent. Churches should both support other churches and sit under the leadership of external leaders. The picture of united diversity within the local church should also be the picture of how local churches relate to one another. This is done through receiving other teachers in and through sending money out. These practices aren't just done off the cuff - they are intentionally built into every member's week. On the first day of the month each Corinthian is invited to contribute to the collection for poorer believers in Jerusalem. And so every saint's life testifies not only to being part of one body but part of an entire movement all across the globe. These actions don't just spread resources, but also draw all of God's people together in interdependent loving relationships. These kinds of relationships are what Holy Spirit loves to bless because they speak unambiguously of the united diversity of the Trinity. In our internet age there are so many ways we can invest in cross-church relationships. Let's ask Holy Spirit which ones we should pursue today.

QUESTION FOR REFLECTION

You are an intrinsic part of God's family that stretches all across the globe and all across the centuries. What does that mean to you?

📖 2 CORINTHIANS 1

Our ears are full of hyperbole. There is so much overstatement in our opinion-soaked world that Paul's mention of despair could slip us by. It should not. Paul was a self-confessed under-stater. He didn't play with words just to make an impact. His yes was yes and his no was no. And so when Paul tells us that he suffered beyond his ability to endure, you know that he suffered. Oh boy he must have suffered. This must have been an extended, exhausting episode of bone-grinding agony. Paul - who had escaped a crazed mob's death sentence a couple of times - tells the Corinthians that he felt the sentence of death. We don't know exactly what happened to Paul and we don't need to know. Paul gives us enough to realise that this great apostle became so weak-kneed, gaunt-faced and hollow-stomached that he called out to his mummy for help and then he kept on wailing. Alright, he called out to God for help, but the reality of Paul's pit of despair should change forever our understanding of our faith. Episodes of extreme pain do not mean that God is failing or that we have failed. These "dark nights" can be times of profound transformation if we respond to them as Paul did. So what did he do? Well I hesitate to answer that straight away because it might sound like God gives instant relief if we do the right things. And that is obviously not the truth. But what we do find Paul doing is setting his hope on God, who raises the dead. "Setting" his hope doesn't feel like a particularly helpful translation. Fighting to keep his hope in God seems better to me because remembering and remaining in hope was not an emotionally straightforward exercise. And fighting is also a helpful word because we can see it was a group fight. The prayers of many helped hold Paul together until God's comfort arrived. Paul did not suffer and "set his hope" on his own. He involved others. Do you involve others when you feel low? Our faith must make space for admission of weakness and pain and begging others for help. Not to do that is not biblical faith. And we also end this chapter realising that our faith must make space for others to express utter agony to us. Let's try to be people who are easy to speak to, who are OK with people not being fixed straight away but who, at the same time, pray faith-filled prayers for their deliverance to come.

QUESTION FOR REFLECTION

There can be long and horrible gaps between our prayers for help and God's deliverance arriving. How can we help people who are trapped in one of those times?

📖 2 CORINTHIANS 2

Paul started this follow-up letter to the Corinthians exposing the bone-grinding agony that he had gone through. Here he continues his disclosure, bringing a new slant to his suffering. We see that in every interaction and moment Paul works to become astonishingly conscious of God. Paul is a bit like a social media addict who is always checking for new posts; except he was only following One Account. Paul refuses to give up looking for comfort directly from God, and so when God makes it available he grabs it and is strengthened by it (1:4). I guess a lot of us do that. But Paul went further. Paul constantly reminded himself that God was watching him. He knows God saw his difficult decision not to return to Corinth (1:23). Paul knows Jesus watched him forgive the Corinthians offender (2:10). Paul knew that God was watching him travel around the Mediterranean and that he even opened a door for him in Troas (2:12). Each of these statements speaks volumes of how Paul's inner mind worked; what he thought about, how he gained his strength, how he viewed every single situation. Fascinatingly we see Paul even claiming that he smelled beautiful to God even though others were telling him differently (2:15). How could he have known such a thing? Well, there is a clue in 1:9 when he says his sufferings taught him to "not rely on ourselves but on God". Paul seems to have allowed his life to cultivate a deliberate reliance on God in every waking moment. Before he opens his lips in reply or before he takes his next step Paul seems to have built a pause, a lag for his Lord. It reminds me of what Bill Johnson has said about carrying the presence of the Spirit; that we should live like we have a dove resting on our head... slowly. And so I'm wanting to slow down my speech. To build in a lag for my Lord. It goes against so much of my natural tendencies but I think it is what I need. If all of us can grow a greater level of awareness of God watching us, opening doors for us, even smelling us then we will find a more robust life. If we can learn to live with a lag for our Lord then we will find a more unshakable life that is incredibly fruitful for Jesus. I so much want to see God all the time. I guess I need to slow down my mind.

QUESTION FOR REFLECTION

How aware are you of God always watching you and responding to you? How could you cultivate greater awareness of Him?

📖 2 CORINTHIANS 3

"We, who with unveiled faces all reflect the Lord's glory, are being transformed into his likely with ever-increasing glory" That is a screensaver verse. It's a verse to lift our spirits when we feel lost or discouraged or alone. Let it encourage you now. The encouragement is two-fold. It tells us we already reflect the Lord's glory. I already reflect God. You reflect God. Now that is quite a statement but Paul is happy to make it about the cranky corrupt Corinthians. And so we know he'd make it about us as well. This is because our reflection of God's glory is not down to our skill or holiness but is due to God himself being a seal in our hearts. From the outside we may look no more "holy" or "devoted" than we did last week, or even than before we came to Jesus. But from God's perspective we already reflect his glory. We look like God to God because he sees his Spirit when he looks into our hearts. This is enormously comforting. And, indeed, any Spirit-filled person will see something of God in me if they look with open eyes. This is because the Spirit of the Living God is writing a letter on our hearts. Holy Spirit is inscribing words and ideas onto you and you probably don't even realise it. What an amazing truth that is. But it gets better. There is more of God that Holy Spirit will reflect in us. There is more writing that he will inscribe each day for the rest of our lives. Each day that we open ourselves to Holy Spirit is a day when God looks down on us and sees a little bit more of himself in us. Simply by Holy Spirit being in us, our mirror that reflects God's glory is incrementally cleaned. And as the mirror is cleaned it changes us - it changes our desires and our inclinations. We find ourselves becoming more like Jesus in our inner being and - like water soaking through a sponge - that eventually starts to flow out of our outer being. God is changing us by his Spirit. And so we can rest secure and be assured. We have sweet freedom from our own self-destructiveness. And we have sweet freedom from the rules and regulations of religion. Our primary imperative is to let Holy Spirit give life to us. And we do that through turning to the Lord and keeping our eyes fixed on Him throughout our day. "Come, Holy Spirit" is a wonderful prayer to pray, especially when God answers it, which he does every time we give him the space.

QUESTION FOR REFLECTION

What do you find most encouraging about this passage?

📖 2 CORINTHIANS 4

This passage is famous for a reason. We love the image of ourselves as an earthenware pot holding lashings of gold. It lodges in the mind and makes perfect sense. God has - in spite of our mediocre means - placed the most fabulous riches inside of us. We have light. We see glory. We are alive. Life is at work in us. We are being renewed day by day. An eternal glory is being achieved for us. The extent of God's ongoing work in every single believer stretches far beyond anything we would imagine. We hold immense bounty. And that bounty now defines us. Far too often we find ourselves looking only at transient aspects of our identity. Our eye and mind is drawn to the chips and blemishes in our pot. Far too often we believe the disdainful glances or the lack of attention that our earthenware vessel receives from others. But when we see how much God is actively doing in us then "we do not lose heart". "We do not lose heart" is a phrase that has flowed like a river from the strange spring of Paul's suffering. The bone-grinding agony of Chapter 1 brought into stark relief for Paul the reality of his existence. Some things in his life were seen. Some things in his life were unseen. And yet the unseen things were the ones that really counted. It is the same with us. The treasure inside of us, God's constant activity in us, how God sees us and smells us are all unseen things. And yet these things define us more than our look, our popularity or even the "success" of our efforts. And so Paul has adopted a deliberate renouncing of things that elevate the seen above the unseen. He deliberately renounced deceptive or distorting ways that prioritised visible success over invisible honour. How could we do the same? I've never found this harder than now. In this age of "big data" so many metrics of my self-worth are based on visible responses to me either on social media or otherwise. I find myself so often losing heart when the data tells me I'm just a jar of clay. I find myself so often wanting to focus on my "visibles", to pander to saying manipulative things so I look more like a sparkly jar. Or to go the whole other way and disengage with everything all together. We need to ask God for his mercy so we do not lose heart but are renewed day by day.

QUESTION FOR REFLECTION

What are your favourite "unseen things" that God is saying over you or doing for you?

📖 2 CORINTHIANS 5

Paul is like the runner who uses a pair of trainers until both soles fall off. He doesn't just think a few theological thoughts and feel encouraged. He doesn't even gasp at God's grace and then raise his hands in worship. No, he thinks about what God has done in him. And then he thinks on it some more. And he keeps on thinking on it until he has run those thoughts as far as he can possibly take them. And then he writes about it. Keeping up with Paul's train of thought can feel like trying to follow a fleet-footed fell runner who is flying along her favourite route. But let's put the effort in; the benefits will be immense. Paul started thinking about death. Which led him to think about how many of God's riches are unseen or unfelt in the midst of this current age. Which made him think about how futile it is for christians just to focus on what is seen. And having done that Paulthen extrapolates those trends to think about the coming Day when the important unseen stuff will become seen and the unimportant seen stuff will no longer be seen. And that gives him courage. And that gives him hope to continue living for the unseen. And even that isn't where he stops. For then he considers how God himself responded to humanity's obsession with "the seen". He feels the love that God expressed in Jesus and he dwells upon that love long enough until it compels him into action. So Paul seeks to persuade men and women of the veiled nature of real riches in this world. Paul makes it his goal to emulate his Lord; to lovingly draw people past a focus on externals and to prize the grace of God which can renovate their hearts. And all of that came out of a time of immense suffering. As I think on this passage this morning I realise how brief so much of my thinking on God can be. I realise I'm more like a runner who nips around the block does a couple of stretches and then is done for the day. And that, I fear, is a sign of my unrecognised obsession with the things that are seen. I'd rather "achieve" something than really understand God. But if Paul is right - if the treasure really lies within and if deep thinking really leads to robust, rich and fruitful action - then even to mull on God's word for extended periods is an act of faith in the value of the unseen. Choosing to read through the New Testament in a Year, doing it slowly, spending time in the day regurgitating the verses - this is a mighty act of faith which God will repay when we meet him on That Day.

QUESTION FOR REFLECTION

What unseen things is Jesus doing in your life?

📖 2 CORINTHIANS 6

Despite all the pain, misunderstanding and rejection Paul received, he still opened his heart wide. This is highly unusual. Having sought to pastor people for over 20 years I find one of the hardest things is getting people to open wide their hearts to others. Whether it is through fear, pain, cynicism or busyness, the "open hearted" believer is a rare one indeed. How wide open is your heart to others? This isn't about having a few good friends or attending certain events. Wide open hearts spend time trying to work out how to put no stumbling blocks in others ways. Wide open hearts speak freely to others out of a deep desire to make them rich in God. Wide open hearts take risks to love others even if the "others" might hurt them quite badly. Wide open hearts are the manifestation of the Spirit making us like Jesus. It was Paul's wide-open heart that facilitated the growth of all the churches all across the Mediterranean. So how did Paul do it? How could he look at a prancing Corinthian who had stabbed him in the back and still choose to open wide his heart to him? As with everything in Paul, it springs out of his calling. For Paul, opening wide his heart is an act of obedience. If he doesn't do it his ministry will be discredited. If he doesn't open wide his heart to the church he denies that now is the time of God's favour. In theological language, Paul's missiology overflowed from his ecclesiology which overflowed from his eschatology. Like with a pyramid of champagne glasses the present experience of abundant grace caused Paul to see that God's future creation was cascading into history, and this present-world grace was now cascading into the church, making it a colony of God's new creation. And this understanding meant Paul's glass overflowed with a wide open heart spilling grace into glass upon glass of Corinthians and Ephesians and Galatians and the like. Paul had to love people because that is what New Creation people do. As temples of the living God, as people living in the favour of God we are yoked to love in every environment, no matter how adverse. Love is holiness made perfect in relationship. So let's ask Holy Spirit to open wide our hearts. Let's push into risk-taking devotion to the people of God.

QUESTION FOR REFLECTION

What would it look like for you today to open wide your heart to others?

📖 2 CORINTHIANS 7

Godly sorrow and worldly sorrow look very similar to each other. One is like a pat on the belly, the other like a punch in the gut. Strangely enough, whether the sorrow is a pat or a punch is down to the person feeling the sorrow, not the one who causes it. Let's imagine you tell me my writing on these passages is superficial and boring. That would hurt me. I've put a lot of effort into these things. I'd feel harassed on the outside and fearful within. I'd feel sorrow. Then in my sorrow I turn to God, seeking his affirmation and care. I also submit my writing to trusted friends, asking them to tell me if your comments hold truth. Assuming I stay in a place of Godly sorrow I will be open to what I hear. Either my writing will improve or I'll realise you are right and that God has other things for me to do. Due to the godliness of my sorrow, your foul and vicious statement (how could you have said such a thing?!) is actually used by the Lord to bring more Kingdom into this world. Now imagine I responded to your statement with worldly sorrow. I'd also start by feeling hurt. I'd also start by feeling harassed on the outside and fearful within. But then, instead of running to the God of all comfort, instead of taking it to trusted friends, I decide to stew on your judgement. Depending on my personality I might feel anger and get bitter or feel crushed and get depressed. Either way I will probably reduce the effort I put into my writing. Almost certainly your comment will have worsened our relationship (I won't be asking you for your foul and vicious opinions any time soon). My response to your statement brings a bit of relational death into our lives. And so, to know the difference between godly sorrow and worldly sorrow is incredibly equipping. A community with a few people who practise godly sorrow is infinitely more healthy than one full of worldly sorrow people. Families with parents who practise godly sorrow can normally cope with most things. Even the harshest response can be an opportunity for growth. Understanding godly sorrow also helps us when we need to confront someone else over some of their stuff. Without giving us licence to be cruel we can know that a wound from a friend can actually be good. If we can help people respond with godly sorrow to our rebuke then we can actually be leading them into life and peace.

QUESTION FOR REFLECTION

When you feel sorrow do you a) try to ignore it and just move on, b) stew on it in yourself or c) process it with God in prayer, leading to growth and Kingdom Come?

📖 2 CORINTHIANS 8

He smashes up our vision of charity. Charity is me giving some of my stuff to someone else in order to help them out. Charity is a good thing. But Paul smashes it up. He does it in two ways. Firstly he tells us our stuff isn't "ours" like we think it is. We haven't truly earned anything. Not our salary. Not any comfort. Not any food or clothes or shelter. All we have has been given to us through the sacrificial act of Jesus. He became poor so that through his poverty we could become rich. This is quite humbling for someone like me - and I guess you - sat under a roof, looking at a screen, having eaten some breakfast this morning, forgiven, embraced, promised all things as my future inheritance. Why has Jesus been so generous to me? When I think about it like this, none of this stuff feels like I can quite call it "mine" any more. I feel slightly embarrassed to have such plenty. And then the second thing Paul does is quote a verse from Exodus. This verse is massive. Paul believes the modus operandi of all the scattered church of Jesus in the world is the same as the modus operandi of the twelve tribes gathered in the wilderness before Moses. Despite our geographical separation we are united as members of the tribe of God. And the riches we have received from God are like manna from heaven - given to us collectively to get us collectively through today. Gulp. We must be careful not to take this too far - I don't think Paul is advocating communism or the abandonment of all savings accounts - but what Paul is saying is that a christian in rural Tanzania or a saint in northern China should be able to depend on having enough daily bread. They should be able to depend on us - as their brothers and sisters - to make sure they have enough daily bread. For us to share some of the manna we collected with them is considered a privilege; as the will of God, as an act of divine grace. Giving to them isn't charity; it is feeding the family, it is passing round the plates at the dinner table. I must admit my stomach knots every time I read this chapter. I feel a conviction from God to be more intentionally generous. Is it even generous, if it's not mine in the first place?? Whatever words we use, the call to action is clear; to push into a life of holding our possessions lightly and to give more stuff to those who are in need.

QUESTION FOR REFLECTION

How might Jesus be asking you to show your solidarity with his global people who are in great need?

📖 2 CORINTHIANS 9

Like the football coach who calls you over to him when you missed the goal, Paul keeps on preaching about giving. You thought the general feedback was enough but no, Paul wants to "get into it some more" with a further head to head. He's an insatiable preacher and don't you love him for it? He keeps on pushing us towards the super-generous God. Paul is determined you see the One who is able to make all grace abound to you so that in all things at all times you will abound in indescribable, surpassing riches of grace. Your cheerful generosity unplugs the bung, unclogs the pipe of God's favour on you. If we give a lot to God we get abundantly more from him. For much of my life I've wanted to believe that truth with a pinch of salt. I've wanted to signal my theological virtue by quickly adding "of course this doesn't mean we should believe the 'prosperity gospel'". I've been like the striker being told he can score huge numbers of goals who nods in agreement while listing all the reasons that won't be true. For once I'm trying just to receive the word as it is. To soak up the deep affection God has for me. To embrace the lavish generosity of his goodness and the abundant capability of his provision. I'm not doing this so that I can become filthy rich. I'm not doing this so that I get more for me. But I've come to realise that my hesitation to believe God's goodness has actually caused me to miss many goals. And the whole team benefits when people score goals. Our God has already gone far beyond what is reasonable in his kindness towards us. Our God is unchanging in his affections and abounding in his kindness. Why can't we just lean on that for a little bit? Paul leant on that a whole lot. Without a caveat or a clarifying comment Paul heaps hyperbole on hyperbole about how much God wants to give us. As we choose to be like our generous God he opens wider the door of his generosity to us. A virtuous circle begins. We give and he gives. We rejoice in giving to him and he rejoices in giving to us. It sounds too good to be true and yet saint after saint has sworn it to be true. And, if I'm honest, I think I'd rather get slightly burned in trying it out than stay nice and safe and score no goals. Our coach is calling us into more. Why don't we trust him and become more generous than we dare? Let's become staggeringly generous, just like our God was in Jesus.

QUESTION FOR REFLECTION

What would it look like for God to make us abound in the indescribable, unsurpassing riches of his grace?

📖 2 CORINTHIANS 10

We all have a sphere of influence given to us by God. Some of us will - like Paul - want to see that sphere enlarged. And that is a good thing. Hmm. That's already got me thinking... But the main thing Paul talks about in this chapter is how he treats those already under his sphere of influence. Parents and grandparents; take note. Teachers, managers and leaders; take note. This chapter lays out for you how God wants you to act towards those under your care. If Paul's missionary journeys had taken him to Rwanda, he would have talked about gorillas. God has made him - and you and I - like spiritual gorillas. We are stacked. We carry immense bulk in the heavenlies. The power in us and given to us could be staggeringly destructive or astonishingly constructive. I just don't think I've engaged sufficiently with this idea. To my shame I realise that I've continually underplayed the authority Jesus has given me. I've been like a gorilla asserting I'm a lemur. Let's not do that any more. Instead let's go and be a gorilla in our jobs, our homes and our communities. But - and this is a silverback-sized "but" - let's do it with gentleness. Let's do it to build up not to tear down. Let's do it not as the world does it but with the meekness of Jesus. Let's protect the field assigned to us by speaking up when we spot bad thinking. If you see someone believing wrong things or making stupid decisions, don't just mutter to yourself. Don't presume you must be seeing it wrong or have insufficient insight. Instead, in love and utter gentleness, step into the situation. Use your heavenly bulk. Trust in the wisdom God has given you. Prayer is massive in this regard. Soak your protective work over others in prayer. When appropriate, step into the situation and gently raise your concern. Even better, when you can, suggest that you pray together. Then stretch out your hand and invite the Spirit to move. Words of prayer were how Jesus exerted so much of his authority. When you fall to your knees or lay a hand on a friend your feeble arm becomes like a gorilla's fist. It has astonishing power to build people up and to set them free.

QUESTION FOR REFLECTION

How much of your God-given authority will you use to build up others today?

📖 2 CORINTHIANS 11

Sometimes it is necessary to "up the ante" in our relationships. Occasionally strong confrontation is essential for people's wellbeing. Knowing how and when to do this is one of the biggest challenges in life. Marriage counsellors see poor conflict management as a huge cause in relational breakdown. Management consultants see poor conflict management as a huge cause of workplace troubles. Pastors see poor conflict management as a huge cause of spiritual shrivelling. Do you know how to do confrontation well? Here are some tips from Paul. Firstly Paul steps back for the very specific complaint to explain his commitment to the relationship and his overall motive for raising the issue. I don't know about you but if someone stresses their care for me and their desire to see me do well I am much more open to what they will say. A statement of commitment in the midst of an argument is like a spray of air freshener in a room with a wet dog. "I am jealous for you… God knows I love you". Ahh! What a wonderful whiff. Let's tell people we love them more. Let's tell people that we are for them. After the statement of commitment Paul lays out in quite emotional language the specific nature of his complaint. He makes himself vulnerable by stressing his fears for the Corinthians and telling them what he wants them to change. When the Corinthians have read this letter they could be in no doubt what the confrontation was about. Paul made it clear for them. As hard as it might be for us to really expose ourselves to people - to really state our fear of where we think their actions are leading - it is essential for us to do so. When we equip them with clarity we enable them to consider our perspective and to come back to us in a way that builds up the relationship, even if they disagree. Finally, as believers, we have the third "C" of Christ which we can bring into conflicts. We can embrace the humble manner of Jesus who was willing to look a fool for the sake of others. We stress that we are struggling for the sake of this relationship. We act in faith that just as God honoured Jesus, he will choose to use us when we ask him to use us as we walk in his ways. So there you have it; three tips for doing conflict well; 1) express affection, 2) be clear what you are worried about and 3) ask God to move to strengthen your relationship. If we do conflict like this, it might seem foolish, but it gives God a chance to really move.

QUESTION FOR REFLECTION
How do you currently manage conflict?

📖 2 CORINTHIANS 12

Paul reaches back over his shoulder, brushes his fingertips on his quiver and selects his final arrow. He has been assaulting the posing, self-interested, fleshy manner of doing ministry... and he has nearly killed it off. As he pulls back the bowstring he has whittled everything down to the simplest of choices. Service or employment. Employment is fine in many contexts but not as a mindset about relationships. Employment is based on an exchange of services for goods - I do this and that for you and you give me something or other in return. That is how the super-apostles did their relationships. They visited and vanquished and vied for affection so they could extract value from their "friends". They built relationships so they could use them for their own ends. But that is not the way of Jesus. Jesus approached the little boy not because he wanted his bread and fish but to show the boy how he could be used by God to feed five thousand. Jesus didn't want money from the rich young ruler; he wanted him to be freed from his superficial obsession with wealth. Jesus invested in the disciples for the sake of us all. And so the mark and mindset of Christ-like relationships is service. It is finding people and really committing to their good. It is saying that I will very gladly spend for you everything I have and expend myself as well. It is a dangerous way to live. People let you down. People you have wedded yourself to can hurt you and embarrass you and humble you. To continue in this kind of life you end up prizing things like thorns in the flesh. You begin to treasure things that humble you because you see that God uses humility to keep you in service. It's a weird thing, isn't it? Weakness feels so awkward and discouraging. Popularity and strength feels so wonderful. And yet Paul let's his arrow fly to kill off the 'super-apostles' obsession with strength because when I feel strong I think I deserve stuff. Jesus sent the thorn in the flesh to puncture Paul's pride in his power. Paul let his arrow fly to collapse the Corinthians capacity for conceit. God wants you humble in your relationships; to serve without demanding stuff back. Where are you at with that? What are you treasuring today? Let's pray for Paul's arrow to pierce our hearts as well.

QUESTION FOR REFLECTION

Do you build relationships with people because of what you can get from them or because of what Jesus wants you to give to them?

📖 2 CORINTHIANS 13

The fundamental identity of a Christian is someone who has Christ Jesus in them. We need to pause on this a while. We need to linger on this doctrine. The defining thing about us is not that we go to church. The defining thing about us is not that we try to live in step with the Spirit or to obey the words of God. The defining thing about us is not even that we believe Jesus Christ was God-made-flesh reconciling the world to himself through his death and resurrection. The defining thing about is that Jesus - the one who touched the blind and they saw, the one who preached the best sermon ever given, the one who never sinned, the one who rose powerful and victorious from the grave, the one who is seated at the right hand of the Father, the one who will be crowned eternal King of every star and galaxy and planet in the universe - that He is in us. I can't do the maths for it. I can barely begin to do the theology for it. But I sure as heck need to believe it. Believing it and knowing it would comprehensively change my perspective on life. It would radically overhaul what I think about myself, about what is possible for me, about what the future will hold, about what I can offer to others. The holy grail of the pilgrimage of faith is to get to the place where you know in your knower that King Jesus is in you. If we can grasp that then we will begin to experience all Paul has been seeking to achieve in this letter; we'll be hugely alert to all God is doing in us; we'll embrace our weakness and scorn all pride; we'll open wide ours hearts to others, be willing to confront others and give ourselves to them in love; we will grow in holiness and beauty in God. It all comes down to knowing King Jesus, God-made-flesh, is now dwelling in us. That's why Paul ends this letter with the famous Trinitrarian prayer that some churches have turned into an awkward ice-breaker (if you don't know what I'm talking about, just be grateful for that). If we can just wake up to the Father, the Son and the Holy Spirit, if we can acknowledge them and grow affection for them and abide with them then perfect peace and perfect love will be in our grasp. Let's spend time today forging fellowship with our God.

QUESTION FOR REFLECTION

Resurrected Jesus the King of all the universe lives in you. How do you feel about that?

📖 GALATIANS 1

It says Jesus rescues us from the present evil age. Up front we must acknowledge that our world is still defined by evil. This doesn't mean that there is no good in the world or that the people around us are altogether wicked. Rather it tells us that something ruthlessly sinister is prowling around with evil intent. When we lie awake at night or mull over the murkier parts of the news, we know this in our hearts and we long for an escape. The nature of our escape route is the question of philosophy and religion and the subject of this letter. In it Paul strains every sinew to stress that human answers to this question will never cut the mustard. All we can do is rearrange the furniture on the Titanic. If we want real rescue our only hope is the God who sits outside of this evil age. The central tenet of this letter is that this God has acted in Jesus to offer us rescue; the gospel of Jesus is God's revelation that sets us free. So we just trust in it, right? We just get in the lifeboat of the gospel, right? Well, one of the biggest issues with this present evil age is the cunning of evil. A bit like the triksy ring in the Lord of the Rings, evil whispers suggestions that the gospel is not real Truth. The Galatians had listened. They were almost convinced that Paul's gospel was one that Paul, or some other bloke, had made up to suit their needs. Very similar suggestions are made on social media every single week. The Evil in this Age whispers to us, trying to deconstruct the gospel as if it isn't from God. Huge numbers of "evangelicals" are buying into this deconstruction project. Galatians shows them how to advance. There is little merit in debating the state of the church or scrolling on social media for a voice that you like. Evil is too good at tricking us when we try to do those things. Instead we need to look at history. Look at the evidence of Paul, his life, and how something from outside turned everything upside down. If you are in this place, make history your friend. Go and read a trusted researcher like Tom Wright or Lee Strobel. Or better yet, get along to church to see the gospel of Jesus embodied in normal people. Our God has intervened in our world. He did it supremely through Jesus and he is doing it right now. If we look in the right places, faith in that gospel can set us free.

QUESTION FOR REFLECTION

What is the gospel that you believe? Is it the same one Paul preached?

📖 GALATIANS 2

Paul seems to betray a lack of regard for the other apostles. He roasts Peter in public like a headteacher with a naughty kid, describes the apostles as those who "seemed" to be important and says they added nothing to his message. He probably refused to wear deodorant when they invited him over for tea. You know… just to make a point. It was a slightly awkward truth for me; that Paul seemed so competitive with the other apostles, but now I see it differently. In this chapter Paul is continuing the argument that he began in chapter 1 - that his gospel is not something created by people but revealed by the One God. To really stress that point he has to show that even the most "senior" preachers are still only witnesses to a revelation that they neither crafted nor are at liberty to change. The apostles are simply the messengers of the master. They simply talk about something that was done to them. Understanding this is hugely important if we are going to grow in our faith. Very many Christians live as if the gospel is a hype-message to help them live better lives. They find the preacher with the best sneakers and the worship band with the hippest haircuts and they simply suck up the succulence that slips from their lips. But the outworking of Paul's understanding of the gospel is that the gospel isn't something smart people use to get you to live a certain way. Instead the gospel is news. It is an announcement that God has come close and he is determined to rewrite your life. Paul puts it like this; "I have been crucified with Christ and I no longer live, but Christ lives in me". God has loved you and given himself up for you. God has caused you to hear his message. Now he bids you let him rewrite everything you know. Let him mentor you into living in a totally new way, just like Jesus did. Why? Not because a preacher can put it well. Not because it feels good when you worship but because God himself - the Most Wise God who crafted you and who cares for you - loves you and gave himself up for you and he is asking you to do that today. Will you set aside that grace and follow what the crowd is doing, or will you gain the beauty of being owned and filled by the God of all grace?

QUESTION FOR REFLECTION

Why not take some time tracing how the hand of God has steered you to himself throughout your life?

📖 GALATIANS 3

Like bank robbers planning their career heist, Paul and the Galatians are arguing over how to get what they really want. What is the plan that will yield them the booty? Already this challenges us. Do we know that the booty in life; the satisfaction of all of our desires is only found in the promises of God? Are our hopes fixed on breaking into the right building? Or are we like schoolboy sleuths obsessing over trying to open the safe in the laundrette while the gold repository next door goes unnoticed? The Galatians may have been bewitched about how to get into the vault, but at least they were seeking the right treasure; the Spirit who works miracles among us and gives us the benefits of the promises of God. To access the vault the Galatians believed they had to dress up in a fake guards outfit, dodge the cameras, enter the complex combination and hope they didn't get zapped by the roaming lasers. Paul tells them they are crazy. In dense and difficult language Paul essentially tells them that that method was only necessary when the alarm system was switched on. Jesus- in his cross- disabled the alarm and invited anyone with faith in him to just stroll up to the safe. So we simply access the treasures by faith (trust) in Jesus, not by works (fulfilling the convoluted plan). The Galatians had believed that initially but then, like all of us are prone to do at times, returned to dressing up as fake guards. Not many of us are tempted to return to the Jewish Law, but we are prone to erecting other "necessary methods" for getting access to the safe. We think we need to be a different kind of person, or to have had a different upbringing, or to have been more successful in life. We once again begin to think it is our attributes and effort that enable us to taste the goodness of God. We - like the Galatians - forget that "there is no difference", that we are all heirs according to the promise if we have faith in Jesus Christ. It is all about Jesus Christ and our receiving of his work. I find I struggle to believe God can really be that good. I find I start to be foolish, thinking it must depend on me… But it doesn't. The plan was always that Jesus would unlock the door for us to have our deepest desires satisfied in God. God really is that good. So let's trust in Jesus' work and allow the Spirit to give us the promises of God.

QUESTION FOR REFLECTION

Is your image of God as good and as generous as God really is?

📖 GALATIANS 4

You are no longer a slave but God's child. And since you are his child, God has made you also his heir. Oh wow. This is another fabulous feast about the favour of our Father. And a further revelation of the frequent folly of his flock. At root the problem with the Galatians is that they don't believe what God has told them. The artisan coffee machine has been installed in their kitchen. Their own personal barista would come at the click of a finger and craft them a beverage that is beautifully bespoke. And yet they aren't drinking the coffee. In fact, they are on the phone to Uber eats to order a greasy spoon's "Flat White". One of the greatest issues in the church today and throughout history has been the unwillingness of Christians to actually draw on the bounty that God has made available. They create a whole range of difficult and boring processes to try to achieve what God is more than ready to give them. It could be people who hold back from receiving prayer or people who create theologies about the gifts of the Spirit not being available today. It could be people who don't receive the free forgiveness for their sins or people who turn a blind eye to the beautiful wisdom of the word. Over and again the problem for Christians has been that God has been dwelling in them, the Spirit has been hovering over them, Jesus has been ready and waiting to pour out his grace on them… and they have spent most of their energy getting stressed and anxious about how they can cope with their life. Drink the coffee! Be filled with the Spirit. Get the bread in your head by reading what God said. Do the stuff; and let Christ be formed in you. God is so abundantly good and so abundantly available. He doesn't do everything you want and to engage with God does take effort on your part but God is abundantly good. God is abundantly available. So live like the child of a great Father and the heir of all things.

QUESTION FOR REFLECTION

What would it look like for you to more consciously live as an heir of all that God owns?

📖 GALATIANS 5

He wants them to cut their testicles off. We could dwell on the fruit of the Spirit. We could compare them with the acts of the sinful nature. That would be awesome. That would give us a good boost in the life everlasting. But I'm struck by the fact that Paul wanted them to cut their gonads off. Not the Galatians of course, but the agitators who had led the Galatians astray. It's worth thinking for a moment what Paul was getting so narky about. Paul was hot with rage over the confusion of the church - Paul was freaking out over doctrine. We know Paul well enough by now to realise that he wasn't some dusty academic - what drove him was the planting of churches and the discipleship of people. So when he is getting so eggy about doctrine it must be because he believed it was absolutely critical to the discipleship of the people. Doctrine was fundamentally important to the health of the church because Holy Spirit moves most when his people are in truth. That's not too trendy a thing to say today, but it probably should be. Doctrine matters because it leads to obedience. What we believe about Jesus really matters because it leads us to Jesus. What we believe about the effects of his death and resurrection make a real difference in the real lives of real people. If people get core doctrine wrong they are spiritually castrating themselves. And nobody wants that. So here's to doctrine. Here's to systematic theology and an obsession with the scriptures. Here's to reading the bible day in day out and revelling in the saving work of Jesus Christ. Not because we want to be able to pass theology tests but because we want to live well. We want to have a correct faith that really can express itself in love. We want to be able to stand firm and not get tied up again in slavery. We want lives overflowing with the fruit of the Spirit of truth. And we want that for the people around us as well. So here's to doctrine. And if anyone starts to preach heresy; well, I'll bring my knife if you will…

QUESTION FOR REFLECTION

Which truth about God most motivates you to live for him?

📖 GALATIANS 6

We get to the end of the letter and find the punch and stroke of Paul's conclusion. We are a new creation, we've started again at Calvary and have already received the most sublime and powerful promises. We live in freedom and love and deep communion with our God. Oh, that feels good. It's like a soothing shoulder stroke while I'm sniffing smelling salts. I can never get tired of those truths. Then comes the punch. We should not be deceived; we will reap what we sow. If we want to grow we must sow. We must sow towards carrying our own burdens and helping others carry theirs. We must sow towards doing good to all people. Even the annoying ones. We must not grow weary of doing what is good. Why? Well there are two reasons here; firstly it is because we ourselves grow in God and towards God when we begin to act like God. God wants us to learn to act like his heirs and co-regents. God wants us to practice what we will practise for all of eternity. We live out now the loving rule of the New Creation that has already been born in us. If you want to grow you must sow. You can't just read the bible and listen to a bit of worship and think you will grow in God. You must roll up your sleeves and really love the others at church. And the second reason is that God cares for the people we are loving. God loves dysfunctional, troubled people and he wants to use us to lift the burdens off their backs. God wants to see grumpy people become more joyful and lazy people become more productive. And the way that happens is through people loving them and helping them and showing them the way to sow to the Spirit and to put to death the deeds of the flesh. The freedom we have is a freedom to help the oppressed and the constrained become fully human again... And yet we (figuratively speaking) all know that we write with large letters; we are like newly born children playing at being kings. And so we know that if people don't listen to us we don't have to feel guilty or think we've done wrong. We will do as much good as we are able, but we won't boast about ourselves, or try to control others, nor make this about us at all. Instead we walk out of this book rejoicing in our freedom and praying grace upon one another as we all boast in Jesus Christ.

QUESTION FOR REFLECTION

What really struck you about the gospel that Paul preached?

📖 EPHESIANS 1

This is a stonking book. While Galatians hammered in on Jesus being the only one to guarantee our freedom now, Ephesians sticks its finger under our chin and tilts our face up higher. We gaze in wonder at our future inheritance and the glorious majesty of the heavenly realms. In that celestial view we discern the vocation for the church right now. We start by being reminded that these heavenly realms are not just a future destination - they have always existed - while Julius was Caesar, while dinosaurs ate cave men and even when wooden church pews were a newfangled craze. And we find that our names have been written there - in those glorious realms - since before the dawn of time. These heavenly realms don't quite sit in parallel to our realm but engulf it and sit over it, always real, always majestic, always rumbling and effervescing with the glorious promise of hope. These heavenly realms have always been fingerprinting the world. But there will be a day - when the times have reached fulfilment - when the heavenly and the earthly will completely become one, under the headship of Christ. That is when our calling - and the creation's calling - will be "filled up"; will have done all it is meant to do. On that day we will become staggeringly holy. On that day we will be completely blameless in His sight and in the sight of all mankind. On that day every nugget and ruffle of creation will be fully and utterly caught up into perfection, into faultless praise of the great King who made it and perfects it and satisfies it in every imaginable way. And we have a foretaste of this day sitting within us now. The Spirit is a deposit paid to us on the point of faith. He is a portion of that future wonder that we can enjoy and experience and be reassured by right now. The Spirit brings that staggering holiness, that unimaginable power and shocking joy and injects it into our current reality. So next time we pray "Come Holy Spirit", let's remember who we are talking to. Before we utter those precious, life-shifting words, let's take a moment to stretch wide our expectations. and ready ourselves to taste hope. For when the Spirit comes He fills us with God's fullness and He does it in every way.

QUESTION FOR REFLECTION

How big is your vision of the vocation of God's church?

📖 EPHESIANS 2

Does your life have a point? Aside from moment to moment virtues of putting food on the table, doing a good job at work and caring for the people around you, is there a bigger narrative and purpose over your life? My heart is desperate for such a purpose - to feel like I haven't wasted this life. Sociologists say our society is increasingly driven by a similar yearning. Even the most godless of people feel a stirring in their stomach to seek justice on this earth. Here we see the source of that longing; it is God. God has created each of us to play our part in his great uniting purpose for this world. He has crafted us like a cog in an engine to purr and spin in harmony and productivity with others. And he whispers this to us even when we are enemies of his being. And so, Paul says, when we have been awakened to our God, when his grace has forgiven us and resuscitated us and placed us on his throne, then we should go the whole hog and let his grace finish its task. The point of our salvation wasn't just to forgive us of our sin but to fulfil the longing of our souls. The purpose of God's work in our lives wasn't just that we should know Him but that we should be fitted together with his people as a well-oiled cog in the engine of God's plans. Together with others we become a productive party of his presence; a grace-made gathering of gladness for one another and the world. The church - made in grace - fulfils the Ezekiel vision of a new temple, filled with the Presence, from where justice and healing flow like a river to the wounded in the nations. So, does it? Do we allow God's grace to go all the way in us? Are we just a person of God or have we become God's people with God doing God's works in the world? This happens when we don't just "attend church" nor even just be "part of a church" but by seeing ourselves, and all other believers, as church. We become church. And we know church is the place where God lives. And we know church is where God's works are done. And so we become an active, harmonious missional church flowing His presence into all of the land. This might feel a long way from our current reality. But what's to stop us stepping into this invitation? What's to prevent us letting grace finish its task in us? Let's pray for God to renew our minds and make us church today.

QUESTION FOR REFLECTION

Are you a Spirit-filled productive party of God's presence?

📖 EPHESIANS 3

For this reason I kneel... I wonder what makes you kneel? What stirs you enough to get you off your natural posture and into a position of pleading? I fear not enough has done so for me. Apathy has been a powerful force in my life. But I'm stirred - in a good way - by our culture. Taking a knee has become quite a thing recently and it has a thoroughly biblical precedent. Taking a knee shows that neither anger nor anxiety will be the primary outworking of my pain and passion; taking a knee is an act of humility and determination. So I want to take a knee much more. I hope you do too? When we do so let's make sure we are kneeling before the right Master. Paul kneeled before the Father. He knew he was kneeling before the one who loved him and was listening to him. Our Father is for us. If we remember that up front it helps us pray effective prayers. And not only so. Let's also remember the ginormous, reverberating, magnificence of that love. These verses about how wide and long and high and deep is the love of God could feel like "old news" if we have heard them many times. But if we pause and intentionally remind ourselves of them when we pray the Holy Spirit will make them real to us and the truth of them will affect us over and again. And then - in case we think the one before we kneel is just a big softie - we would do well to fill our lungs, stretch wide our eyes and consider the uncontainable capacity of our compassionate creator. He can do immeasurably more than anything we could mumble as we kneel before his love. And so, well set, in a position of humility and determination, before the mind-bendingly kind and capable one... we are ready. And then what do we pray? Well, the joy of our freedom before God is that we can pray whatever we want. But the prayers that he really loves are prayers for his Church. Not just for our "church" - those we already know and love and do life with, but for His Church of all ages and all nations, some already called in and some yet to be called in. And he loves prayers for his fullness to fill us all in every way because that is his plan that he made visible in Christ. And that is his plan that he will bring to fulfilment in the end. And when we pray into God's plans, we agree with our great God and we open wide the door for him to do more than we could ever imagine.

QUESTION FOR REFLECTION

Do you care enough about God's church to kneel for it?

📖 EPHESIANS 4

I can't remember the last time I urged someone to do something. Maybe it was when I urged my wife to buy me more chocolate. We don't tend to go in for 'urging' other people to do things - let alone something as potentially guilt-inducing as urging someone to live a life worthy of their calling. What could have possessed Paul to do it? I think that there are two main pillars undergirding this urge. The first pillar is a real desire for God to be given glory. Paul seems to have been far more obsessed with that than any person I have ever met. Paul was constantly driven forward by a desire to see Jesus acknowledged as the boss in the church right now. Paul wanted the future supremacy of Jesus to be acknowledged by all the church in all their lives all the time and Paul pursued this above everything else. I so much desire to emulate him in this. The second pillar undergirding Paul's urging is a near-unlimited expectation of what God can do through people. His litmus test of success in the Christian life was not clinging on until the day you die. Paul didn't think the management of a bit of sin and the giving of a bit of time and money was the highest peak of the Christian's walk. He actually believed - nay expected - the rank and file to be filled with the whole measure of the fullness of Jesus. Paul operated on the assumption that every half-wit and rogue who came to his churches would one day be living their lives as if they were Jesus. He believed that through the power of God and the work of his church all of us could become fully mature, beautifully holy, staggeringly powerful, overwhelmingly loving, changers of the world. Paul's vision for people was immense because his vision of God was immense. If we could only get half way towards emulating Paul in this it would have catastrophic consequences for the mundane and ordinary existence that many of us call Christianity. If we could emulate Paul in his zeal for God's glory and in his vision for people then we would really see what it is like to live in unity and live well. I urge you to start praying for this vision to fill our minds and our church.

QUESTION FOR REFLECTION

If God answered all of your prayers and desires for other people, how much would it really change the world? How could you expand your vision of what you pray into others lives?

📖 EPHESIANS 5

My brother used to speak to me with psalms, hymns and spiritual songs. I wanted to smash his face in. I suspect we both needed to be filled with the Spirit. But, thinking back, I realise that he was doing something really wonderful and revolutionary; he was seeking to stretch his faith-growing routine beyond a 90 minute slot on a Sunday. For too long my view of christian practice was restricted to Sunday mornings and then - when I felt really keen - a bible study "quiet time" at some unearthly hour of the morning. If we are to truly be filled with all the fulness of Jesus and to live up to this staggering vocation of seeing all things united under his lordship then we must find more life-giving rhythms that draw the supremacy of Jesus all across our lives, all through the week. In the Vineyard we know that the Holy Spirit is utterly foundational for this. We must be filled with the Spirit. Stop reading this right now. Ask again for Holy Spirit to fill you. Ask not just that you have a quick quiver in your liver or even begin to shaker like a Quaker. Instead ask Holy Spirit to grip you and mould you and remain upon you every second of this day. You collaborate in Spirit's work in you by speaking words of worship and pursuing paths towards purity. The place to start is the home. So let's get real. Filling your mind with some stuff, choosing to speak out other stuff is foolish, it is unwise; it will leave you half asleep. What you watch and fill your mind with forms who you are. A habit of listening to worship at home will help cure an addiction to pornography, or lust, or an awkwardness in romantic relationships. A daily dose of the peace-loving Word of God will make you less prone to anger. Silence and stillness will undercut your greed. If you are struggling in your marriage, or just want a better marriage, or you are struggling as a parent.. don't give up. Jesus' fullness can fill up anything you lack. But you don't get there by focusing on what your spouse (or kid) is doing wrong. Instead, simply establish rhythms of grace that sprinkle the mystery of the Messiah into the murkiness of the marriage. Find regular, repeated ways to enable those around you to hear of the love Jesus has for them and for the hope they can have for their lives. Prioritise practices that enable your loved ones to be filled with the Spirit. Some effort is required to do this. It won't always be easy. But the payoff is delicious and Holy Spirit does most of the work. So why don't you establish some new habits today? They will wake you up to all that is good, and drench your life in Jesus' love.

QUESTION FOR REFLECTION

What habits do you have in your home?

📖 EPHESIANS 6

Like an American football team "embracing the process" that leads to excellence, Paul has spent this letter advocating for the excellence of the imitation of God. We can become a productive party of God's presence, a grace-made gathering of his gladness. We just need to embrace the process of lifting our eyes to him, taking the knee in prayer and adopting rhythms of grace. The overcomplication of the spiritual life - the cluttering of our calling - is something that baffles me. There are a few niggles and nuances along the way but the thrust of the process is clear and clean; see how astonishingly great God is, ask him to change us and then repeatedly do things that help that occur. Then you will be strong in the Lord. Having laid out the process with inspiration and urging, only now does Paul bring in talk of match-day. A day of opposition and evil will come. And when it comes, just trust the process. To "stand" is the defining verb of our battle. Standing doesn't mean being passive. Standing means trusting the process- standing means to lean back with confidence on the grace that has already worked in you. Standing means to trust that the measure of God is already in your midst. Pretty much all of the armour metaphors used refer to this one simple truth - God is astonishingly great, he has helped us and he is with us right now. That is the truth around your waist, that is the righteousness on your chest, that is the gospel on your feet and the salvation on your head. In Kids Church we make the kids act out all these things like they are separate pieces, each of which could fall off. But they are really one; the simple, freeing truth that our God is a great coach. Our God has trained us well enough to cope with this foe. Our God has put all the components we need in us and we just need to trust in the process. And so that brings us back to prayer. Prayer is the mighty act of advance in the faith. We pray for the saints to trust their God and to do as they should. Prayer really makes that more likely. And so I finish this book once again wanting to pray some more. I want to pray more for my church and more for my friends. For prayer is the process by which God's fullness flows into his church and makes us the force for his glory that he himself is praying for us to be.

QUESTION FOR REFLECTION

What has struck you most about Paul's immense vision for the church?

📖 PHILIPPIANS 1

For me it is a triple-chocolate muffin or a caramel slice. For Paul it is dying to be with Christ or staying alive in prison. All of us have our little dilemmas about what we would prefer more. But whereas I get a little grumpy if I feel I've made the wrong choice Paul just seems incessantly joyful no matter which way it goes. He is so filled with joy that he doesn't even care that people are preaching Jesus just to give him hassle - "what does it matter?" he asks. Is that a cracking attitude or what? I'd love to see more of that joy-filled laid-backness in my life and in the church. Not a laid-backness about seeing the kingdom advancing - Paul was always praying for that, he was longing for that, he was rejoicing in that and eagerly expecting that. I'd love to see a laid-backness about what troubles or stresses come our way. "So I'm in prison today - big whoop, at least it means the guards get to hear about Jesus". "So I'm in hospital for a few days, well that's a great chance to get to testify to some other patients". "So things are a bit quiet at work at the moment - what a wonderful opportunity to spend some more time in prayer". "So a bloke is giving me a really hard time - I'm chilled out about it - it gives me a chance to show grace and to learn to forgive". This kind of laid-backness can only be fostered in Jesus, it can only be found through embracing his perspective on our future and our past. Jesus feels affection for me. Jesus died for me and rose from the dead and he's told me I'll do the same. If we think about it, what else can really matter after that? If death is promotion and life in the body is guaranteed fruitfulness then everything else is incidental. Isn't it? I'd love to be the one believer in ten thousand who really lives like that is true. I'd love to be "That Guy" who is so incessantly, irrepressibly joyful that nothing can shift me away from giving thanks. So I'll keep reading Paul's letters and keep fixing my eyes on Jesus; the one who sparks more joy than any caramel slice.

QUESTION FOR REFLECTION

Do you know the joyful contentment that Jesus is offering you?

📖 PHILIPPIANS 2

It is the second humbling that is the real challenge. One level of humbling ourselves is bad enough. The second level is what really tests our resolve. Jesus humbled himself once by not clinging onto his equality with God but choosing instead to become a human. This involved a huge sacrifice of his eternal authority. It involved him giving up unbroken intimacy with the Father and the untold riches of the heavenly realms. Jesus had the perfect life but he chose to humble himself and give it up to become a human. That was the first humbling. Then, as a human, he chose not to use his unmatched intellect or his dynamic charisma to build his own career. He chose not to see his unparalleled resources as things for his own benefit. He resisted the urge to use his breath-taking skills to get a wife, a life and free himself from strife. No, he chose to humble himself a second time choosing to die a reject's death watched by only a handful of people outside of a city where thousands were thinking about something completely different. This second humbling puts my jaw on the floor. This second humbling shows me that my attitude is so very far from being like that of Jesus Christ. If I ever choose to humble myself once I tend to feel a bit smug and thank God for my virtue. Have I even considered humbling myself twice?? Going beyond just giving stuff up but really choosing to do what is best for others even if they don't notice it and I get no recognition?? I really want to be able to do it but it just seems so hard. I take comfort from the fact that the Philippians were no better than me and yet Paul believed they could do it. I can indeed find encouragement from the fact that I have now been united with Christ. If I place myself before him with "fear and trembling" then he can help me. Nothing is impossible with God. I can do all things through Christ who strengthens me. I can find joy and gladness and live a real life of pure love when I will myself to act in solidarity with the Son.

QUESTION FOR REFLECTION

What would double humility look like in your life?

📖 PHILIPPIANS 3

It's like a huge athletics centre racked with state-of-the-art equipment and every contraption for helping you reach your peak. Philippians 3 is a spiritual mega-gym. It is stacked up with line upon line of muscle-enhancing concepts. If you want to be spiritually mature then Philippians 3 is a room you should live in. That's right. Spiritual maturity doesn't come through having been a Christian a long time. Spiritual maturity doesn't come through consuming a lot of worship or listening to a lot of talks. Spiritual maturity comes from living the word. It comes from taking the bible's view on life. It comes from wanting to know Christ, from working hard to know Christ, from choosing to see everything else as crud except the joy of knowing Christ. Spiritual maturity comes through giving our own achievements - or lack of them - or heritage - or lack of it - no regard. It comes from forgetting all that stuff and instead choosing to strain towards what God has in store for us. The clear practical step in all of this is for us to check our role-models. Who are the people you aspire to be like? Who are the voices you value and the lifestyles you leer at? Some of them will be dogs. They will look cute and attractive and then tear at your flesh. Watch out for the ones whose god is their stomach. Don't just follow anyone. Don't just listen to anyone. Watch out for the dogs. Instead actively pursue the mature in Christ. Follow the example of those whose extended patterns show they really know Jesus. Press forward to get to know those who abound in joy in Jesus, who model the humility of Jesus, who really walk with their God. And don't just listen to their words; live according to their patterns. Grasp hold of all Jesus wants you to be by appenticing yourself to those who have apprenticed themselves to him. That is a great way to grow in maturity. That is a great way to live up to what we have already attained.

QUESTION FOR REFLECTION

Who are your role models? Are they people who abound in the joy and humility of Jesus?

📖 PHILIPPIANS 4

Another treasury. Another chapter we could explore for months and still have only just begun. I'm tempted to focus on the repeated image of our lives being fragrant offerings to God - it is definitely something I need to press into, I think it is a defining theme in Philippians. But instead I just want to think about 'rejoice'. I will say it again: "rejoice" (I like the way Paul does that so I thought I'd copy it - it is about the closest I'll ever get to being apostolic). For all the straining and pressing and doing Paul has been on about you could start to think of him as just a little bit earnest. Maybe he starts to seem a bit like that annoying boy at school who, when answering questions, put his hand up so hard that he lifted himself off his chair. And Paul certainly went the whole hog for Jesus. But an over-earnest bloke was not who he was. He was incredibly enabling of others. He wasn't trying to prove himself as better than others. He was trying to help others do better in life. He rejoiced in what others could do well. He encouraged them to do the same. He encouraged people to focus on the good and the excellent. He called people to copy him and to emulate his pursuit of God and at the same time to laugh and to celebrate and to gaze in wonder at great stuff. Paul wanted to spread joy, deep joy, lasting joy in the Lord. Paul wanted those things because that is what Jesus wanted for us. That is what Jesus still wants for us. He wants to give you the secret of being content in all circumstances. He wants to give you his fountain of joy that gives you strength in your troubles. Jesus wants to meet all your needs according to his glorious riches so you feel amply supplied even when no one shares a single thing with you. Jesus wants you to experience so much of his grace and his peace that you cry "ah, what does it matter!" no matter what happens. So Jesus is calling you to meet him in prayer. And to meet him in thanksgiving. And to meet him in his rejoicing. So let's respond to that call and actually choose to meet with Jesus. If you make that your life goal, you will find not only joy and peace but also the riches of the glory of the grace of Jesus Christ.

QUESTION FOR REFLECTION

Who and what is good and praiseworthy in your life? How could you increasingly thank God for those people and things?

📖 COLOSSIANS 1

Think of it like trying to build a tower with a deck of playing cards and a big concrete block. Unless you put the concrete block on the bottom, a lot of things are going to break. To realise that is wisdom and understanding. For much of history the problem of humanity was that they couldn't move the concrete block, nor even touch it and it wasn't in the right place or at the right angle for them to build. They were constrained and condemned to towers that break or fall or fail. Then Jesus came along. Magnificent Jesus. Concrete Block Jesus who had promenades-worth of concrete in him, and yet could prance like a pony and tickle children under the chin. Jesus changed everything. Now, through Jesus, people could build a tower that would not break. Wisdom could be lived if cards were stacked on Christ. In these glorious verses Paul waxes lyrical about the monstrous magnitude of Jesus; Jesus is the image of the invisible God, the firstborn over all creation, all things were created by him and for him. Just in case any of the Colossians had forgotten; just in case we had forgotten; Paul reminds us all that Jesus is frightfully massive - the concrete block of all of life. And in these glorious verses Paul giggles gleefully about the generous graciousness of our self-giving God; he has rescued us, he was pleased to bring us into his friendship, he has put Christ in you, you now have the hope of glory. And so we come out of this chapter wooed towards wisdom. We come out of this passage - if we have skimmed through it sufficiently slowly - wanting to build our tower of cards upon the concrete block of Christ. The short-hand summary of such a life is this; love. Fruit-bearing. God-pleasing. Progressing towards perfection. Love for all the saints and love for God is the pinnacle of wisdom, it is the glorious riches of his grace. So will you pray for more love-inducing wisdom into your life today? Will you labour for love? Will you lean into love defined by and built upon Supreme Jesus; the Royal revelation of the fullness of wisdom of our self-giving God?

QUESTION FOR REFLECTION

Are you trying to fit Jesus into your life or are Jesus' personality and priorities what define all you are and seek to be?

📖 COLOSSIANS 2

When you live rooted upon Jesus you have all you need to get more of God. And more than that; building your life on Jesus gives you the power to live the wisdom that all of us seek. And yet maybe you, like me, have those agonised nights when you struggle to believe that what you have is "really it"? The Colossians seem to have done this. Wracked with insecurity the Colossians began to doubt that their experience of Jesus was up to the task. So they started trying to do "serious" and "spiritual" things to achieve the upgrade they desired. They followed their culture's idea of "spirituality"; prescribing severe treatment of the body and lots of restrictive rules as the way to really being fulfilled. This was a very un-Jesus-like method of getting more of God. While I don't suppose many of us have bought into that particular heresy today, I recognise how quickly we can adopt our culture's solutions for trying to do well in life or to grow in God. Paul is clear; the route to getting in life is the root of Christ. If we want to grow we should fix our eyes on him. We should want to know him so that we can become like him. He is the embodiment of our best life - of humanity 2.0. Don't just grab any clever sounding soundbite by a social-media savvy sage. Ask the question - is this something Jesus did? Is the action they are recommending an action Jesus took? The truth is that in our world right now there are so many podcasts and preachers, books and articles that beckon us into more. These can be inspiring and helpful prompts. Let them spark your hunger. But don't follow them just because they resonate with you. Don't start doing something just because it sounds virtuous. The majority of voices lack power to get things done. Instead apprentice yourself to Jesus. Continue to live in him by doing the stuff he did. It takes time. It involves moments of doubt. But if we keep on keeping on then we will become glorious illustrations of the redemptive power of our God. When you want to move into "more", it's to Jesus you should go.

QUESTION FOR REFLECTION

What particular part of your life looks most like Jesus?

📖 COLOSSIANS 3

Since we have been raised with Christ.... Hold on a second, let's just take that in. As far as I am aware none of the Colossian church were wrapped in strips of linen and laid in the tomb with Jesus and, as far as I am aware, there was only one bloke in the garden who Mary thought was the gardener. Only Christ was raised, only Christ appeared to the disciples and showed them his wounds. So how can Paul say the Colossians have been raised with Christ and, more than that - how can we read this and take from it that we also have been raised with Christ? One day my grandfather discovered he was at war with Germany. My grandfather didn't declare war and he didn't do anything to bring about the war but he got carried along by the decision of his Prime Minister. One day I was raised with Christ. I didn't beat death and I didn't do anything to bring about my resurrection but I got carried along by the redemptive resurrection of Prime Minister Jesus. Jesus rose from the dead and when I made him my king I became part of this growing band of barbarians, Scythians, slaves and free who have been raised from the dead along with him. This has enormous implications. Just like the "at war" version of my grandfather was different from the "at peace" one - he travelled from Yorkshire to India and from being a gas man to leading a band of men - the "raised" version of you is different from the previous "worldly" version of you. You are now a person defined by love. You are now a version of yourself clothed with compassion and gentleness. You are in India even if you have a Yorkshire pud in your belly and the North Sea still feels like it is tingling your toes. Why not take some time to speak that over yourself? If you are struggling with behaviour, rather than rules and regulations that lack power, remind yourself of who you now are. Imagine yourself full of humility and gratitude and then keep on asking Holy Spirit to help you live that out. You have been raised with Jesus. That is the power in your life. That sets the vision for your life. And your joy really comes when, through the power of the Spirit, you live the raised life in this moment, right now.

QUESTION FOR REFLECTION

How has being raised with Christ changed your life?

📖 COLOSSIANS 4

I'm so grateful for being in a church. I so deeply appreciate the love and care and encouragement that my brothers and sisters minister to me. But there is one thing that others do for me that I think I appreciate more than any other; they pray. When people say they pray for me I want to kiss their knees. They are carving out my future, they are smoothing my ride, they are strengthening me and establishing me. Their kneeling, their bleary-eyed beseeching, their trying to concentrate but getting distracted and trying again helps me bed into wisdom and live the raised life. So when Paul says we should devote ourselves to prayer he is calling us to do a beautiful and powerful thing. Prayer helps our friends. Prayer wafts wisdom over our friends. Prayer wins battles for our friends. If we want to see others do well, if we want to see them grow and prosper and move closer to Jesus then there is really nothing finer and more potent that we can do for them than pray. Of course praying doesn't often feel like that. Praying can often feel like wrestling, as it did for Epaphras. And of course we are talking about Roman wrestling. Roman wrestling wasn't the glamourized, fancy pants, flashing lights, cheering crowd type of wrestling we have today. Roman wrestling involved long periods in contorted positions being almost suffocated by smelly blocks of muscle. That kind of wrestling is very draining and takes significant determination (I'm sure our modern wrestling does too, if we look past the flashy veneer required to make it entertaining). And prayer does often have that difficult, grubby wrestling sort of feel to it. But it is worth it. When we pray for others, we add to the firmness of their stance. When we bring others before God we usher them into maturity and into assurance. Faith is built on prayer. The church is built on prayer. The Kingdom is built on prayer. So I want to pray. I hope you do too.

QUESTION FOR REFLECTION

Who are you wrestling for in prayer?

📖 1 THESSALONIANS 1

If you want to explode your vision of what is possible then digest this; Paul planted the church in Thessalonica in a single month. One month! It can take us that long to order a new PA cable. The staggeringly speedy formation of the church happened because Holy Spirit moved in power. Holy Spirit added conviction to Paul's words and sparked joy in the new believers. But I'm convinced that the effectiveness was also due to Paul's clarity. In these short letters from Paul we find some of his simplest and clearest explanations of our faith; turn from idols to serve the living and true God and wait for his son from heaven. Choose each segment of this glorious sentence and suck up the sustenance it brings. "Turn" - the message is for us to act, to do something different, to press into something. This isn't passive reflection - this is a surge of energy to spark something new. "From idols to serve the true and living God" - this isn't obligation but freedom. The gospel calls us to be free from bondage to fear or misplaced attachment to things that lack power. The gospel works on our inner being; it shows us the inclination of our hearts towards destructive or unsatisfactory stuff. And it enables us to lean instead on the true one, on the one who is always right, always good, always insightful. It bids us to yield to the one who is alive, stewarding and serving all of creation, tinkering and transforming, bending and breathing. The gospel connects us to the empowered, true and beautiful God. "Wait for this Son from heaven". Waiting admits that now is not all there is. Waiting acknowledges the grubby battle in which we now stand… but it does so with sincere hope and joy. Waiting knows that we can rely on another - a much stronger one - for our destiny. Waiting knows that Jesus will come, in his way, when he decides; that he won't leave me hanging like a child forgotten after school. And in that sense I think waiting is probably a way of living - an attitude more than an activity. It is a slant towards reliance on another and grateful expectation of a good thing I could never earn. When the gospel is presented as clearly, and as attractively as that, it's no wonder a church was formed in a month. What might Holy Spirit do through you this month, if you can speak with the clarity of Paul?

QUESTION FOR REFLECTION

Which aspect of Paul's summary of the gospel grabs you the most?

📖 1 THESSALONIANS 2

"You suffered from your own countrymen...". For the last 40 years most of us in the UK haven't suffered much from our own countrymen, unless it has been the ignominy of watching them getting smashed in a penalty shoot-out. This benign incubator for our faith has subtly persuaded many of us that the joy and power of the gospel are best experienced in pleasant places. But it has rarely been so. The New Testament experience shows us that lives filled with the Kingdom and glory of God are most likely to be lived out in environments of strong opposition. And the hardship needn't affect the joy and power in any meaningful way. You can feel hard pressed and overlooked and still abound in all joy and worth. But it doesn't just happen. We do some stuff to make it possible. Paul calls this "stuff" father love and mother love. Showing and receiving both mother love and father love are essential if a church is going to thrive in persecution. Mother love is the coochie coo kind of love that delights in time together. It tickles cheeks and strokes hair. But mother love also works hard to provide; it sacrifices and scrapes things together to nurture and nourish the little cherubs it cares so much about. When you receive mother love you know it; you glow on the inside and you grow in stature. (Just in case you are offended by Paul's gender-defined language, remember Paul himself showed the Thessalonians "mother love", so it isn't something he is saying only women have to do.) And then you also need what Paul calls "father love". This father love isn't so much about physical provision as verbal encouragement and direction. Father love cheers "that's great" and urges you to "keep going". It looks at you, acknowledges your progress and lovingly encourages you what you can become if you keep doing the right stuff. Father love points to the dizzying delight of doing things like the divine and assures you you can achieve it, if you continue to trust in him. Each of us probably leans more naturally towards showing "mother love" or "father love". In Jesus we can grow in the other type as well. And when we do, we can, together become a church truly worthy of our God - thriving, growing and overflowing with joy, even in the midst of hardship and trial.

QUESTION FOR REFLECTION

What kind of love do you show most often? How could you cultivate it and show it even more to Jesus' people?

📖 1 THESSALONIANS 3

What really counts in the faith? What is it that will bring us glory in the presence of Jesus? Paul asked that question a lot. And every time I ask it I find it liberating and inspiring. Because the answer is not how many books we have read or people we have converted or how long our quiet times have been. It is relationships. It is love increasing and overflowing for each other and for everyone else. And that is something all us can do if we lean on the leading of Holy Spirit. What sparks staggering joy in the presence of God is saints we have edged up to and prayed for and put an arm around and spoken words of encouragement to. Blamelessness is being a believer in Jesus who mourns with the mourners and rejoices with the rejoicers and builds up others in the faith. Holiness is hugging and holding fast to others for their growth and their maturity in Jesus. It is house-group and prayer groups and people we have spoken to at coffee on a Sunday. It is quick messages or long listens or agonising alongside and not really knowing what to say. It is bearing with and choosing to forgive and cheering on. It is food together and drink together and sitting and not doing much together. I think you get the point? When Jesus comes back all the work we have done for others in the spiritual realm will suddenly be exposed like UV rays under one of those special glow lamps. And people will walk up to us and say "thank you so much for praying for me that time", "thank you for helping me understand a bit more of who Jesus was", "thank you for challenging me about my addiction and my sin", "thank you for helping me become a Christian". And it will be a source of huge, huge joy for us. We will see the work that the Lord has done through us and it will be like a sparkling crown we place on our heads. Building others up - that's what really counts in the faith so let's devote ourselves to doing it in our town.

QUESTION FOR REFLECTION

Nurturing others often goes unappreciated. How can you keep reminding yourself of its value?

📖 1 THESSALONIANS 4

And so we will be with the Lord for ever. That is a phrase worth repeating over and over and over and over. It was a phrase Paul used to encourage a persecuted church. It is a phrase that encourages any saint in any space who stews on it. Will you stew on it? We will be with Jesus. Forever. The kind one, the wise one, the healer will while away week after week with us as his friends. This hope sets such a liberating context to our lives that I want to tattoo it on my soul. Whatever life looks like now, no matter how beautiful or how savage, it will all fade into nothingness when He comes. And no matter what risk comes off or doesn't come off, no matter what venture triumphs or fails, our future fate is now found with him. That is the pastoral purpose of this powerful passage. Much has been debated about the rapture language of these closing phrases (the word rapture is a translation of "caught up" we see in verse 17). Lots of theologians have written really insightfully on this if you want to explore it further. But don't get distracted by that fairly marginal idea. Focus on the main and plain. Don't miss the centre of the throbbing encouragement that Paul thrusts upon his early churches. All the saints will go marching in and we will be in their number. We will go into the kingdom of Jesus to join him in his flawless eternal paradise. Whether we die or remain alive, whether we are ugly or beautiful, knackered or full of beans we will be swung into his victory parade to dance arm in arm with people from every century and nation and people-group and culture. And he will be over us all and close to us all and fulfilling us all and smiling at us all. Let's encourage each other with this thought. Let's encourage each other with these words; we will be with the Lord forever.

QUESTION FOR REFLECTION

How is your eternal future affecting how you live right now?

📖 1 THESSALONIANS 5

Again we see Paul talking about the return of Jesus and saying "therefore encourage one another". And, if we are honest, we probably want to ask "encourage one another to do what?!" Most answers in evangelicalism have been around encouraging each other to attend church, or to do our quiet times, or to do some evangelism. Paul rarely says such things. Instead his encouragement is much more relational. Or we could say he is much more specific in his call; don't just attend church, respect your leaders and honour them. Don't just show up for services but warn the idle, encourage the timid and help the weak. These calls usher us past activity to attentiveness; we look for how to honour a leader, we try to spot someone in our community who is fearful or weak, we wrestle with how we can helpfully warn the idle. And these things are all worth doing because the King is coming. The King who helped the weak will come and celebrate those who have emulated him. The King who warned the idle will come and congratulate those who emulate him. The King who appointed the elders will be grateful for your desire to honour his choice. And so we are encouraged by his coming. His coming makes small choices especially significant. So let me ask you a question today; lovely person who is reading this passage; are you encouraged today? Discouragement is a toxic trick of the enemy. Are you falling under the spell of his strategies? I've fallen into discouragement so many times. I can flop down crestfallen in so many ways that I can't quite explain. If you are, I say to you be encouraged. Think about Him. Our Coming King. He won't come to chide or to condemn. He is the God of peace. He is faithful to his word and he never flakes out on his flock. He will return suddenly and gloriously, wrapping you up into his majestic beauty and delight. So I pray that this God - our God - will grab hold of your whole spirit, soul and body right now - and he will encourage you and keep you pure and persevering in joy. I pray the grace of God to be upon you today.

QUESTION FOR REFLECTION

Are you encouraged?

📖 2 THESSALONIANS 1

So here is the doctrine of heaven and hell. God will be glorified in his holy people but will punish with everlasting destruction those who do not know God. There are surprisingly few verses in the whole Bible about what happens to those who don't live as if they know God. So it is worth us dwelling on them here, especially as the popular conceptions about heaven and hell are so far from the biblical picture. On the one side is everlasting destruction and a shutting out from the presence of the Lord. There debate over whether the destruction is everlasting in its duration (i.e. people are constantly experiencing destruction) or everlasting in its effect (i.e. it happens in a few moments but can never be overturned - the idea of annihilationism). I currently prefer the latter as I think it makes better sense in the overall sweep of the narrative of the Kingdom and the character of God. But I am conscious that either way, the fate of those who refuse to know God Is Not Good. I find that tricky. I suspect we all should find it emotionally tough. But among that tough emotion I'm determined to do two things; to still commit to understanding exactly what God has said and to find a way to celebrate its goodness; as the just and right actions of a stupendously good and loving God. So what does Paul actually say? Well, the dividing line in eternity is the presence of God. Those who in this life showed they wanted it will be fully in God's glorious presence forever and ever. Those who in this life showed they didn't want it will get what they wanted; eternal separation from the presence of God. (C.S.Lewis has created very helpful images of hell based on this primary concept of the absence of God in his book The Great Divorce). Looking at eternity this way helps us see how wonderfully good this truth is. Delightful juices can surge though our bodies at the achingly beautiful image of what is in store for us who are in Christ. He will come to be glorified among us. Jesus chooses to let us share in the most captivating and soul-soothing worship time that we will ever, ever know. And that will just be the start. Who knows what pleasure-filled stratosphere we will go into from there. And all we have to do to get this is believe the testimony of God's word that the presence of God is the greatest joy we could ever know.

QUESTION FOR REFLECTION

How much does your life testify to your delight in the presence of God?

📖 2 THESSALONIANS 2

Rebellion. The man of lawlessness setting himself up over everything. Counterfeit miracles. We didn't tend to talk or think about these things in the kinds of churches I was in. When someone raised them we gave each other "knowing looks" and quietly reached for the biscuits. But the incredible thing is that Paul had only spent a month with the Thessalonians and this was stuff he had told them about (2:5). The End Times was routine fare for the early church. And so I've been working hard at trying to claim this stuff back from the yelling fringes of Youtube. I wonder if you could do the same? Could we start talking about a coming "Day of the Lord"? Could we discuss - in a nice way that still involves our brains- the "signs of the times". Paul tells us that towards the End the general attitude of "lawlessness" will culminate in a single individual or project which celebrates atheism. This project will achieve such success that it will penetrate even the heart of God's church. Many have identified this movement with a Roman project or the Communist form of government or a particular Papal decree or even wearing masks in church. People have loved to point the finger at a hundred things that other people are doing… But the huge benefit of this passage is how it links lawlessness to the breaking of God's laws that have always been in place. The man of lawlessness isn't so much going to try to make us get a vaccine as try to make us remove God from the scene. Lived idolatry and practical Atheism have always been the scourge of God's people. They are so subtle. We should beware them sneaking into the churches we agree with, not berate the way they are seducing the churches (or people of the world) we don't agree with. Every time we hear reports of such things "out there" we can use them to lean more firmly on God "in here". A general sense of lawlessness needn't cause fear in us. Instead it can cause us to turn to Jesus more, to trust Jesus more and to gather deep encouragement from Jesus some more. If Jesus predicted it then he is not phased by it. He knows what he is doing. And he can give us more than enough strength to stand firm and to keep doing good in every word and in every deed. The encouragement and strength that comes from understanding the times is why Paul preached it even to new believers, and why we should do as well.

QUESTION FOR REFLECTION

When you hear major bad news in the world, how does it affect your relationship with Jesus?

📖 2 THESSALONIANS 3

Paul has waxed lyrical about the majestic riches of the coming kingdom. He has cautioned the church about the signs of the times and chaos that the man of lawlessness wants to cause. He has urged the Thessalonians to encourage one another with the ecstatic glory that is ahead. And then, without any obvious change of gear, he says "settle down and earn the bread you eat". Throughout my life most Christians have been very focused on this "settling down" and "earning the bread". Because of the circles I've been in I've also met a few who have spent their days gazing glassy-eyed at the distant clouds pondering the beautiful perfection of the heavenly realms. But I've not met many - like Paul - who seem to comfortably and easily do both, at least in the Western world. I think that it is because the western view of life is so disenchanted. We see this world as fairly flat, only populated by humans and animals with God, perhaps popping in every now and then. But the Jews and Christians inhabited a densely populated world with spiritual realities being bumped into in every moment in every place. For them, it was totally obvious that the God who made bread and could be encountered through bread would want his people to settle down and earn some bread. For them it was totally obvious that catching a fish or lending money or writing a message would have a profound spiritual aspect to it that would go on for all eternity. Their enhanced awareness of this reality caused them to engage in doing good right now in this world. Paul saw huge value in his canvas business as a beautiful reflection of the beauty of God's Kingdom Come. He wasn't trying to escape for it or apologise for it - he was encouraging others to emulate him in his labour. I wonder if you have a biblical view of your work, of your salary, of your good acts in society? Most of us spend most of our time working and much of what we do there will be reflected in the coming age. We should pray for a spiritual imagination to grasp that. Let's pray that our earning of cash and our late night work efforts become not a distraction from our faith but beautiful embodiments of our hope in the coming age.

QUESTION FOR REFLECTION

Do you understand the immense spiritual significance of your work?

📖 MATTHEW 1

Clearly no-one told Matthew that listening to someone else's family history is less interesting than filling out a passport application. And yet, in it we see the bewildering arc of God's grace, stretching across kings (Solomon) and prostitutes (Tamar), adulterers (David) and asylum seekers (Ruth). On reading this stuff, barely anyone could think they are ineligible to be included in the family and plans of God. And after putting that awesome inclusivity out there, Matthew quite happily switches into one of the most understated paragraphs I have ever read - a virgin to give birth, an angelic appearance and a promise so great the English language can't do it justice. "To save people from their sins" - in six words to define the predicament and remedy for every individual in the whole of history. In six words to sum up the huge imbalance of all Christian faith - that we bring the sin and Jesus brings the salvation. In six words to reassure all struggling believers that they are in the hands of One who has come to rescue them. Now that's a message for our stressed out, lonely, confused world if ever I've heard one. And what does the message invite you to do? To read on. To consider these things and maybe - just maybe - give your whole life to embracing Immanuel.

QUESTION FOR REFLECTION

You have been invited into the ancient, unstoppable arc of God's grace. How is that affecting you?

📖 MATTHEW 2

It seems strange to me that Herod - the Jew - had so much vested interest in finding out who this King of the Jews was but he couldn't even be bothered to head down to Bethlehem to check him out for himself. And it also seems strange that God allowed these very wealthy, very foreign, probable astrologers - the Magi - to be some of the first to be overjoyed and overawed by this new baby king. But I guess that is the way with God - the most unlikely people get to play jubilant parts in His redemption narrative if they will just seek after Him. And those who seem best qualified end up bitterly angry and tragically rejected because of their arrogant complacency towards Jesus. Matthew shows right at the start of this gospel that Jesus runs a dividing line through every community in history... but the dividing line is not between the good and the bad or the qualified and the unqualified or between this race or that race, but between those who are inclined towards the worship of Jesus and those who are inclined towards rejecting him. The good news for you is that if you are reading these notes then you are almost certainly on the 'inclined towards worship' side of the dividing line. Will you stay there? The Magi's journey was neither short nor simple, it wasn't always clear where it was leading but they held the course. Our pursuit of the presence today is similarly grubby and at times down-right baffling. But awe and joy lie at its end. Will you hold the course and make pursuit your priority? Or will you, like Herod, find more important things to do?

QUESTION FOR REFLECTION

How do you feel about the fact that Jesus draws a dividing line right across human societies?

📖 MATTHEW 3

You can just imagine Jesus coming out of the Jordan river, hair dripping wet, white robe clinging to his skin in a few embarrassing places, maybe there was even some algae hanging off his right ear. This was the One who was showing everyone what God had called his people to be. This was the one who had come to fulfil all the promises of the prophets. Many in Israel had turned the 'call of God' into a status symbol. They had become like celebrities flaunting their credentials around. They would never have been seen dead with wet clothes clinging to their buttocks. So many in Israel thought living for God meant impressing others; putting on good show after good show... but never bothering to sort out their hearts. John the Baptiser had slated them for it and, by his baptism at John's hands, Jesus throws all his weight behind John's judgement. As Jesus comes up out of the water he shows that God's real people, God's real hope is not about trying to look good but about raw, honest humanity humbling themselves in a flood of repentance and then calling for the Dove - the Spirt from God - to transform them from the inside out. This is the oxymoron of our faith. If you want to be God-like you need to look like a moron every now and then. The thing we need - the one we need is the Dove who will transform us and empower us, and the Dove only comes after the Flood.

QUESTION FOR REFLECTION

Are you a fool for Christ? Are you willing to humble yourself in repentance; seeking all that God wants you to be?

📖 MATTHEW 4

This is a pretty mega passage. Jesus just won't accept single bible verses as convenient proof texts to get to do what he wants. Instead he chooses to lay his desires aside and submit his way to the prevailing winds of the whole counsel of God. And that is a challenge - to get beyond just snatching at bible verses that seem relevant to our situation and instead letting the Word dwell in our guts and change our whole perspective on the world. To do that takes time and to do that takes effort. To do that involves days reading passages that don't make a whole heap of sense but which we trust somehow will go to work on our innards. If we were just able to do that, if we were just willing to consistently do that then our churches would be very different places. They would be much more joyful places. They would be much more free places. Because if we wrestle with the whole counsel of God then we will allow it to re-work our whole perspective on the world. This fundamental re-working of how we view the world is at the core of what Jesus meant by "Repent, for the kingdom of heaven is near". Repentance is letting the Word shred our self-centred, insecurity-driven approach to life. Gold-plated repentance is letting the Word assault our judgmentalism and savage our pride. Signs and wonders are the Kingdom of God come near. Wow, oh wow, there are so many of them on offer in the Kingdom. But the Kingdom of God come near is much more than that. To acknowledge that the Kingdom of God has come near is to drink deep of the life-giving, hope-creating and freedom-finding Word, letting it dwell in you richly, to strengthen your compassion and assure you of your adoption. Jesus' extraordinary ministry and his astonishing fulfilment of all the hopes of Israel were birthed and suckled and weened on the living word of God. We would be crazy to think that we be close to the kingdom in any other way. We need to get the bread in our head.

QUESTION FOR REFLECTION

Are you just trying to feed on the word or are you really letting it form you?

📖 MATTHEW 5

O the awesomeness of these phrases. I must have read them 20 to 30 times in the last few days and yet every time I feel like I'm getting claxoned in the face by another surprising truth. Jesus calls 'good' a lot of things that I like to keep at arms' length. It says it is a glorious thing to feel the inadequacy of spiritual poverty, to be wracked with the sorrow of mourning, to constantly be feeling like you are wanting and needing more. I don't want any of those things. I want to sit pretty and smile smugly and be patted gently on the shoulder by one man and his dog (if only my dog could pat my shoulder- now that would be a wonderful thing). But Jesus seems to be saying that is not how the kingdom works. The rich and succulent pleasures of the kingdom are reserved for those who have struggled and strained and reached the end of themselves. The Kingdom is for the humble - for those who spend their life on their knees, knowing that their help comes not from themselves but flows from their King. And when the King brings help, he wants to drum the beat. Our King wants us to do what he says. It's actually a bit embarrassing how strong Jesus is on this point. Why is he like this? Isn't he meant to be "LOVE"? Well, Jesus is the lover who knows better than us. He knows what we get wrong and he wants to help us get it right. And so, if we let him actually be our King we discover, perhaps surprisingly, that central to his Kingdom are quality relationships. How we treat those around us really matters to Jesus. Even more than things like reading Christing books and re-posting posts of the latest 'hot' preacher. Many of us could bring far more pleasure to God if we exerted more energy on reconciling ourselves to our family and dreamed more dreams about carrying others' burdens. Keeping oaths isn't sexy. Praying for annoying people isn't glamorous. But these are the places where mourning comes in, where spiritual poverty and purity are forged and where blessing chases us around like a stray dog on heat.

QUESTION FOR REFLECTION

If you obeyed everything Jesus says in the sermon on the mount do you think you would be happy?

📖 MATTHEW 6

This reminds me of the game chubby bunnies - where you have to stuff as many marshmallows in your mouth as you can and then say "chubby bunnies". Jesus has packed as much rip-snorting, life-flipping truth as possible into this ever-so-short sermon and then we, with our souls straining with the effort, try to apply it to our lives without our brains bursting out and sliding onto the floor. Even the greatest minds the world has ever known have found the Sermon on the Mount to exceed their abilities. What chance do we have? And yet I do think that this monstrous and intricate sermon has several fundamental principles which even a child could understand. Jesus seems to be building an argument on four basic convictions: 1) that God is real 2) that God acts as our Father 3) that God sees all we do and 4) God will ultimately determine how our life works out. Each one of these principles builds upon the other and, if we are honest, each of them is probably something we struggle with at times. And no wonder. The God of this Age - Mammon, or whatever other form he chooses to appear in - screams in our faces that God is not real, that he does not want to nurture us, that what is secret is irrelevant and - perhaps most of all - that he (Mammon) has the keys to our fate. Do we really believe that our secret prayers and our unrecognised obedience and our quiet service are building our future? Do we value these above the comments of our bosses and the statements of friends and the £££s in our pay-packet and the looks we get on the street? It is a challenge. I find I am so much influenced by the latest fad or the latest meeting. I want to be where it is at and I want to be recognised there too. When earthly success (which generally revolves around numbers) is all around then I am happy as Larry but when it begins to fade I find myself scrabbling about for a quick fix. But God is real. God is my Father. He sees what I do in secret and he will ultimately decide my fate. I don't need quick fixes. I need to trust Him. I don't need earthly success, I just need to give Jesus my heart. For if I make Him my treasure and if I give him my prayers and if I seek Him first then I need to worry about nothing. For I may not be 'successful' but I know I'll be safe.

QUESTION FOR REFLECTION

How could you forge more of a secret life with your Father in heaven?

📖 MATTHEW 7

Live different. Don't just go with the flow. Don't conform to the pattern of this world but continually mark yourself out as children of your Father by responding to situations and people in a radically different way. I find it easy to approach people - all people whether I know them or not - with one overriding question; "what can you do for me?". Whether it is my wife who I want to listen to me or my friends who I want to entertain me or a random stranger who I want to keep out of my way on the train, I am pretty good at asking the question and finding an answer for what I want people to do for me. It is almost like that question is engraved on my soul. And also engraved on my soul is a rampant bitterness and frustration that all these ignorant people don't live up to my expectations. My wife has to go and do something else, my friends get distracted trying to deal with their problems (how dare they?) and the stranger on the train talks infuriatingly loudly on their mobile phone. This is how I find life is naturally lived. But Jesus wants to wipe this away. Jesus wants to fill in all these engravings and carve something almost entirely opposite in their place. Jesus wants us to ask not "what can you do for me" but "how could I help you out today". Jesus wants us to look into other people's lives not to work out what we can plunder from them but to work out what we can shore up in them, what we can encourage in them and, at times, what we can challenge in them. How can we do this? How can we start to be truly generous towards others, even if they steal our seat on the train? It comes through knowing beyond doubt that we have a Father who will give us all we need. It comes through realising that we are one of the favoured few who have found the narrow way. It comes through looking at the cross and the resurrection and realising that what God did for us there is more than enough to sort us out for this life and for eternity. And so we don't need to put our expectations on the people around us because our expectations have already been more than exceeded by our God. Instead we can genuinely give ourselves to others, trusting and praying that as we do so, they will come to see that God can exceed all their expectations as well.

QUESTION FOR REFLECTION

What does your behaviour suggest is engraved on your soul? What would you like to be engraved there?

📖 MATTHEW 8

Authority. In some ways it has been torn down in our society. But in other ways it is more highly regarded than ever. People pay small fortunes for a lunch with Warren Buffet in the hope that they can learn some invaluable investment tips. TED is awash with "experts" on pretty much everything. Our deference to experts is an acknowledgement of authority; that some people have particular spheres of life that they know everything about. If you have a particular problem in a particular sphere then all you need to do is employ the right expert and they will sort you out. It is this kind of authority that Matthew speaks into. Jesus, he says, is your expert par excellence. If you are being battered by a storm and you want to know how to survive, This One Man will help you stand firm through the trials. Whether your storm is disease or loneliness or family issues - this same expert will see you through your malady. Matthew is making this One Great Claim; Jesus has authority. Jesus is the expert. Jesus is the Master Teacher for life. Jesus is the Great Physician, Jesus is the best counsellor or advisor or healer than you ever could find. And - this is the really cool bit - he is willing to work for all at no initial charge. I think we need to recapture our confidence in this basic idea. We need to re-convince ourselves of the expertise of Jesus, of his unrivalled knowledge on life. Each and every person we see today would find their lives dramatically improved if they sat at the feet of Jesus. And how do we re-convince ourselves? I think it is by testing it out. Give his words a try. And consistently and gently encourage the people around you to turn their ears to Jesus. Don't just treat him as a comforter but as a captain. Don't just ask Jesus to give you strength to get through, but also ask him what you should do in order to get through. And then do everything he says. If we do that I think we will pretty quickly be convinced; seeing the sick healed is quite a convincing thing, seeing changed lives is quite a convincing thing. It all starts with listening. And then giving it a go. Will you do that today?

QUESTION FOR REFLECTION

What particular teaching of Jesus are you trying to learn to obey at the moment?

📖 MATTHEW 9

When Jesus says "your faith has healed you" to the bleeding woman it sort of sticks in my throat a little bit. I mean it wasn't her faith that healed her; it was Jesus. If she had gone and touched the cloak of one of the Pharisees with the same level of faith I don't think she would have gotten much back from them, except maybe a kick in the head for violating the purification laws. So here's the thing; Jesus should never have let this lady touch her; it officially made him unclean for the rest of the day (or longer I can't remember the specifics I think they are in Leviticus somewhere), and yet when she did so, not only did he heal her but he also praised her for her understanding of where to go for help in this world. The "faith" that Jesus lauded was an appreciation that Jesus is the New Wine and to come to him for help is the New Wineskin. Jesus is the one and only place for people to turn and receive real transformation. The bleeding lady saw that and acted - and this is what Jesus was celebrating. Matthew is celebrating it too. He wants you to embrace it. He places the bleeding lady alongside multiple miracle stories and bustles them around Jesus' new-wine-saying like paparazzi around a celebrity. All eyes on the New Wine. Why? Because the New Wine is the New Way to receive New Results. Humble trust in Jesus as New Wine makes you a heretic to who you once were, acting in ways that seem preposterous and even offensive to people who are still trusting the old wineskins. But it opens the door to a bounty of blessings. So what are you leaning on to sort out your problems? What wineskins are you using to seek to do well in life? What rules won't you break because they are the cultural norms? No matter what you used to do, and no matter what those around you do, if you keep coming to Jesus with humble trust that he is the solution to your trouble, you may cop some flack from others, but you will see miraculous healing and he will praise you for your excellent faith.

QUESTION FOR REFLECTION

When you are in trouble, what coping mechanism do you use? Is it one that Jesus advocates?

📖 MATTHEW 10

And then Jesus comes out with "everyone will hate you...you will be called Satanic...I've not come to bring peace but a sword... whoever loves son or daughter more than me is not worthy of me". Did Jesus never attend 'Vision Casting 101'? Does he not realise that seekers might be sensitive to such severe statements? Jesus has a disturbing desire not just to win people to his tribe but to win them to a Way of Life. He doesn't just want their allegiance; he wants them to act like him. And so, in a brazenly straightforward manner he lays out the challenge of Kingdom Living in this Age. What Jesus demands in this context is a bit like a recruiting slogan for an aid worker to be sent into the Russia-Ukraine conflict. Jesus wants his people to live in a form of missional warfare - relentlessly releasing freedom and hope to people while being assaulted on every side by misunderstanding, abuse and harm. And - most crucially - to never let those assaults their commitment to the cause. That's what I find hardest; to remain utterly resilient in the face of rejection. If you are like me, you would do well to mull over this chapter and its grubby reality of our calling. But don't miss the golden bits. Don't miss the bits that make all of the resilience and mission and grubbiness worth every penny. Don't overlook what Jesus says about the attentive, constant care of the Father. Don't skid past the fact that this care may not remove all harm right now, but it does remember it. Every bit of it. And - when the time comes - it will reward every good act in this war. As I think about this today, I wager that the biggest difference to my resilience and effectiveness in mission will come when I actually pause long enough to let the tendrils of this truth tunnel themselves down into my heart and my soul and my mind. Will I accept and believe that my Father - while totally uncompromising in what he wants from me - does indeed see me and does indeed love me and is itching to release rewards to me when I administer his freedom to his world.

QUESTION FOR REFLECTION

Are you ready to give all Jesus asks you to give?

📖 MATTHEW 11

When the builder rubs his chin and says "this is going to take a lot longer than you thought" you wonder whether you've called the wrong tradesman. That's what John the Baptist was going through. He was expecting an extreme makeover with instant results and he was getting... well, something else. This, my friends, is a perfect illustration of the theology of the Now and the Not Yet of the Kingdom. What John wanted, and what people always want from God, is an instant assertion of his transforming greatness upon a situation; ripping out all that is wrong and whacking it in the skip. Then, in the same weekend, an unveiling of a glamorously upgraded "house of our dreams" in its place. Like leaving our job as a cleaner to be appointed the next day as a Non-Exec Director of Dettol. But God doesn't do it like that... much to John's befuddlement. Of course, the reason God doesn't do it like that - the reason Jesus did just clap his hands and release an instant makeover of the world - is that people get hurt that way and people get proud that way. Instead, painstakingly and persistently Jesus brings a chance at transformation to people. Piece by piece the Kingdom Comes. A leper- who would have been out in the skip - can have glimmering skin instead. A blind man and a bleeding woman and some poor overlooked people get to experience the Kingdom Transformation in their lives. So do some tax collectors and Very Bad People who would certainly have been ripped out if the transformation had been instant. But not all people get the transformation. As was always expected, some will indeed be removed and sent away. Just not yet. Not yet. And not at all if they choose repentance and take on the yoke of Christ. We live in the age of invitation. The age when Jesus approaches people full of bad intent and rather than ripping them straight out he rubs his chin and says "well this is going to take a lot longer than you thought".

QUESTION FOR REFLECTION

What are the painstaking and persistent pieces of transformation that Jesus is bringing to your life in this time?

📖 MATTHEW 12

Jesus healed a man who was both mute and blind. I must confess that I've never seen such a thing, and yet the guys who hung around Jesus saw it all the time. And that is why Jesus speaks so harshly about blaspheming the Spirit. While the Son of Man had something slightly veiled about him - he looked like a normal bloke and spoke in parables that obscured the truth - the Spirit exposed the Kingdom as readily as a naturist on a nudist beach. So while you could listen to a parable and go away wondering what it was all about, you could only walk away from a healed mute thinking that it was a work of God or a work of evil. And to consistently plump for the latter, even when the result of the healing is manifestly good, would be a deliberate act of disbelief; it would be a conscious choice to harden your heart. And to harden your heart against the Kingdom of Heaven is a blasphemous act that cannot be forgiven. What does this mean for us? Well apart from warning not-yet-Christians about sweeping under the carpet the manifest evidence for God, it also presents a challenge to those of us who already follow Jesus; it warns us that the works of the Spirit are not like a fireworks show. The Holy Spirit doesn't work to make us go "oooh" and "aaah" but to change us. Jesus demands that we respond to God's work not just with a note of appreciation but with hearts and minds becoming more responsive to him; with a greater commitment to letting him convict us and mould us and let his Spirit define everything we are. This is the great call of discipleship; that the more Jesus shows us the more we choose to trust him and the more we choose to trust him the more we work to become like him. To refuse to walk this path ultimately leads you to blasphemy; it is claiming to worship God, but refusing to let him mould your life; you claim to love him and yet in practice you are hard towards him and all he wants to do.

QUESTION FOR REFLECTION

What do you do with these very challenging statements of Jesus?

📖 MATTHEW 13

As we press deeper into Matthew we see more of the character of Jesus. Here is one part of him I think is often overlooked - everything he did was expertly crafted to provoke. He couldn't have annoyed more people if he had grabbed a megaphone and bellowed into their faces. What he says to people is accept me or reject me - but what you can't do is be ambivalent towards me. Will you see yourself as my field and beg me to make you good soil? Will you agree my kingdom is worth everything and trade all you have to gain it? Will you accept I'm going to separate all people in a harvest? Are you getting what Jesus is saying in these parables? Are you really get them? He is saying He owns you. He owns you and me and every single inch of this earth and how you respond to your owner will determine whether he accepts you or rejects you. We find this hard to swallow. Our culture has hard-wired us to footnote God's rejection out of the gospel. Our daily dish is a warm dose of God's approval slopped in everyone's direction. Jesus wants to be your lapdog and all of that stuff. Nope. Like an annoying butler, day after day Jesus serves up the difficult to digest dinner of God's Lordship of our universe. These lovely stories that we teach to our children are actually asking them this - will they accept that Jesus is the Director of their whole life, letting him tell them their part, provide them with their costume, prompt their lines? If they (or we) say no - then what they are actually doing is writing themselves out of the script. There is only one director, and his name is Jesus. But - and this is what Jesus wants you to do - if you do accept Jesus as Director and if you ask him to help you play your part in his play then you will be hugely fruitful, you will receive great treasures, you will be overcome with joy and will shine like the sun.

QUESTION FOR REFLECTION

Is there any part of your life where you are rejecting Jesus or being ambivalent towards his call?

📖 MATTHEW 14

Herod was King of the Sadducees - the landed gentry of Israel who claimed that their rule was the fulfilment of God's promises in the Old Testament. They frollocked at parties, swapped wives and ate food off silver platters. They were right proper poshies. But - like many posh people today - their whole lives were governed by fear; fear of the people, fear of their guests, fear of their wives. Their value came from what others thought of them and they spent their lives running after the approval of men. Compare that to Jesus - the real Promise-fulfiller. His life is not governed by fear. His actions aren't fickle and fleeting to fit the fancy of his fellows. No. Jesus is driven by one major emotion - Sweet Lady Compassion. That truth deserves dwelling on in silence for 20 seconds. Jesus - our God - is driven by compassion. When people seek Jesus he can't help but show them compassion. The crowds gather round him and he can't help but heal their sick. The crowds hang around him all day and he can't help but feed them. The disciples get scared and he can't help but comfort them. Peter wants to try something impossible for humans and Jesus can't help but encourage him and lift him up when he fails. When we look at this chapter we often focus on the implication of Jesus' miracles - Jesus surpasses Herod, surpasses Elijah, surpasses Moses as The One From God. That is correct. But, let's not lose sight of Jesus' compassion. It is his inclination towards compassion that makes his Kingdom so stunning. In 25 years of following Jesus I'm sad about how rarely I have actually expected to experience Jesus' compassion. Forgiveness? Maybe. Marching orders, yes. But, if I'm honest, I've often related to Jesus as if he was a King like Herod. Or - even worse - I've thought of him just as a bland bystander in my life. But Jesus is not like Herod. Jesus is not just a passive viewer. Jesus is relentlessly compassionate towards those who are seeking him. Jesus does miracles for people who are seeking him even if they are dumb, bad at planning or are biting off a bit more than they can chew. And that makes me love Jesus. That makes me want to be really super attentive towards Jesus. It makes me want to try crazy things for him and to expect him to do crazy things through me. Jesus is Compassion. And so what have I got to lose?

QUESTION FOR REFLECTION

If you knew Jesus would do any miracle for you, what impossible thing would you try for him?

📖 MATTHEW 15

Jesus praises soft hearts, not clever lips. It's actually quite hard to tell the difference. The Pharisees' tradition sounded clever. They spoke in a way that claimed softness towards God, even special fellowship with God. But Jesus saw behind the surface. Jesus knew that despite all their fanfare, the Pharisees were propagating a hard religion which was happy to overlook needy family members. God looked at their hearts and he saw cold hard pride. But what of the Canaanite woman? Why does Jesus treat her like he does? The woman initially seems to be bringing clever lips. In her foreign accent she copies the words spoken by Israel's crowds. Jesus shows he is not a magician - he does not respond to correctly spoken spells. But he also hangs around long enough for her to be able to approach him and expose her heart. And she does just that. Her actions show her soft heart; her really soft heart towards the true God of All. So Jesus breaks all the rules to release healing to her daughter. Matthew pieced together these passages to prompt this big question; "where is your heart?". You might be able to repeat clever words, but where is your love? Hearts are funny things. They can so easily drift, their affections can so quickly flutter onto some other things. Does your heart burn for Jesus right now? Does it urge you to kneel before Jesus and beg for his touch? Is your heart close to him? If so, expect mercy - expansive mercy - to be pushed in your direction. If not, beg for God to soften your heart to Jesus, ask the Spirit of God to cause you to be deeply attracted to God again.

QUESTION FOR REFLECTION

What do you love most about God?

📖 MATTHEW 16

My atheist mate thinks v28 shows Jesus being wrong. "Jesus claims the world will end within a life-time of him. It doesn't. The supposed "all knowing God" doesn't know much. The church has never recovered from this embarrassment." My atheist mate is wrong, but then so was Peter, so there is still hope for him. The mistake of my atheist mate, Peter and billions of people since is to make the "Son of Man coming in his Kingdom" synonymous with the "end of the world". With this framework, when Jesus comes into his glory, cellos play, clouds break, calves skip and all that is wrong is instantly turned right. It's a vision of global cataclysm and universal delight all rolled into one Big Moment. It's a bit like what we saw John the Baptist expecting back in chapter 11. It's a bit like what Peter now expects - the glorious, victorious Age of the Messiah comes instantly and totally, bringing destruction of all evil, elevation of all the righteous and freedom from all suffering before you can even blink your eyes… right? Wrong. What Jesus wanted to teach Peter and what the Holy Spirit wants to teach the church is that the Son of Man coming in his Kingdom looks small and foolish, and is in the midst of an opposing Kingdom that is louder and brasher and hence gets all the headlines. In short, the Coming of the Kingdom of Jesus looks like the cross - it is like one seed falling to the ground in a vast forest, but with that seed one day becoming the biggest of them all. Delight is arriving but it is easy to miss because evil is allowed to carry on, for now. Jesus' Kingdom came in the resurrection, and yet the resurrection came into the midst of a wicked and adulterous generation who systematically ignored it, opposed it and tried to shut it down. We still live in such a time - a time when Jesus Kingdom is Now here and Not Yet fully here. In the future, the consummation of the kingdom will occur, and then All Will Be Made Right. But for now we live as Kingdom people in the midst of another Kingdom. And so we should expect sparks to fly as the other kingdom jostles against us. We should expect hardship and mistreatment and being misunderstood. But we should also expect glory. Jesus' kind of glory; the glory of perfect obedience in the midst of corruption. The glory of losing your life for Jesus sake even while everyone else is fighting over the world. That is the abundant, authority-filled life in this age. So are you perfecting obedience in the midst of your hardship? Or are you, like my atheist mate, letting your mistaken assumptions about how God works, push you away from real faith?

QUESTION FOR REFLECTION

When God makes his Kingdom available to you, how will you spot it?

📖 MATTHEW 17

More stuff on the Now and the Not Yet of the Kingdom (see notes from yesterday). Jesus' Kingdom is coming and remaining in the midst of a generation that is unbelieving and perverse. No instant gratification, no easy wins. No bowing of every knee and confessing of every tongue. Not yet. So what do we do? What would Jesus have his people do who live in the choppy waters of these two contradictory currents? We've already seen "perfect obedience in the midst of opposition" is our new definition of faith. We nurture the mustard seed that is growing within us. We trust the yeast to do its work, over time. We listen to Jesus and we see incredible things happen like a demon-possessed boy being delivered. But there is another aspect to living in this age that is less often spoken about; what do we do with the Other Lot? The "unbelieving" and "perverse" ones? How should we treat them? Here's the shock; The Kingdom of Jesus does 3 things to unbelievers in this Age; 1) it puts up with (v17) 2) it tries not to offend them (v27) and 3) it does miracles for them to rescue them into the Glorious Kingdom of Life (v18). This task of Jesus' people is, by faith, to grasp hold of the transformative power of Our Kingdom and then use it to exorcise people from the Other Kingdom. That's the focus of our interactions with people who do not believe. And that's the context in which the fascinating parable about mustard seeds and faith must be understood. Mustard seed faith believes Jesus has the desire to rescue perverse people out of unbelief. Mustard seed faith believes Jesus has the power to rescue unbelieving people out of unbelief. Mustard seed faith gives Jesus the chance to rescue this unbelieving person right now. I wonder if you are using that kind of mustard seed faith? I wonder whether you even see the two kingdoms at play? The bible itself tells us this perspective takes time to develop. But it also tells us that Jesus is determined to get us there - he will accept nothing less. She who has ears, let her hear.

QUESTION FOR REFLECTION

Jesus did miracles for people who he described as perverse and unbelieving. What do you make of that?

📖 MATTHEW 18

Mercy is a fine word don't you think? It's one of those words that isn't used too much so it still has some potency. Mercy is the common theme in this chapter. Following Jesus, and living in the church is always about looking out for others, trying to find ways to keep them close to you and in touch with God. It really pains me that so many Christians shy away from the grubby reality of our faith - rubbing up alongside people, being inspired and offended, supported and wounded by them. We seem so quick to take a step back and not really throw ourselves into friendship with the church. We often say the problem is with the church being too institutionalised or too full of difficult characters, or too "out of touch". Is the real truth that we are just not good at forgiving others' sin? If we are serious about following Jesus we have to get stuck into the local church, doing life together with the other "little ones", challenging them and then forgiving them, showing them mercy and asking them to show us mercy too. Over and over again. All this effort is not just to play happy families; it is the forging of a people in the pattern of the Prince. Awkwardness in the Assembly is God's Anvil for our Awakening. A church that has forged mercy has immense power to bound and loose forces in the world. A church full of mercy is a dynamic fount of blessing for the wandering sheep in the nations. Because a church full of mercy is a church that has asked for mercy from the Lord and has received that mercy and abundant things beside.

QUESTION FOR REFLECTION

How are you showing mercy in your interactions with others in Jesus' church?

📖 MATTHEW 19

When I first read about being a Eunuch for the Kingdom I choked on my cornflakes. The thought of Jesus forcing that on me (or anyone else) seemed impossible to digest. Today I ate my breakfast just fine. Here's what I've learned: when we read the bible we are not just to take the verses about divorce or sex or any other commandment, whack them on a handout and try to do whatever they says. That is not an adequate approach - it will likely underplay both the high desires of God and instil a kind of judgementalism towards those who haven't "followed the rules". Instead, we read in order to step into the poetry and the history, the law and the prophecy to meet our God and be re-moulded by him. This is what Jesus is getting at with the rich young ruler; he may have been following some of the rules of God's book, but he hadn't really met God in the book and so he wasn't really following the Ruler. If we want to read the bible like Jesus we need to read to discover the One who lies behind it. When we come to the bible in this way an encounter takes place. In this encounter we become captivated by God himself. We begin to realise that not getting divorced, choosing sexual celibacy and giving away possessions are challenging and beautiful paths to greater intimacy with the joy-filled God who wafts life around like a cheap perfume. When we throw down the thrones in our hearts that we have built for sexual satisfaction, for financial wellbeing, for positions of power we realise that there is a better one to put on the throne, a better Way to find life, a more pleasing allegiance than accumulation, masturbation or manipulation could ever provide. True comradery with God feels like treasure worth 100 sexual encounters or 1000 new toys. We start to live a totally new life from deep convictions that have been rewritten in our souls. It is this "Presence-seeking" approach to the bible, rather than proof-texting and rule-defining, that we are trying to model all throughout this New Testament Journey. It is the approach we see all throughout the New Testament church and is the only one that seems to be worthy of our ridiculously awesome God.

QUESTION FOR REFLECTION

How has the beauty and wisdom of God rewritten the deepest desires of your heart?

📖 MATTHEW 20

Jesus so often subverts the conventional wisdom about how to pursue God. Most Jews believed physical blindness to be a barrier to communion with God. The more merciful members of the community may, potentially, have prayed that a prophet would come to bring healing to the blind so that they could be accepted into the temple of God. But surely none of them, not even the most compassionate Jew, would have thought that God would approach a blind man and ask him what he could do for him. Surely no-one would have believed that God would even tolerate the presence of a disabled man, before his imperfection had been taken away from him. And yet Jesus, God incarnate, while he is in the middle of something, while he has a crowd around him calling out reverence and request, stops, turns, and looks at the blind men. And when he says "what do you want me to do for you" you feel like he is taking all the world's religious establishments, turning them upside down and shaking them all about. He is putting himself, the all-powerful, all-conquering master of the universe at the service of two blokes who don't even know whether they're wearing odd socks. Jesus' complete lack of presumption and his unquenchable desire to hear from people must have felt like a warm summer breeze to those who had been frozen out of the religious community for oh so long. And his ability to follow through on their requests and actually bring them healing looks like a haymaker following the left-hand uppercut that Jesus has just landed on the chin of everyday religious life. This is a crazy wage being paid to the dismayed. This is a whole new fate being offered to those coming late. This is the parable of the workers enacted in our midst. Oh I so much want more of this empowered openness in our church. Oh I so much want more Jesus in my life. I so much want to be like this God who will welcome anyone into his presence, and then serve them up miracles for their deliverance. Please come my King. Oh please come and have your way in our land.

QUESTION FOR REFLECTION

What would you have felt and thought if you were in that crowd, seeing Jesus stop and respond to the blind men and then see them healed and following him?

📖 MATTHEW 21

You know the story of Jehu - the wild-riding maniac who Elisha anointed to destroy the house of Ahab (2 Kings 9)? Think of him times seven. You can discuss Jehu over the dinner table, you can even nod approvingly at his zeal... until he comes at you with a whip. And that is exactly what Jesus does in this chapter. Jesus's prophetic actions (donkey-riding, temple-sacking and tree-withering) and his prophetic parables (two sons, tenants and wedding banquet) are his Jehu-like assault on the House of Religion. Jesus tosses over the ramparts any idea that he can just be the prophet of "those people over there". He curses any suggestion that vague religious conformity is to his taste. Instead he approaches every human on this planet and he says "fall in behind me"; do what I say or be thrown into the sea. I wonder if we really do this justice? We teach our children about Jesus on a donkey. We even teach them about the sacking of the temple (although we often make it about his anger at commercialism in the church). But when do we present Jesus as a zealous jealous King riding hard in our direction, demanding allegiance and obedience? When do we ask ourselves which son we really are - the one who actually does the work, or the one who does not? Hear this - and you need to really listen to this - Jesus wants you. He wants all of you. Jesus isn't just a rabbi wanting to warm you with his wisdom. Jesus isn't just a healer wanting to coddle you with his kisses. Jesus isn't just a prophet wanting to inspire you with his insight. Jesus is King. Your King. And as Your King he wants you - all of you - to fall in behind him, to work his vineyard, to invest his talents, to dress in his wedding clothes. Will you bow the knee? Will you march to his beat doing his work on his terms for his glory? It's not an easy request. But an easier request would take us away from this faith where we find joy, and fruit and a share in the beautiful banquet that is to come.

QUESTION FOR REFLECTION

In what ways has Jesus demanded your allegiance? How are you getting on with responding to his demands?

🖺 MATTHEW 22

The Sadducees were the culturally engaged wing of the religious world. They probably read the Guardian and worked in the civil service. The Sadducees had chopped Isaiah onwards out of their Old Testament and so focused on making good of this life for this life, using the principles of the Torah as "a bit of a guide". The Pharisees farted in the Sadducees general direction. They hated the idea of woolly compromise with the corrupt. They were looking for the destruction of evil society and the establishment of a new Davidic Kingdom for Israel. They totally believed Yahweh would resurrect the righteous to live in this Coming Kingdom and they were determined to be righteous enough to get into it. Even if it killed them. Or killed you. More likely you; with stones or something. Jesus rebukes both. The Sadducees and Pharisees both came to scripture to gain proof-texts for their preconceived ideas. Jesus says they never knew scripture at all. Both came to God for a leg-up in their pre-adopted agenda and so they never knew God at all. God doesn't do proof-texts or leg-ups. God does God. Better than David, more majestic than Torah, more delicious than marriage and sweeter than Caesar - God is God. And while we might not be quite like the Sadducees or the Pharisees it seems that one of the hardest things for us humans is to let God be God. We love to grasp hold of God and twist him towards our intentions. We love to cast God in our image, to squash God into our box. Let's remind ourselves of this - the Coming Kingdom will all be about God. In that day, in that world, God will be all in all. So the best way to spend our days in this kingdom is getting used to God; humbly apprenticing ourselves to God. Engage with society, hope in the resurrection, seek righteousness, do a good job for Caesar, but do it all like God. Not what you think God is like but what God is really like. What God says he is like. Let God be God.

QUESTION FOR REFLECTION

How would you know if you were trying to squeeze God into a box?

📖 MATTHEW 23

Roasted by the Redeemer. Even rap battles scarcely serve up such a succession of syncopated slam-downs. Man ain't happy with the Pharisees. You learn a lot about a person when they are angry; what riles Jesus reveals as much about God as the miracles do. So the 7 woes listed here are ambient revelation of our God; they show us what God really cares about. Firstly he cares about His Supremacy. Everything the Pharisees do is for men to see. That is not good. God wants his people back; he wants them to do things for him. The Covenant God wants his Covenant People to hold to their Covenant Promise and give attention to him as their Covenant Partner. Secondly he cares about Ordinary People. The Pharisees had raised the bar and shut the door so many times that the ordinary workers, the hungry sinners, the mediocre masses felt they couldn't get to God. Pharisee religion was one for the elite. And God was vexed. God wants the ordinary, the normal, the mediocre, the failures. And thirdly God cares about Reality. The Pharisees found all kinds of ways to tinker with the trimmings, to pretend people could paint purity onto their person. But they couldn't. You can't paint healthy arteries onto your chest and claim God's given you a heart transplant. Well, you can, but God doesn't want you to - he actually wants to fix you. So let's talk about your faith. Is it marked by God's Supremacy? What do you do that is just for Him to see? Does your faith open doors for the ordinary and the mediocre? Are you intentionally building friendships with people who are slightly annoying? And what about Reality? Are you exposing your true self to God for him to meet you and redeem you there? Jesus rebukes the Pharisees and then he wails over them. He wants them still, despite all their sin. If God is convicting you today it is actually his mercy; yield to him, entrust yourself to him because he cares for you - he wants to gather you under his wings and show you his love.

QUESTION FOR REFLECTION

How does your faith open doors for the ordinary and the mediocre to access your God?

📖 MATTHEW 24

Preachers have done a lot of weird stuff with Matthew 24. Part of the problem is chapter divisions (which were only added to the bible in the 16th Century). Chapters make you think you can look at chapter 24 in isolation from the 27 chapters around it. Madness that way lies. Jesus' prophetic declaration about the temple (v2) which sets up this whole chapter is the simple follow-on from the prophetic actions and parables we've seen over the last few chapters. The Son of Man is bringing the end of something as well as the start of something. Jesus' references to betrayal, love growing cold, "the abomination that causes desolation", shaking ground, the Son of Man appearing like lightning and the gospel being preached to all nations are then played out in chapters 26-28. If you flick back and forwards you will see an amazing parallel of language between these chapters. The predictions of Jesus also continued to be played out between the resurrection and the destruction of the physical temple in AD 70. Jesus said they would happen within the generation and they happened within 40 years. Not bad prophetic insight. So does this chapter have anything to say to us today? Firstly we must follow it in awe and wonder to the cross and resurrection. We see Jesus' work there not just as forgiveness of sin but as the birthing of a new age for the whole earth. Think about that. And then we must follow Paul, Peter and the New Testament Apostles in hearing in Jesus' words a promise of the Master's return after a long time away. Overwhelmingly, universally, the Apostolic preachers spoke of This Return not as a scary prospect for the church but as a wonderful hope - not as a murky terror rolling in from the distance, but as a delicious consummation of what was started in Christ. And they repeated Jesus' urgings of v42-47 - be ready, don't let your love grow cold, be faithful. It will be good for you if you do that. So good. You'll inherit all the earth. You will co-rule with Christ.

QUESTION FOR REFLECTION

Where would others say your hope lies?

📖 MATTHEW 25

There is much comfort in this chapter. And a wry smile or two when you think about it. Jesus says he will be late. Jesus says people will be so bored waiting for him they will fall asleep. Jesus says he will be gone such a long time even his servants will start thinking he isn't worth the effort. Jesus gives the church a theology of absence. And even since then we've been trying to give it him back. Matthew 24 furnished us with a vision of the tribulation around the time of the cross. Matthew 24 was mainly about our past. Matthew 25 speaks starkly into our present. And Jesus says this - our biggest trial in this time between Jesus' two comings is how we cope with his absence. Of course Jesus knew he would give his great commission spiel about being with his disciples everywhere, Jesus knew he would send his Spirit. And yet, despite the glorious gift of Jesus' presence to the church right now there is also the trial of his absence. The two mingle together like chocolate and milk. We don't like this, but it is His will for this age. How do you respond to Jesus' absence? I know I am terrible in it. Here is the comfort - Jesus knew we would be. He gave us these parables to help us. Firstly he urges us to equip ourselves to cope with his absence. The jars of oil might just be part of the story or they may point to deliberate habits to invite more Holy Spirit into our lives. Whichever it is, the question the parable asks you is this - are you intentionally preparing yourself for times when Jesus seems absent? The talents and the sheep parables come from another angle; will you obey only when Jesus seems close, or will you faithfully and repeatedly do what he has asked even when there is no whiff of his presence? We are a presence-loving people. Our church enshrines practices that seek the Presence of the Prince. Come Holy Spirit is our cry. And yet we must also emulate earnest endurance. We must promote simple faithfulness to the last, the least and the lost. In fact, when Jesus returns one of the biggest things on his radar will not be what we did when he was close, but what we did when he seemed absent - that is where true loving faithfulness is forged.

QUESTION FOR REFLECTION

How do you get on when God seems absent?

📖 MATTHEW 26

As emotional roller-coasters go, this is a Big One. There's the room-filling ecstasy of fragrant worship and the untellable exhilaration of unveiling the new covenant. But then heart-stabbing betrayal, soul-crushing isolation and the sourest swill of being let down by your best friend. Never can we think of Jesus as a detached, emotionless God. He knows what it is to be human. In particular it is the description of Gethsemane that I struggle to get my head around. The level of emotion that Jesus displays and the enormity of the situation is a little too much for my task-centred brain to process. I tend to just look at the end result and experience a fleeting moment of sadness over the fact that my beloved saviour was roughed up by some upstarts. But taking this passage on its own for a moment forces me to dwell a little in this agonising garden. And as I sit here I feel myself starting to well up at Jesus' declaration "my soul is overwhelmed with sorrow to the point of death". Why would Jesus let himself feel such sorrow over the world? How does he not run from such deep emotion as this? And how - having embraced such emotion - could he then still drink from the cup for our sakes? I'm completely floored by the emotional health of our God. That he could care so deeply about our sin that it would nearly kill him and yet he could still get up from that prayer and let sin kill him. This is an emotional God whom we serve and yet in his emotion he never swerves from doing utterly faithful things. I'm desperate to better ride the emotional roller-coaster of life. I want Jesus to help me embrace the ups and downs, finding intimacy with him in both the highs and the lows. And I also want Jesus to help me stay strapped into the Father's will, no matter how I feel. Still choosing every time to drink the cup the Father puts before me.

QUESTION FOR REFLECTION

Do you drink the cup the Father places before you? Even when you don't want to??

📖 MATTHEW 27

What Matthew masterfully shows is how each of the different sets of people at the crucifixion have received some revelation about who Jesus is but have refused to re-engineer their lives around it. It has been the repeat theme of his gospel and it reaches a climax here. Pilate is told that Jesus is the King of the Jews and his wife has been warned in a dream but he carries on with his activities as normal, thinking, bizarrely, that giving his hands a quick tinkle in some water is sufficient response to the fact that he is about to crucify his Maker. Others, such as the soldiers and the crowds, have glimpsed Jesus' kingship and saving power but prefer to stand themselves above or outside of this claim, mocking him for it or suggesting that his supporting evidence isn't quite strong enough to gain their approval. What a disgusting thing this is. How stupid to think that we can watch God in a detached manner and pass judgement on Him according to our own rules and opinions. Matthew's provocative demand is that we climb inside this narrative and submit ourselves to the revelation of God that is taking place in this Place of the Skull. We have to walk this ground with humility and openness, prepared to be completely undone and remade by this history-quaking and earth-shaking event. Life can not go on as normal after we have truly understood the cross; either we choose to drink its blood and follow its call or we close our ears and live forever with its blood on our hands.

QUESTION FOR REFLECTION

Are you walking the ground of the cross with humility and openness, letting it undo you and remake you?

📖 MATTHEW 28

It's such an abrupt ending to the gospel that you feel like you are dropping off a cliff. We only just got our heads round the fact that Jesus died and then, before we have time to take our bearings, he flash-bangs a couple of soldiers, cheekily greets the women while they are sprinting down a track, issues the great commission and, well... that's it. I guess Matthew feels like he can cut things off so quickly because his application points are self-evident; if Jesus has actually been raised then the whole world must be told. Matthew hasn't really explained what it means to make disciples, other than to do what Jesus did, and he has barely name-checked either the Holy Spirit or baptism throughout the whole of his volume. But I love this because it reveals Matthew's assumption that you will be involved in the church. It exposes Matthew's demand that you read the rest of the New Testament. Matthew hasn't tried to answer all your questions or to provide you with a compendium of faith. No. Instead he has put together a gospel to convey one overwhelming message; You Must Act. All the stuff about the Kingdom, all the parables, all the miracles, all the excuses, all the rejections, all the questions and all the calls of Jesus point in one direction; You Must Act. The Victorious Resurrected Christ wants you to become a fruit-bearing Kingdom disciple. Jesus wants you to be immersed in a Trinity-filled community and to press hard into His Kingdom agenda. Jesus wants you to leave the nets of your old way of doing things and come be a fisher of people. There is a lot of the year left and a lot of the New Testament left and a life-time of stuff still to learn but will you act on this? Will you act on what Jesus says? It's shocking how rare it is for someone to really try to do everything Jesus commanded. It's shocking how rare it is for someone to really know and live as if Jesus is with them everywhere. But why don't you and I be some of those happy few? It's Matthew's prayer that we would. It's Jesus' prayer that we would. Let's make it our prayer as well.

QUESTION FOR REFLECTION

How has the gospel of Matthew changed your life?

📖 HEBREWS 1

This is a complex book with intricate arguments. You may have noticed that it doesn't address a particular church, nor is it signed by a particular author. But it can break you down and re-make you much stronger if you take the time to get inside its logic. Hebrews is an invitation to soak in the herbal essence of consummated Judaism. Hebrews takes all the promises, all the longings, all the inclinations of the children of Abraham and pours out Jesus upon them. It goes crazy for Jesus. It celebrates the Old Testament revelation, it honours angels, it bows to the practices of the past. But it shows they were just shadows, or signposts, or carefully-cultivated cravings. It pours out Jesus as the longing and answer and glorious consummation of every one of them. It shows that Jesus is and has always been and always will be the superior majestic glory in this universe. In the end, if we look at it rightly, everything wise and good and beautiful points to him. Jesus is the heir of all things - everything ultimately will sit in his house and he will do with them what he likes. Jesus is the sustainer of all things. If you or I stopped working for a few weeks almost nothing would fall apart in the world. Sabbath confirms that to us. But if Jesus stopped working for a second, even for a nanosecond, everything would melt into chaotic emptiness. Whether you acknowledge him or deny him, whether you worship him or reject him; if Jesus pulled back from your life even for a second you would disintegrate. He sustains all things. And Jesus was the source through whom all things were made. The fabric of life passed through him and was pieced together in him. He is vastly superior in the past, in the present and in the future. And, to top it all, he is the radiance of God's glory and the exact representation of his being. Jesus shows us God. Perfectly. All the time. So, here's to Jesus. Let's raise a toast to him and not to anyone else. There are many wonderful things in our world. Technology and creativity, nature and personality. And we do right to give it some honour. But no-one else could be more worthy or more magnificent than Jesus. This book calls us to fix our eyes on Jesus, to approach Jesus, to stand close to Jesus, to revel in Jesus. It is a rallying cry for a worshipping church.

QUESTION FOR REFLECTION

In what ways are you conscious of Jesus sustaining you?

📖 HEBREWS 2

This passage is more tightly packed than a flamenco dancer's trousers… but don't let that put you off. Everything in it flows from a single premise; Jesus has brought us the greatest possible salvation. As a word, 'salvation' is bashed around by Christians like a squash ball on a court. It is easy for us to do the same; whacking it around without a second thought about what we actually mean by it. That diminishes our faith. Grasping what Jesus' salvation actually gives us - and why it is much better than any other salvation - will bring us immense benefit. Let's catch this salvation word and have a good look at it. Here is how Hebrews puts it; Jesus - the vastly superior Jesus - allowed himself to be made lower than those he was greater than. That in itself is quite extraordinary. It says so much about Jesus' character and commitment to us. He will do things beneath him. He will do things that stress him and cost him. Hebrews tells us that Jesus then suffered at the hands of men and died. He died to make us holy. He died to call us brothers. He died to destroy the devil. He died to free us from our fear of death. Each of these four facets of faith fidget with fruitfulness. Are you appreciating the enormity of them? Are you paying attention? Jesus died to make us holy. By holy we should understand "whole" - restored to perfection - humming with the harmony of the Spirit of Life. You can't get that "peace" in many places. Jesus actually gives it to us. That is how great his salvation is. Jesus also calls us brothers. A brother is a bosom-fellow. A brother is a collaborative adventurer. A brother is a co-inheritor. To be called a brother (or you might prefer the word sister) by a great human would be surprising. To be called a brother by the heir of all things is utterly astonishing. Space prevents us from doing this stuff justice but to know that Jesus' salvation rendered a death-knell to the devil is perhaps the greatest of all his achievements. Satan is the horrific and horrendous power that makes life suck. If Jesus' salvation really does destroy the devil that would have seismic consequences. How can I even think that through? Hebrews begins to help us do just that. It urges us to analyse it - and in doing so to conclude that Jesus is the greatest possible provider of the salvation we so desperately need.

QUESTION FOR REFLECTION

What aspect of Jesus' salvation of you have you thought about the least?

📖 HEBREWS 3

He is talking to Jews. As the name of the letter shows, it was the Hebrews that he was addressing. And their temptation was great - they could so easily just drop this Jesus-bit out of their religion and it would make life so much more comfortable. People were getting persecuted for the Jesus-bit. People were getting ostracised for the Jesus-bit. People weren't getting let into the synagogue because of the Jesus-bit. So maybe it would just make sense to nudge the Jesus-bit somewhere to the back of the draw and instead focus on the faith-bit and the love-bit and the God of Abraham-bit. There is a similar temptation today. We can be tempted not to talk about God as a person called Jesus, not to assert that there is more to our faith than a vague spiritual reality. We can face a strong temptation to speak of Jesus as a fluffy friend (or a "spiritual" belief) rather than a real person with defined opinions, who is opposed to some stuff and in favour of other stuff. It can be tempting to compromise or fit in or just tone down what makes us stand out. But then we depart from the bible. Then we err from this call to fix our thoughts on Jesus. Then we lose sight of the greatest part of this whole thing. Jesus is the worthy one because he is so unusual. Jesus deserves the greater honour because he is so much more than a "religious figure" or a subject of belief. Jesus is the faithful one who is building us into his house. Jesus is the one in whom we share life and all that is right. If we get this then we know that we can't just hold loosely to a kind of Jesus-saviour. We become Jesus-freaks. We become Jesus-ists and Jesus-obsessives and Jesus-dependents and Jesus-worshippers. Everything becomes about Jesus. Or it doesn't become about him at all. That is the core conviction in this epistle to the Hebrews. You can't nudge Jesus to one side of your faith. You can't be a Christian and not have Jesus as your focus, your Way, your light of life. So I leave this passage wondering whether Jesus does indeed get the bulk of my focus? Am I really a Jesus freak? Does he punctuate my days and fill my thoughts in the night?

QUESTION FOR REFLECTION

How often do you think about Jesus?

📖 HEBREWS 4

Way back near the start of time, in an aeon now shrouded in mystery, a story emerged about God creating and then resting, delighting in what was good, having peace with what he had made. Many understood this story not just as a justification for a working week but as an expose of God and his character, and of his trajectory for his cosmos. We go back to that now. Hebrews confirms to us that the Seventh Day is a tantalising promise for how life could be. The Seventh Day is a glimmer of Shalom; of rest, of peace, of delight, of the sweet-scented aroma of everything being good. This is Sabbath. And now, the writer of the Hebrews, declares that that promise has been fulfilled and that glimmer has shone bright - we can have rest, we can see everything is good - if we remain in Christ. The one who sat there on that seventh day is right here now offering us his rest. If we remain in him. The sabbath is not a day - it is the mood of the kingdom. The Sabbath of peace is not 24 hours of inactivity but a lifetime of beautiful encounter. Sabbath is lived out every moment of every day in the Kingdom of our God. It is peace with God, it is peace with creation. It is marvelling at all that is good and delighting in all He has made. We can enter it now to some extent and we will enter it fully when he returns with his Kingdom. Do you know his rest? Does your soul reverberate with harmonies of encounter? This is what this chapter invites us to. To know His Rest right now and to remain in him so we can know it fully when he comes.

QUESTION FOR REFLECTION

What aspect of God's diverse creation brings you the clearest glimmer of the shalom he intends for us all?

📖 HEBREWS 5

I'm glad the writer has much to say about Melchizedek because to be honest - I've not nothing. He seems like an obscure character used to answer a question that I've never asked. But the stuff about maturity hits me between the eyes. Maturity is about being able to distinguish between good and evil (v14). That's a powerful definition I'm going to try to remember. If we can just sneak across into chapter 6 we see that such maturity is built upon the elemental teachings of repentance from bad acts, faith in God, baptism, laying on hands, the resurrection, and eternal judgement. These teachings seem to follow the narrative of the Christian life as it should be lived. You repent and turn from idols to God, you get baptised, you are empowered and filled with the Spirit, and then... oh, what's this stuff about resurrection and eternal judgement? We don't seem to talk about those very much. Certainly not as the foundation of things. But resurrection and eternal judgement seem to be the two linchpins of the Christian mindset after being filled with the Spirit. They lift our eyes to a day in the future - a day beyond our current experiences - where momentous events will occur and destinies will be set. For centuries they seemed to be used like prefects supervising (sometimes a little too keenly) the activities of Christian pilgrims, scaring them into behaving for fear of future rebuke. But they needn't be seen that way. They can be seen as a glorious hope of justice and peace. They can be seen as the consummation and full enjoyment of the slithers and snippets of the kingdom that we get to experience today. They can be seen as fundamental truths about life, without which maturity cannot be reached. They set the context for our life - they help clarify the things that are worthy and the things that are useless, the things that are good and the things that are evil. It is hard to be mature in faith if you don't ever think about resurrection and judgement. So can I encourage you to think about them some more; they warrant your time more than musing about Melchizedek.

QUESTION FOR REFLECTION

Do you really know the difference between good and evil?

📖 HEBREWS 6

I often feel like I need an anchor. I am prone to drifting with the tide and getting very close to some rocks. My soul sometimes fades. It sometimes exudes about slightly dubious things. So I'm very grateful for the anchor metaphor in verse 19; it really helps me. I realise that sometimes I need to consciously fix my thinking around a defined constant. Sometimes I need to resist the ebb and flow of my emotions by deliberate thoughts about the permanence of God. God never changes. God's purpose never changes. God has deliberately shown us that he would bless Abraham and give him many descendants. The inclusion of the gentiles was always going to happen. God's project was always going to rumble on in an ever expanding manner. Sometimes slow and sometimes shudderingly fast, but an increase in God's government has always been God's plan. Sometimes I just need to remind myself that God knows what he is doing and his family will keep on growing no matter how I feel, or even what I do. God's commitment to blessing is also deeply reassuring. I don't know about you but there are times when I lose sight of the simple goodness of knowing this God. On dark days the wind of worry can blow me off course and threaten my ship. On those days I need to remind myself that God is good; he has always done good. Sometimes we can see it and other times we can't but all of us now share in God's blessing to Father Abraham. So, how do you feel today? If it is a good day, run your hand around this anchor. Get used to its feel; it will be more easy to use when the waves begin to hit. And, if it is a bad day, let your anchor fly; think of the permanence of God and how his purposes never change.

QUESTION FOR REFLECTION

When and how do you consciously cling to God as your anchor?

📖 HEBREWS 7

Jesus always intercedes for us. I wonder what he is praying for me right now? I wonder what he is praying for you? That's quite something isn't it? To think that the Big Man of space, time and everything else is spending his days uttering words of petition for us. It is deeply humbling. It is hugely inspiring. When you are peeved, he is praying for you. When you are intimidated he is interceding. When you are wayward He is wrestling for you in prayer. What a love. What a faithfulness. What a commitment to you and to me that Jesus - the King of Creation - refuses to be passive as we tumble and trip through life. He prays for us. He goes on praying and fighting in the heavenly realms. Jesus didn't stop fighting for our salvation after the cross; he is still grappling for us right now. He is working in prayer that we might receive grace and goodness and the fullness of gladness in God. Reading that this morning makes me love Him again. Reading that gives me hope in him again. And so I want to see those prayers fulfilled in me - no matter what they are. If the one through whom all things were made has got some desires for me then they must be pretty raspingly beautiful. I want to lean on those prayers and let them take my weight. I want them to carry me into the banquet hall of the kingdom. Yes, Lord God, whatever you want for me - I want it too! Your will be done, O God. Let me hold onto your hope and see all your prayers come true.

QUESTION FOR REFLECTION

What is Jesus praying for you right now?

📖 HEBREWS 8

Let me get this straight. God called a man - a pretty ordinary sort of man - and made ridiculously generous and long-lasting promises to him. Then the man messed up. But God passed these staggeringly generous and long-lasting promises on to that man's son and then on to his sons until all these sons messed up so bad that they got themselves enslaved in Egypt. So God responded to this abject failure on the part of the sons (now called Israel) by walking them out of slavery in Egypt and then making even stronger and even more ridiculously generous promises to them (from the top of Mount Sinai). And then the house of Israel messed up. Again. And again. And again. And then God repeated his ridiculously generous promises over and over, again and again until one day the house of Israel had gone so far that these ridiculously generous and long-lasting promises were no longer tenable. So how did God respond? He made new promises to them. Except these promises are not scaled-back, slightly-less-risky, minimising-potential-losses promises. No, these are so staggeringly, incredibly generous and so epically, gong-resoundingly long-lasting that they make the previous ones look pathetic by comparison. He makes himself our high priest. He takes his heart and gives it to us. He takes all of his being and places it at our disposal. He does this for us even though our track record is terrible and our future prospects are quite puny. He does it because that is who he is. Our God is the God of ridiculous generosity, of unflinching faithfulness, of relentless determination to do good to his earth. Let's remember the jaw-dropping personality of our God. Let's rejoice in it, cling to it, be staggered by it and worship him because of it. In fact I need to pop off and worship him right now.

QUESTION FOR REFLECTION

How has God shown himself to respond to human failure?

📖 HEBREWS 9

The acted symbol of the temple showed Israel again and again that the culmination of their hopes, the pinnacle of their dreams, the foundation of their identity was to be with God. Each time they sacrificed animals, sprinkled blood, or passed by the tent they were reminded that Yahweh Elohim was their map, their mentor and their maker. The sacrificial system was a rhythm of reminders to come and be with God. A lot of Israel were like blind men or stiff-necked animals - they failed to follow the symbol to its source. "Where is the man who seeks God?" the psalmist wailed. But for those who were alert to God, the rituals of redemption led them again and again into repentance towards God, hunger for God, devotion to God. Tabernacle worship was good as far as it went. But the symbols created a demand they could not satisfy. Like passengers on a perpetually circling aeroplane, they could see the airport out the window, but couldn't land or disembark. Then Jesus came. The revelation of Hebrews 9 - the revelation it revels in - is that Jesus landed that plane and opened wide the doors. True forgiveness of sins was now achieved. Anyone could now enter the actual Holy of Holies. So do we? Most of us have ditched the rhythm of reminders and rituals of redemption. That's OK if we are actually entering the presence. So are we entering the presence? Are we coming to God and finding him as our map, our mentor and our maker? Modern life seems to have such a bias away from being with God. Are we forgetting what it is all about? Are we being stiff necked or blind men? He has come so we can be with him. He will come so we can be with him, if we are eagerly waiting for Him. Oh I want being with God to be my passion once again.

QUESTION FOR REFLECTION

Are you stiff necked?

📖 HEBREWS 10

Encouragement in the faith comes not just from Jesus. There is huge encouragement from him; His character and his identity and his provision for us is immense. The last 9 chapters have called us to dwell on them and fix our eyes on them and be encouraged and strengthened and fuelled by them. And they have been good. They have been great. But that isn't the end of it. We also encourage one another. God has put the world together in such a way that people depend on people, brothers and sisters in faith depend on brothers and sisters in faith. The calling of every man and every woman is to spur one another on towards love and good deeds. We have in our souls an intrinsic need to meet one another regularly and consistently, to give of ourselves to encourage one another and strengthen one another. That is how God has made us. And yet we naturally shrink back from it. For a range of reasons we shy away from meeting together (when we say meeting together what we mean is actual open, honest, generous engagement rather than just being in the same room). We come up with explanations of why it is best for us (or even for others) if we don't go today or don't share this or that particular thing. We find ourselves swaying towards isolation. But that way is death. Life is found in leaning into one another, in attending small group, in praying with two or three others, in coming on a Sunday, in daring to speak out, in daring to expose ourselves and let others expose themselves to us. Meeting together is saying "I am a filthy sinner" and having others say "yes, that is true, but you are also loved and you are also being made pure. So take up your forgiveness and grasp hold of your inheritance and get back out there and do what God is calling you to do." Let us not give up on meeting together like this. Let us not give up on pressing into this. Life is found leaning into one another. In one another is encouragement in the faith.

QUESTION FOR REFLECTION

Have you been making decisions that lead you to the death of isolation? Could you choose to expose your true self to others in church and let them expose their true selves to you?

📖 HEBREWS 11

The now and the not yet. Recently we've started reclaiming the now - and, if I could, I would turn a few backflips for that. We have boldly approached the throne in worship. We have carried the presence into our streets. We have contended for healings and for ecstasies of His peace. We must keep pushing hard into the now. But our faith must also retain the 'not yet' or it is not faith at all. Now let's be clear that focusing on the Not Yet is not about lowering expectations. Now and Not Yet faith looks at what is now and delights in the salvation of our God made manifest among us - it expects people coming to faith, people being healed, people being set free, love being shown. But faith in the Not Yet also regards today with slight disappointment. Faith that understands the Not Yet says 'Is this it?' and faith knows that while it might be, for now, it won't be for ever. That is why true faith longs for that better country, the heavenly one that is not yet here. True faith is willing to sacrifice in the Now for the Not Yet. It can take the hurt because of its hope. Faith sacrifices the first-fruits and builds arks and leaves homelands and lives in tents and admits that this earth (as it is) is not our home. Faith is willing to leave rewards and longed-for-results and desired-satisfaction until a future time. Faith ultimately invests its efforts in this current age for the promise of the future age. I feel like I've only just started to understand real faith. I feel like I've just begun to say with integrity that I have entrusted things to God for Him to give back to me on That Day. I wonder if you have got there yet? Have you accepted hurt because of your hope? Does your Way of Life not make sense if this is all there is? If you have - and I suspect you have - then the world is not worthy of you. If you have - even in a small way - then God is not ashamed to be called your God.

QUESTION FOR REFLECTION

What is stopping you from becoming a hero of the faith?

📖 HEBREWS 12

I think it is really interesting how the writer of Hebrews approaches lifestyle issues. With Paul, everything is pushed back to our identity in Christ - he continually assures us that we are a new creation in Christ and therefore should live in the new creation kind of way. This writer doesn't do that. This writer looks at the problems and struggles in this life and then compares them with the problems of the past. This writer always shows how now, under the new covenant, we are so much better off than our forefathers and therefore can't really complain or make excuses about not living right. And having done that this writer then turns our attention to God. Not so much God in us and who we are in God but who God is in Himself. This writer paints a continually expanding, glorious fresco of the Almighty God of All Ages. You get the idea that this bloke is still so completely overcome by the wonder of it all. You get the idea that this writer bounces up and down on his chair and then flings himself face-down, awestruck like the thousands upon thousands of angels in his vision. You get the idea that this writer sees himself continually standing in bold trepidation upon the most holy ground of the City of the Living God, always edging closer to the judge of all men, hearing the cry of welcome and yet daring only to edge forward all the same. You get the idea that this writer is continually putting down his pen to weep and to spread-eagle himself again at the wonder of it all. He knows his God is a consuming fire. He knows his God spoke and the whole earth shook. And, as he sees that, as he thinks on that, he knows with joy and certainty that all he wants to do is cling to his God and give himself to his God and worship his God. I think I would like to follow him in that.

QUESTION FOR REFLECTION

Jesus endured the cross for the joy set before him. Is your vision of God joyous and awesome enough to sustain you through hardship?

📖 HEBREWS 13

We saw in chapter 12 how, when it comes to lifestyle issues, the writer to the Hebrews runs a slightly different form of argument to Paul. I love the diversity this exposes - Paul was the apostle to the gentiles and this writer (who I personally suspect might have been Apollos... but what does it really matter?) was focused on Messianic Jews. They both wrote in different ways with different vocabulary and with differing emphases. And yet among their diversity they had so much in common. They were both mates with Timothy and were happy to use him as their representative. They both celebrated love, they both called their churches to show hospitality, they both strongly warned against sexual immorality, they both advocated the formalised expression of church, they both fixed so much of their attention on the kingdom to come, they both waxed lyrical about Jesus. Jesus was their hero, their role-model and their friend. That is the beauty of the early church that we peer at through these apostolic writings - they were a huge range of people; rich and poor, educated and uneducated, Jewish and Roman and Turkish and Greek and every blend under the sun. They were male and female and young and old and new converts from paganism and life-long observant Jews who had found their Messiah. And they all hung out together. They all fixed eyes on Jesus together. And because of Jesus they all were united on an incredible range of issues. Because they all knew that Jesus was the same yesterday, today and forever they gradually became the same, while remaining vastly different. I love the diversity of our church. I'm more and more convinced that united diversity is an essential marker of a real work of love. Enacted love is the work of his peace. And so let's do what all those early apostles did - let's pray for the peace of God's presence and the work of his grace. Let's fix our desires on Jesus and let him equip us to do every single good thing that will bring pleasure to him.

QUESTION FOR REFLECTION

What struck you most from the letter to the Hebrews?

📖 JAMES 1

When Paul and the other apostles were pursuing the mission to the nations, James probably stayed in Jerusalem pastoring a church of converted Israelites. So he writes with a pastor's heart and a delicious, spicy Jewish flavour. This flavour could be summed up with the verse "do not merely listen to the word and so deceive yourselves. Do what it says." (1:22). Obedience and action were ground into the Jewish understanding of religion - sacrificing at the temple, taking care of family members, controlling your diet, celebrating the festivals. Religious life meant doing God's things in all of life. That was just how it was. Most of us have grown up in a cultural blend of Greek and Romantic thought. In Greek thinking ideas are beautiful. You can dwell on them, debate them and devote yourself to them, all the time reclining on your klismos nibbling olives. On the other hand Romantic thought has taught us to celebrate epic moments of inner joy and ravishing acts of beauty. Much modern worship services doff their beret to the French Romanticism of the Enlightenment. Neither Greek thinking nor Romantic thinking are wrong, but they can lead into immaturity and error unless they are tempered with the Jewish mind. So it is worth us digesting as much of James as we can. It is worth us reading James as if he is a foreigner we are trying desperately to understand. Let's get him to speak slow. Let's repeat back to him his sentences to make sure we've really understood. Some of James' lines seem simple and instantly applicable. Tame your tongue. Be quick to listen. And yet, with the Jewish mindset we realise their huge power. We come to them like sporting drills to be practised and practised again to make us do God's things. I want to be someone who sucks all the juice out of my faith. I want to be someone who delves into all the riches of all that God has for me. I want to delight in thinking about God. I want to enjoy feeling God. And I also want to act like God. And so I'll try to practice this book like a coaching manual for life.

QUESTION FOR REFLECTION

Are there things you believe that you struggle to live?

📖 JAMES 2

This passage is laced with the spicy Jewish flavour we saw in chapter one. Faithful Jews always knew that they must be defined by their God. Religion was not a segment of the grapefruit of life; sectioned off to certain practices on certain days. No, religion was like the chocolate in a chocolate milkshake; mixed into every aspect of every day. If a Jew looked at one small part of a person's life and saw no evidence of faith in that moment, it would be like them taking a sip of a chocolate milkshake and not tasting chocolate; "have you served me the right drink?!" they would cry. This is what James is talking about when he calls faith without works "dead". James knows that if you have any of God's grace in any of your life then it will seep into every part of your life. Or at least it should, if it is genuinely God's grace. James wants everyone to know that the power that reverberated in his little brother really changes people. James wants God's grace to have full effect in our lives; to make us perfect and complete in him, doing all God wants us to do. Here is what this means for us; we let God make us people who every waking hour of every day clearly live out of the reservoir of God's grace. Forget the attending of church services or reading of the bible which only happen in certain moments of a week. Think about the stuff you do all the time; how you treat people, how you use your words, how you make your plans. If we want our milkshake to taste of chocolate then these are the areas where we let God's grace go to work. And that is where "faith" comes in. Faith - for James - is cooperation with God's efforts in our lives. Faith is saying "yes" to God making us like him. If we let God have his way in us then we naturally start to treat all people well, to recoil from cursing others or making vain boasts. Real faith means something inside of us shifts and becomes like God, even when we don't know it is happening; even beyond anything we could achieve by our own efforts. And so, this Jewish flavour actually expands the sense of adventure we have in our faith. We realise God wants to redeem all of us; to make us clean and pure and beautiful and joyful in every single droplet of our lives. That is what it means to be rich in faith and a real heir of the kingdom.

QUESTION FOR REFLECTION

What are you letting God change in you at the moment?

📖 JAMES 3

How we make decisions shows who we follow. Every choice casts a vision of what we love. It breaks down like this. What we love, how we think things actually get done, what we run from, fuse together into what we could call our "wisdom for life". This "wisdom" is the sum total of all our conscious and unconscious desires; it is our playbook, our "code" to help us get where we want to get. And so - whether we realise it or not - this wisdom acts as the hidden umpire of our minds; determining how we act or respond, how we plan or let things slide. Many believers do not have Jesus as their umpire; their "wisdom for life" is unaffected by their faith. They may show up in the right rooms and use the right phrases but the seat of power in their minds is still occupied by the same old loves. So they say stuff and do stuff that is "vile". James' agenda is to unseat the old umpire and put Jesus in his place. What would it look like to do this? Well, it may take effort. It may take time. The first thing to focus on is the purity of Christ. The priority of a pilgrim is purity of heart. Stop a minute and think on that. When considering a job offer, or which coffee to buy, or how to reply to a child, the first instinct of immanuel is "which option will make me more pure?". Purity here is about all pointing in one direction; it is about a life that isn't frayed at the edges or conflicted in any way. I buy a coffee and speak words that most advance my pursuit of God. Trying to rewrite our decision making habits to make them pure like this will take time and effort. Something like 95% of our decisions are made subconsciously. But if we start with the 5% we are conscious of, then our "wisdom" will begin to change. And so for thirty days or so we push into purity; we ponder on it and play around with it. We imagine how our day might look different if we were totally pure. And then we choose to act that way as much as we can. And God, in his mercy, will speed the change along.

QUESTION FOR REFLECTION

What decisions could you make today to pursue even greater purity?

📖 JAMES 4

It's about now that I suddenly start to feel like James is just a tad harsh. He is speaking to Christians and he describes them as adulterous people, sinners and double-minded. He says they are just a mist that appears for a little while and then vanishes, and he says they boast and brag and do evil and sin. Phew! Would you want a pastor like that?? But, you know what, I think I would. Because good old James had lived with holiness his whole life. He had probably shared a bed with holiness - sleeping alongside his brother Jesus who never sinned and was the epitome of purity. He probably watched in gob-smacked wonder as his older brother gave away and turned from the things of the world, humbly entrusting himself to God. He probably stood next to Jesus as people slandered him and Jesus just smiled in response. He probably received rebukes from his brother about boasting about his future or thinking too much of himself. You see, I don't think James was down on people - he loved people, he gave his life to pastoring people, he wrote his letter to people - I just think that James had a very realistic perspective on what people were really like. When you have spent your life with brilliant white, slightly light brown just doesn't seem that great. So James would be a great pastor. Because James would always show us there's something more. James would lead us into holiness and equip us for leading purer lives. If you are a leader or you want to be, the best thing you can do is emulate James - the best thing you can do is get such a clear and vivid image of Jesus that nothing else seems that great. It is a life-time's work. But a life-time is what we've got. Let's draw near to God and share a bed with holiness; it will expand our vision of how delightful life can be.

QUESTION FOR REFLECTION

What is most staggering to you about Jesus' holiness?

📖 JAMES 5

"Be patient until the Lord's coming." I can't remember ever really engaging with that idea. Even today I fleet-footed past this verse to get to the stuff about prayers of faith. But I feel drawn back to verse 7, as if the Spirit is highlighting it to me. Why haven't I ever focused on this before? I know that patience is not something I am good at, but I don't think that is the main problem. I think the main problem rests in my theology; do I really believe that Jesus is coming back? And, more than that, do I think it would be a good thing? James certainly did. Paul certainly did. As did Peter and the writer to the Hebrews. In fact the whole ruddy lot of them were convinced that the Lord was coming back and it was going to be awesome. And - if we do think about it - it is going to be awesome, isn't it? It is going to be awesome because Jesus sees good stuff you do that never gets noticed by your peers. It is going to be awesome because all you have sown-to and cultivated will spring up into verdant, eternal life. This time is more grubby than we would like. It is a time of planting and tilling. But then is when the harvest will come. Then is when abundance will abound - and the abundance will link directly to our purity right now. This perspective on the struggles in life helped the church grit their teeth and remain faithful through their suffering. It helped them not get distracted from the delight of devotion. I want to learn from their example. I love Jesus. I deeply deeply love Jesus and know he is the epitome of goodness and joy. I am so richly satisfied when I fix my eyes on him and do stuff that invests in the harvest on his return. So, Holy Spirit, please would you hammer into my thick skull the truth that even small acts of faithfulness are worth it. Please would you help me wake up in the morning wondering whether today will be the day when the ploughman overtakes the reaper. And then please would you give me patience - a patience to stand firm and not grumble and keep going for goodness in the grubbiness. For when Jesus returns it will be astonishing. The glory of his Kingdom fully come will make it all seem worthwhile, and will surpass even Elijah-type prayers in this time.

QUESTION FOR REFLECTION

What part of James' letter struck you the most?

📖 1 PETER 1

I suspect that all Peter's life he kept coming back to that moment on the beach, broiled fish in his belly, when Jesus told him to feed His sheep (John 21:17). This letter shows us what Peter did with that. For Peter, feeding sheep meant telling people how small they are... and how big God is. On some days I know I am puny (particularly on bin-day - ooh my arms ache after having to drag those heavy bins to the pavement). On some days I see the transience of my life. But I spend a lot of the time avoiding that particular topic of thought. Peter, however, rams it back in my face - I am like grass (1:24), I wither, I am a child (1:14). I need my ego bashed. I need to know none of this could possibly depend on me. I need to know that moving a recycling bin is just about my limit. That is food to my soul, as perverse as it may sound. And then I need to know that God is the Father, that he foreknew us all and he keeps things in heaven. He is rich in mercy, He is holy, He is the impartial judge, He is the one who raised Jesus from the dead. In short, He is very very big. His little finger stretches further in every direction than the arm-span of all of humanity standing side by side. I could stretch my mind back in time to the very dawn of the Age... and He would have been sat there, enjoying the view. I could gather every person together of every different culture and time... and He would have watched every one of us grow; he would have been the Father of us all. And we could gather up every fragment of gold and every diamond and every treasure of every nation... and it would just seem like a piece of belly-button fluff alongside His riches. God is so big. And He has chosen us. He is shielding us with his power. He is sanctifying us with his spirit. He is showing us that he is good. Oh what an amazing meal this is. Oh what a miraculous catch of fish Peter is serving up for us. I am so deeply grateful to him. But I'm so much more grateful to Jesus.

QUESTION FOR REFLECTION

So much in our culture wants us to focus on our own self-esteem. Are you building your identity on what you are good at, or on how tiny you are compared to God?

📖 1 PETER 2

How to thrive in exile is the major theme of 1 Peter. Exile is disconnect from the presence of God. Exile is struggling to see God's purposes coming to pass. Exile is being surrounded by people given to other gods, who seem to be getting along better than we are. For the Jewish nation, exile was disaster. Exile was a siege, squeezing out hope. And ever since, us newborn babes in Christ have interpreted feelings of exile the same way; they have cramped our chests, suffocating our souls. Peter the Pastor - Peter, the feeder of the lambs - addresses us here. He tells us that we were chosen. The Father chose us. He didn't have to. He certainly didn't need to. He didn't do it because he felt guilty. It wasn't a half-hearted act. He chose you because he wanted you. He wanted you. And so he chose you. He didn't choose everyone - some are stumbling before him - but he did choose you. So, little lamb, don't let your attention get distracted by everyone else. Instead, remember the mercy the Father has shown you in Jesus. By his wounds you were healed. Through the death of Jesus, your spiritual exile was ended. And, so you can never be disconnected from God again. You belong to him and he is choosing to shepherd you. He is choosing to oversee your soul today. He - through Jesus Christ - is fulfilling his purposes in you every time you come to him. He is forging you and many, many others, into the population of his Kingdom. More than that; he is expertly and patiently crafting you and I together into a Holy Spirit House - a new temple - a place of His relentless rejoicing presence, even in the midst of the prospering "pagans". That is a meal worth eating slowly. That is food that we want to digest well. For this food can transform our whole experience of life. This food can underpin a whole sense of identity. It gives us capacity to thrive spiritually in the midst of our physical exile. Fierce words, fickle friends, feelings of the forlorn cannot change what He Has Decided. Our Shepherd stands strong. And so let's come to him. Let's listen to his instructions and walk in his ways. Let's choose to be different, letting the healing of his wounds go to work on our souls.

QUESTION FOR REFLECTION

In what ways do you feel like you are in exile? What is God's response to those feelings you have?

📖 1 PETER 3

In the last chapter we exiles were reminded that we were chosen. In the grubby days of disconnection, that light shines bright in our hearts. This beast of a man (I always imagine Peter to have been a big bloke for some reason...) shows us how this light brightens even some of the most shadowy challenges we face. In the Vineyard we have summed up a common cause for these shadows; "people do people stuff". Some people, often people to whom we are very, very close, haven't yet believed the word and look down on the way we live. Other people, often people who have believed the word, are just plain evil to us. Husbands may be dismissive of our devotions. Bosses may bash us when we are blameless. Church members may crush our fragile dreams. These things do cast shadows onto our soul. If we are not careful they can lead us into disillusionment and despair, anger and plotting of revenge. So Peter - this beast of a Pastor - gives us the antidote; "in your hearts revere Christ as Lord". What he means by this is that we should actively lean on the shoulder of Jesus and respond to these shadows in the same way that he did. What did Jesus do? He lovingly died a thousand little deaths - and then one big death - because he knew he would be made alive in the Spirit. If we think on this properly and revere Jesus in our hearts we will begin to trust that where he has gone we will follow; through suffering and then into God-fuelled resurrection. What this does is take away fear. What this does is remove our frightened thinking that we will be mistreated for eternity and that suffering will define us. It won't. Resurrection will. And so we can put up with hardship. We can turn the other cheek when accused. We can even love our enemies and give gentle and loving responses to their demands. This kind of equation - people give us all kinds of nasty stuff and we give them all kinds of lovely stuff - is the equation of the gospel. If we have the huge vision of God that Peter cast in chapter one and if we are certain that this huge God has chosen us (like Peter said in chapter two) then living out this equation becomes not only possible, but normal. Jesus - the exalted King - gives us all the strength and all the stamina we need to be kind to people who are not kind to us.

QUESTION FOR REFLECTION

When people are not kind to you, how do you respond?

📖 1 PETER 4

"You have spent enough time in the past doing what pagans choose to do - living in debauchery, lust, drunkenness, orgies"... Wait a minute. Am I the only one who hasn't spent time in the past doing orgies? Debauchery - yes. Lust - unfortunately yes. Drunkenness - to my shame yes. But orgies?? I once went to a party where some people were kissing in the corner but I don't remember joining in. Maybe that means this passage doesn't apply to me? Sadly I think it does. In this description of the flood of dissipation it is shocking that the only one that has an added adjective - to set it apart is the worst - is idolatry. And that cuts me to the core. I have looked to idols like the worst of them. Idolatry was neatly summed up by Augustine as any disordering of our loves. Idolatry is loving a good thing above the best thing; working so hard that I neglect my other God-given responsibilities, wanting to be liked more than wanting to do what Jesus wants, meditating on my phone when I'm trying to meditate on the word. Idolatry is a subtle sin that we can convince ourselves is not present... until we begin to suffer. Suffering is about our nightmares becoming real. We suffer most when what we love most is attacked. And so suffering always exposes our idols. That is what Peter means when he says "he who has suffered in his body is done with sin". If, when we are in real physical pain we can't love others deeply, we begin to realise where our priorities really lie. If, when we have been slighted, we use our words to get them back, then we realise how our honour is more important to us than Jesus'. And these revelations help us; they show us a new area when God wants to set us free. Living in exile and having people do people stuff to us can actually help us become holy. As long as we use all of these revelations as prompts to prayer. Because none of us have the strength to beat idolatry on our own. But through prayer - prayer that commits us to our faithful Creator - the unspeakable strength of Saviour seeps into our souls, sustaining us in goodness and reordering our loves.

QUESTION FOR REFLECTION

How has suffering led you into prayer, and then into holiness?

📖 1 PETER 5

We thrive in exile by leaning on the strength of Jesus. In him we remember we have been chosen by God. Through prayer unspeakable strength seeps into our souls. But there is one last factor, one last problem we need to be aware of if we really want to thrive. We call him the devil. The devil is real and exile is his domain; he prowls around here trying to devour people of faith. Which is a bit tricky, because we can't even see him. And so we are called to be humble; to constantly look for guidance and help from the One who can see him, from the One who has our back. It feels a bit like soldiers on the ground being guided by the officer watching both them and the enemy from the satellite in the sky. If we remain in communication then the devil will not succeed. If in humility we cast ourselves upon the Lord, if we never trust ourselves to understand anything too fully or to be able to cope with anything independently, but rather always look to Jesus and his scriptures for direction then we will do well. If we understand movement towards hardship to be Jesus way of saving us from an ambush and frustrating delays to be his way shaking off a tail, if we turn from any hint of pride by always assuming that God knows more and sees more than we ever could possibly do, then we will be resisting the devil - the father of the proud. If we always keep in our view the fact that God is the one with the mighty hand and we are the ones who are puny, well, then we will receive grace in the 'now' and a crown of glory in the 'not yet'. Humility is recognising that we are in a battle and that God is the only one who can get us through it. Humility is acknowledging that only in Him can we fulfil our calling. Humility is always resisting the temptation to not read the bible or worship or pray or love our neighbour or bear with the difficult person in housegroup by acknowledging that the One who knows better has said that these are the best things to do and it would just be plain stupid to not listen to him. And if we continue to say and to show that we can't live without Him then he will restore us. He will make us strong and firm and steadfast. And He will bring us into his eternal glory in Christ our King

QUESTION FOR REFLECTION

What shocked you most in Peter's first letter?

📖 2 PETER 1

As with every excellent meal, there is a good portion of seconds. And this second portion from Peter has a strong aroma of humility. Peter says that by the death and resurrection of Jesus we have already received everything we need for life and godliness. That is actually quite a shocking statement. We have already been given all we need to ace this test. Many of our prayers suggest we don't believe this… when we beg or plead for stuff we already have. But - in case we lean too far out of that window - this is not a push to "mega-faith" or self-reliance. If we think we apply this truth by focusing on ourselves (our Spiritual Pedigree, our Faith, our stuff) then we will end up far away from the "love" that is the climax of our faith. Rather like a blind lady receiving a guide dog, we should see the provision of the cross as a helper for us. The divine power walks alongside us helping us do what we could not do. We remain unable to see with our own eyes, but we can now ride the bus, go to the shops and work our job because the dog sees and the dog becomes our eyes. In the same way God's divine power is already with us, enabling us to live the kind of Christ-like life that was impossible for us before. We couldn't be joyful in suffering. We couldn't hold a sound mind in every strife and storm. We couldn't abound in affection for our enemies. Our hearts couldn't see and grasp those things. But the heart of Jesus could grasp those things and - by his power and his promises - his heart becomes our heart. Now if I was blind, it would be obvious how I would be led by the dog. But how am I led by my God? Peter points to the God's promises. He tells his people to pick them up or hold them tight. If Peter - who met Jesus, who walked with Jesus, who was made the boss by Jesus - calls God's promises very great and precious then I think they warrant my time. Will I be humble enough to give them it? Will I put in the effort to find them in the scriptures and score them onto my soul? Will I accept my tendency to be short-sighted and so adopt a way of life that trusts the nuzzling and nudging of the dog over the resonance of my own heart? I so much want to be like God. I so much want to see my faith give birth to love. I need to start to learn the promises of God.

QUESTION FOR REFLECTION

Which promises of God guide your day to day walk?

📖 2 PETER 2

"I watched a really good video online the other day. This preacher from South Africa was opening up some really deep truths…" Sound familiar? With the increasing availability of all kinds of teaching on the internet this chapter is more important than ever. Continuing the guide-dog metaphor, a genuine risk in exile is that you accidentally grab the wrong lead. Perhaps someone will even put the wrong lead in your hand. And then, led by a wild dog of sensuality or pride, you end up in destruction. You may think that melodramatic. In our culture - even among other church leaders - I've found people are shockingly blaisee about the risk of false teaching. To be bothered about false teaching is to be like a prig. Or a fusspot. We'd rather focus on "what we are for". But ask yourself this question; who knows more about the risks and rewards of genuine discipleship - you or the Apostle Peter? No disrespect, but I'm going to go with the one Jesus called The Rock. So, how do you protect yourself from false teaching? Well, Jesus said "By their fruit you will know them" and Peter drills into this a bit more. He encourages us to follow the trajectory of a teaching. Is this dog leading me towards humility? Strutting speeches about special revelations are seriously suspect. False teachers use such language to promote their church, their teaching, their insight over against the rest of the body of Christ. They use phrases like "When you've seen what I've seen..." and "the problem with the rest of the church is...". Preaching should enlarge our vision of God but their preaching enlarges our vision of them. Beware of such people. Please. Develop a very strong antenna for preaching that leads you away from humility. And then drop that lead. Return to the humble guys and girls who preach the main and plain message of the Messiah. Beware also of dogs headed towards sensuality. If they tell you to "be true to yourself" or to "live your dreams" be careful. They may just be immature. Or they may be leading you to a plate full of dog vomit. Good teaching helps us be true to our King. Good teaching helps us step into his dreams for us. Good teaching celebrates holiness as a beautiful possibility and revels in humility before the Great and Awesome God. Give your ear to those preachers and you will thrive in exile and be fruitful in your faith.

QUESTION FOR REFLECTION

How do you discern if preaching is "false teaching"

📖 2 PETER 3

One thing we have not yet pulled out in 2 Peter is the fact that living in exile is a choice. You choose to live as an exile rather than assimilate to your host culture. It's like Brits living in the Costa Del Sol nipping off to the English Pub for fish and chips every day. Except with Christians it is a Christ-like character and values and a certain type of behaviour that you make your daily bread. And making it your daily bread is a must. Because living as an exile is a choice. It is a choice that attracts stares, derision, and even some persecution. Why - Peter asks - should we continue to make this choice? Why don't we just adapt to our environment and live like the rest of them do? Because "The day of the LORD will come like a thief. The heavens will disappear with a roar." Exile will end. Peter really stresses this point with a huge amount of figurative language. A thief, a fire, a deluge and a fire (again). All of these point not to the smashing of this good earth but rather to an irreversible universal transformation by God. Think of Noah and the flood, except maybe a bit hotter. The fire language in particular shows God's action will be purifying and refining; destroying things that do not conform to his desires and bringing to purity those that do. To continue the metaphor Peter is saying that one day Britain will invade Spain and the fish and chip boozers will be identified and celebrated, while all those tapas bars and olive shops will be shut down. So you should get yourself down the pub. Exile will end and all you have lived for and hoped for, all you have believed in and trusted in, all those promises in the scriptures, all those instructions in the scriptures - every single one of them will be shown to have been utterly brilliant, resonating with truth. The Word of the One - even the tricky letters of Paul - will be proved devastatingly accurate in the end. And so do not give up. Do not fail. Peter - good old Pete - knew what it was to fail. He had a pastor's heart born out of his betrayal and restoration. And out of this heart he calls us friends. He knows that the wait seems long and our flesh is weak and so he calls us friends. As friends of his and friends of one another we learn to persevere. We learn what it means to really have hope. And we grow in the grace of our friend; Jesus the King.

QUESTION FOR REFLECTION

What did you get from 2 Peter?

📖 JOHN 1

A jumbo jet has landed in my garden. It has wrecked the house and the fuselage has squashed the garage. The roar of the engines still pops in my ears. I had felt pretty stretched and challenged by the 3 Synoptic gospels (Matthew, Mark and Luke) but then, out of nowhere, the hulking monstrosity that is John has just been thrust on me from above. And that is what Holy Spirit intended. John lived late into the establishment of the early church. The "disciple who Jesus loved" played grandfather to the swelling ranks of Jesus-followers, and he rapped his gnarled knuckles on the table of awe. Awe at Jesus and love of brother. Perhaps the newer, younger believers had become a little too familiar with Jesus. The inevitable dilution of wonder had gone just a little too far for the apostle to stay schtum. And so the old boy clears his throat, girds up his loins and unleashes heaven. "In the beginning was the WORD". Forget your birth. Forget this universe. There is one in our midst who preceded it all. "Through HIM ALL THINGS were made." Talk about expanding our horizons. Talk about invading our small preoccupations with a hulking beast of an idea. The challenge in John is to read it slow enough to let the Spirit penetrate our souls with the tiniest increment of these enormous, explosive truths. Awe. It's a rare commodity in any immature church. We need to slow down to catch it. And yet, while stretching towards awe we must also see that the baggage of this plain was an abundance of grace. Grace that leads to love. God is so great we must fear him and God is so loving that we must befriend him. The old man John champions a life lived in this tension. The angels of God descended to earth as well as ascended. Jesus didn't just pass by John's two disciples but asked them to "Come and see". Jesus didn't just leave for Galilee but he found Philip and asked him if he wanted to turn it into a road trip. The awesome Son of God, the everlasting, all creating one was here... and he was completely obsessed with spending time with people, with drawing into intimacy with his creation. The church's recent obsession has been sung worship, and quite rightly so. But Jesus coupled worship with relationships that went beyond a quick coffee after church. And so, if we truly have had this jumbo jet land in our garden, if we truly let Old Man John speak the Word into our hearts then we will become people who worship our socks off, and then go find our neighbours socks and wash the feet that was wearing them.

QUESTION FOR REFLECTION

Has a jumbo jet landed in your garden?

📖 JOHN 2

Considering John said he had way too many anecdotes about Jesus to include in his gospel it could seem strange that he starts with these two. Everything suggests they happened several years apart in totally different parts of Israel. One shows Jesus reluctant and discrete, happy to enable revelry and excess. The other shows Jesus ferociously zealous, totally uncompromising about God's house of prayer. Christ - a captivating cocktail of quasi-contradictions. When reading John we should see him as an early-day Quentin Tarrentino, weaving together a complex patchwork of scenes from the life of Christ to create a heart-thumping, dramatic picture of the man. The purpose of the gospel is not an orderly report (like Luke's gospel was) but a window into the central figure of any real faith. John writes to Christians to help them have life. Real life. He writes so you may know the invasion of the real Jesus into your ordinary everyday life. These two stories show the intent and implications of the invasion of the I Am. Firstly Jesus invades your life in a gentle, surprising way - flooding your human celebrations with a merry and enriching presence that makes them better by far. This is the slow creep of the gospel into your gut. This is the smile-inducing intimacy of Jesus' New Wine presence. Even now as you read this Jesus is coaxing you into tasting his presence. Even now Jesus is directing angels to serve you surprisingly sweet sustenance of his grace. Will you drink? Will you sit back, settle your mind and receive? It's easy to overlook. Then comes the second invasion; when Jesus throws the furniture around. In this second invasion Jesus demands reverence, he kicks things around in your life to foster purity and obedience. This second invasion hurts as much as the first one soothes. It is an invasion for repentance. And when this invasion comes it is easy to recoil, to front up, to look longingly back at Cana and pretend the temple can still stand as it is. "Oh, sweet Jesus, please just give me another drink!". And he will. He will. But he will also keep on sacking and keep on tipping until he has holiness and prayer and sparkling purity and manifest justice enshrined in our hearts. John shows us right up front that life - real life - embraces both invasions of this glorious Messiah. It's both love and awe. It's both soothing and convicting. It's both death and life. Will you open yourself to this contradictory King?

QUESTION FOR REFLECTION

Will you welcome both kindness and rebuke from Jesus?

📖 JOHN 3

You could scarcely get a more impressive witness than John the baptizer. But, as John himself said, he is not the focus here. John, the first among men, the most-desired conference speaker of his day, the dynamic Elijah-prophet of God... is a mere side-show, a meagre warm-up act compared to the One Who Came From Above. What does this mean? Well, look at Nicodemus. Jesus takes every human concept of greatness, he pulls perceptions of prowess to his person and he chops them off at the knee. Now that Jesus has come, the discernment of rabbis is not enough. Appreciation of miraculous signs just will not cut it. Re-tweeting a touted teachers talks falls tantalisingly short. Jesus suggests that all our measures of what it means to be "spiritual" mean diddlysquat unless we climb back up the birth canal and hook ourselves onto a whole new placenta. This gospel isn't about life improvement. It is life replacement. You have to be born again. You have to rearrange and reorganise your life to draw life and sustenance from a totally different place. I still find it staggering how hard and how rare it is to really be born again. Over and over again we think the Christian life is about tweaks and two-steps. We meet Jesus under the cover of darkness and hear that God so loved the world. And we go away encouraged. Maybe we tweak our schedule a little bit. And the rest remains unchanged. But John doesn't do that. Crazy John. What a hero. He saw the lamb, he pondered his words and then he changed-up everything. "He must become greater; I must become less" he said. It's like an entire company rebranding around a new logo, throwing away the old things that defined it and putting this new identity at the centre of its communications, its properties and its workforce. Sounds OK, until you realise that the old logo is you. Your face, your reputation, your "image" is the one being "binned" and replaced with the face of Jesus. But. Of course. The new life is so much better than the old one. It's a beautiful life now lived around a sure and certain truth. It's a truly free life that tastes of eternity and lasts as long. It's a life knowing you were loved so much that the King died for you and would do so again if he could. "It's my joy" said John. I want it to be my joy too. I want it to be yours. Will you really be born again today?

QUESTION FOR REFLECTION

Have you been born again. Or have you just tweaked a few things?

📖 JOHN 4

It is really interesting that Jesus stayed two days in Sychar. Jesus was merely passing through Samaria on his way to Galilee, so this is a fairly major departure. I'm sure Jesus had plenty of really important things that he was going to be doing in Galilee but he chose to postpone those (or perhaps even scrap them) in order to press into what he saw his Father doing in Samaria. I find this flexibility challenging. I fear I regularly surge on past Sychar and thereby miss out on seeing "many more become believers". If it was me, I'd have been off feeling smug and telling everyone about my encounter with the woman at the well. But in doing this I would have failed to see that God wanted me to press in further. I would have missed a whole village coming to faith. I need to be more willing to let God mess up my timetable. I want to be more open to how much He actually wants to use me. Why? Because Jesus is not just my truth. He is not just My Jesus, My Saviour. Jesus is the Saviour of the whole world. John is very clear to point this out; he started his gospel showing Jesus offering salvation to a few men of Israel, but has swiftly and deliberately shown how Jesus also included Samaritans in his call. And this is the crucial point - these "outsiders" are brought in through our willingness to drop our "normal" life choices. That is what "love of brother" actually means; we spend days in Sychar. This might be moving some things on our schedule but it might also mean being willing to let some of our cultural preferences slide. In his conversation with the Samaritan woman Jesus conveys such freedom of access to the Father - just to worship in the Spirit and truth. There is huge scope for diversity in the kingdom. Which sounds so jolly until someone prays in a way that annoys you. Or they want to sing songs you don't like. Or say something that strikes you as rude. Let's be honest. It isn't easy to stay two days in Sychar. But, it is crucial if we are to walk in the paths of our king. As Paul says in Ephesians, the desire of God is to bring all things together under the one head. God's vision is for his Kingdom to be an extraordinary, life-filled, brimmingly diverse family. And he invites us to be door keepers and ambassadors for this family - going the extra mile and smiling that extra smile in order to welcome in those who we never would normally have known.

QUESTION FOR REFLECTION

What would "staying two days in Sychar" look like for you?

📖 JOHN 5

John has exploded this extraordinary man into our consciousness. He has shown Jesus to be Lamb of God, to have power to perform mind-bending miracles, to be the one around whom all nations should form, to be the one who is above all. But, for many of John's early readers there would be a problem with this. As any good Jewish boy would know, there is only one who is above all and His name is YAHWEH. John tackles that problem here. He doesn't provide a doctrine of the Trinity but rather quotes Jesus' own words about how he relates to the Father and, crucially, what the Father has given him to do in the world. (By the way this is a pretty cool example of how we can advocate for Jesus - just quote his words and talk about what he is doing in the world.) John shows the Father has given Jesus a commodity to trade in. The commodity is real, unadulterated, soul-shaking life. But Jesus doesn't sell it and he doesn't just distribute it willy nilly. He bestows it on certain people, and it gives him great pleasure to do so. This is an incredible image of Jesus; a bit like a company rep who is sent onto the street to hand out free goods to build a good reputation for the company. Except the company is the most prestigious you could ever find, the goods are so precious no money could buy them. And the motive is genuine concern for the crowds rather than self-interested publicity. Jesus has been sent by His Father not just to give some people a temporary, jolly boost but to determine destinies That is what all the talk of judgement is about. And the reason Jesus is so trusted a company rep is that he is utterly in tune with the Father in every single way. He does exactly what the Father asks him to do. All the time. Which begs the question - am I in tune with the Father? Are you? We could never be totally like Jesus. But we could be more like Him than we are. That is what Old Man John is showing us. Jesus shows us what our life could look like if we chose to make it so. If I soaked my life in prayer and made every effort to obtain the praise that comes from God I could actually look a bit like Jesus. Because of the Spirit, you and I can now live a life utterly in tune with the Father. We can become people whose every word is a word that God himself would have spoken. We can become people who do extraordinary things because our hands and mouths become willing instruments of God's intentions. I'm hugely motivated by that idea. I hope you are too. Let's choose to increase our commitment to prayer.

QUESTION FOR REFLECTION

If you stopped right now and asked God what he wants you to do in this next hour, what would he say?

📖 JOHN 6

This is like a massive contraction in the latter stages of labour. Things have been building for a while but this is a big one; the knuckles are seriously whitening and the midwives are putting on their gloves. Everyone is thinking "Here comes the Kingdom". Everyone except Jesus. He has pooched off to a mountainside to have some time on his own. To the crowds this feeding of the 5000 looks like one of the last major signs of the end of exile. The long promised heavenly banquet is being served up and the king is being unveiled. Surely enemies are about to be vanquished and friends bequeathed into a glorious time of prosperity and peace? No. Or at least, not quite. Jesus is the King and he is ending this exile but he hasn't yet shown the people the full expanse of his kingdom. People haven't yet grasped that his domain is not just Israel's friends but some of her enemies as well. And they haven't grasped that Jesus hasn't come just to vanquish people but to transform them into better versions of themselves. So Jesus walks away to let the people cool off from their passions. These people aren't yet ready for this baby. And then Jesus walks on the water. Jesus subjects nature to his mastery. He is God incarnate, I AM here among us. "Fear not" he says and indeed we shouldn't. For while Jesus confounds our simple minds and sometimes seems to dash our hopes, we can never doubt his greatness. Jesus shows us here twice that he is too majestic for anything to threaten or overthrow his magnificent intentions for the world. And so we know that our true hopes can never be dashed, only the ill-formed ones that are too small or incomplete to hold all the bounty he is pushing our way. Jesus may have seemed to walk away from your prayers, but keep your eyes on the water because he is going to calm your fears when he walks to you across the sea.

QUESTION FOR REFLECTION

Some of Jesus' teaching is hard teaching. Some of his treatment of us isn't what we expected. Will those things cause us to depart from him?

📖 JOHN 7

The trouble is, it is a ridiculous idea that God would walk on the earth. If you are honest you will agree that, ever since the sin of Adam, we have all hidden from the idea that God would actually be found among us. We happily buy into the idea of holy people, we even look for human 'saviours' who will get us out of our latest problem or give us a push up the next rung of the ladder. Many buy into the concept of a divine force out there somewhere that we might be able to tap into like a Jedi. But the idea that the Almighty and Eternal One could actually appear before us and look pretty normal - well that is plain crazy. And that was the problem of the crowds at the festival; they were looking to give things to God, they were even looking for God to give things to them - primarily a new powerful king messiah who could set them free from their problems - but they just did not seem to conceive of God himself coming to them. As human beings we all have this same problem - we think God wants us to give him stuff, or that God wants to give us stuff and we miss the fact that God wants to come to us and befriend us. God wants to come to us and change us. God wants to come to us and put living water in us so that we might constantly feel fresh, constantly feel enlivened and constantly press into friendship with him. How are you doing on that one? How are you doing in putting aside your pessimism and false sense of religious obligation and really perceiving God approaching you in shockingly intimate ways? How is your friendship with God? I must confess I constantly struggle with the blasphemous feel of the whole thing. I constantly find myself wanting to hide in the trees and put on a fig leaf and watch God rather than have him come to me and minister my heart with his truth that sets me free. But every day Jesus is here. Every day Jesus is speaking to me his divine truth. Every day Jesus is beckoning me to come and drink of his love. The ridiculous thing would be to stay hiding in those trees.

QUESTION FOR REFLECTION

How is your friendship with God?

📖 JOHN 8

The devil is a bit of a background figure for the majority of the bible but he has a massive impact on the whole redemption story. I wonder how much you are aware of him? One of the biggest changes in my faith in recent years has been a growing awareness of the realness of the devil. In this passage Jesus calls out the devil as an enemy who needs to be defended against. Jesus then shows how the devil has bodies on the ground; although the agents he has (the Pharisees) don't even realise they are working for him. Jesus' beef with the pharisees was that they echoed the devil's song that prevents people from building their identities on the loving words of God. The devil advocates for us to base our identity on our history or our performance. The devil loves us to think our salvation ultimately depends on ourselves. The devil will put people around us who tell us that real life is found in us being true to ourselves, that the key to a better future is us believing in ourselves, that you can do "it" if you try hard enough or are smart enough or if you get that lucky break. These people don't realise they are echoing the accusations of the Accuser. Unwittingly they are making us slaves to a law that we can never keep; they are heaping up burdens on us that will crush us in the end. Even the best wisdom - like that of the Torah - ends up killing us because we are broken humans who cannot achieve our own salvation. Any identity based on what we find within or on what we can achieve for ourselves will carry that same brokenness inherent within it. We need One to come from outside to liberate us from the brokenness we feel but cannot diagnose, from that crushing slave master that looms over us but we cannot shake off. Jesus comes to bring that intervention. He was sent to us by the Father of all and he knows what our true problem is. Jesus holds eternal wisdom about our greatest problems and how to see them resolved. And so the fight in this age is to build our identity on him; to decide who we are not by what others say about us - whether good or bad - or by how good or bad we really are, but to follow his light and to gladly listen to every word that he speaks.

QUESTION FOR REFLECTION

How much does the opinion of others affect your identity? Who does Jesus say you are?

📖 JOHN 9

It just seems so illogical. Why wouldn't you want to go to Jesus to get life? Jesus has healed a man born blind. Eyes that were not properly formed in the womb have had their creation process completed by Him. Jesus has shown that he can mould, sustain and extend matter. Money can't do that. Fame can't do that. Even Keeping up with the Khardashians can't do that. Any sane person who is looking for life would at the very least want to explore Jesus some more. If Jesus can tap the power behind creation then who knows what he can do for you. Maybe that six-pack is not out of reach after all. Maybe he could sort out that cellulite. Or maybe he could renovate your heart and ignite your soul and renew your mind and give you a peace and a joy and a taste of something that you never dreamed possible. But some people bizarrely choose not to explore him. Some - like the man's parents - are so strung up in the opinions of others that they deliberately shield themselves from Jesus' life for fear of looking bad. How dumb is that? And then others, like the pharisees, are so intent on preserving their puny little lot that they deliberately obscure the truth about who Jesus is and cling to what they have. You couldn't make it up! And then finally there are others who are just not using logic at all - they are so caught up in their prejudices and wrong-thinking that they just can't even be bothered to think about what they are seeing. This is the clear message John is giving through this passage; don't be swayed by the naysayers, don't be upset by the opponents. Press on. Press on to gain life in Jesus. And encourage others to do the same. Encourage others to use their eyes and use their minds and explore this man. For, if they do, they will find him re-creating their very selves.

QUESTION FOR REFLECTION

In what ways has Jesus renovated your soul?

📖 JOHN 10

I must confess that the ability of demons to open the eyes of the blind is a topic that I have never heard discussed in a coffee shop. I suspect that many of my friends would think it is a retrograde view that comes from another age. But the activity of demons, incredibly, is not the thing in this passage that is most likely to prompt the gag-reflex. That honour lies in the offensively exclusive statements Jesus makes about himself. Jesus raises his eyes to the crowds and, without the faintest whiff of irony or self-aggrandisement, informs them that he is their only hope in life. He eyeballs men and women and tells them that without his love... they are screwed. The legacy that Jesus established and John passed on is defined by exclusive statements about Jesus. It is a legacy we have received but that we seem to shuffle our feet in fulfilling. We are not called to be nice. We are not called to make people happy or to educate them or to heal them. We are not called to bring world peace or write good books. At least, that is not the sum of our calling. That is not the root or the foundation or the framework of our task. These are really good things and things that we hope for. But, ultimately, our calling is to help people find Jesus. Our calling is to show people the good farmer who gives overflowing life and who came back from the dead. Our calling is to help people make a decision about what they are going to do with Jesus. Our calling is to expose the death that lies outside of the kingdom and to offer the life that is found in the King. I feel like Jesus needs to be talked about more. Not in a sappy, or an arrogant or an un-natural way, but as the watchman who opens the gate to life. As the one who calls out every single person's name and invites them to come in and find peace.

QUESTION FOR REFLECTION

How could you talk about Jesus more?

📖 JOHN 11

With three words he raised a man. And one of the words was restrictive; if he hadn't named Lazarus who knows how many wrapped bodies would have emerged from the tombs? It was quite a display of power. It could make you feel very intimidated. But he also wept. He wept. I must confess I have never wept over someone else's misfortune. I've cried over the depth of my sin and blubbed with joy while trying to give my wedding speech. But feeling someone else's pain to the extent that my heart breaks a little? That requires a depth of empathy beyond anything I have acquired. I like to feel that I'm the one who can get the job done. I've got the stiff upper lip that helps me make the right decisions even in the difficult situations. Jesus makes that sound stupid. He wailed like a baby and sorted out the problem. To have in one man both the epitome of supportive friendship and the pinnacle of transformative power, well, that man would have to be a liberator of epic proportions. And so we can come to him - the Son of God who has come into the world - both with trepidation and with boldness. We shuffle towards God Most High, towards the One who wields intoxicatingly potent power. And we fling ourselves heavily upon the extended embrace of the Lord who Sees Us, the one who came to build solidarity with us. We know that God feels raging sorrow over the pains that plague us. We know that the Almighty Maker and Restorer of All is not unmoved by our plight.

QUESTION FOR REFLECTION

Have you ever felt Jesus weep over you or with you?

📖 JOHN 12

There are two statements in this chapter that rub against one another like tectonic plates under California. The friction between them sends shockwaves through my soul. Firstly the statement is God's; "I have glorified my name and will glorify it again" (v28). The phrase is imbued with confidence and hope. It speaks of a hulking beast unthreatened by the future. It sounds like Tyson Fury at a pre-fight weigh-in he already knows he will win. And yet - a bit like Tyson Fury - the crowd who heard it went away baffled; they heard the talk of glory but they thought it was thunder. Get this; God will glorify himself in his own way and he will be remarkably unphased that the world will misunderstand it. And then the Jewish leaders; "This is getting us nowhere" they say (v19). And that reveals so much. The leaders want glory, but their view of glory is defined by the masses. They need the people's approval and recognition and following and praise. And so they swap and change what they are doing, becoming increasingly desperate to try to grasp hold of the glory they desire. They will try whatever is necessary to get the following of their fellows. Two tectonic plates shifting against each other - one secure, defined but misunderstood - the other insecure, fleeting and desperate to "win". The way John sums up the conflicting stances is like this - one prefers the praises of people, the other prioritises the praises of God. And this is why it sends shockwaves through my soul. Because I am so often like the Jewish leaders - aren't you? I hate being misunderstood. I flee from obscurity. I quickly lurch in new directions if I think that will win me more friends. Ultimately I lack the confidence that God defines glory. I want to become like Jesus. I want to prefer the praises of God to the praise of any man. Addressing this very question Jesus tells us to walk in the light while the daylight remains (v35). I take that to mean that I should hang around him and listen to his words. I should keep on doing New Testament Journey and meditate on those passages where Jesus is speaking to me. That will settle the ground. That will place me on the solid rock where no matter how people treat me I will stand secure, imbued with confidence and filled with hope.

QUESTION FOR REFLECTION

What does it mean to be praised by God?

📖 JOHN 13

Jesus tells John in advance that Judas is the one who will betray him. This little whisper across the dinner table could have put the whole cross and resurrection plan in jeopardy. What if John had jumped up and started berating Judas? And yet Jesus takes that risk for the sake of deepening his relationship with John. He loved John so much that he told him his secrets. It almost feels reckless. I believe Jesus is equally committed to pursuing deeper relationships with us. If we would just recline next to him and ask him questions we may be gobsmacked by what he discloses. It is all part of the 'new command' that Jesus is giving. Jesus demonstrates with John the kind of love he wants all of us to have as the defining mark of our discipleship. Wow. I know there are many people in church really seeking to love one another. We have been overwhelmed by how much people have loved us in church. But I still want to press into this more. I want to give people more time, more encouragement, more support and more of the Father. I'm such an amateur in this. Especially if the people I'm meant to love act stupid. Some betray Jesus. Some deny Jesus with their actions and their words. Lots of them misunderstand Jesus and keep on asking questions that make no sense. Yes, lots of people are just like the disciples were, and they are just like me. And that is why Jesus' love feels quite so reckless. That is why it is noticed by the world. Because a love that washes feet, reclines together and trusts others with information, a love that knows about betrayal and loves the betrayer anyway - that is the kind of love that is different. That's the kind of love we all want to receive and Jesus invites us to give. I have so much more to learn from Jesus about how to really love. Oh God would you please help me to become more like Jesus and to lavish love on my fellow followers in the way.

QUESTION FOR REFLECTION

What is Jesus whispering to you in this time?

📖 JOHN 14

Sometimes you wonder whether Jesus was trying to be as confusing as possible. If we've seen him then we have seen the Father and yet he is the Way to the Father. He is representing the Father and the Spirit will represent him but they are all One and while he is going away he will come back again. And Father Son and Spirit are all in one another. This is Jesus explaining the Trinity to us in a way that we might be able to understand and, for 2000 years, we humans have stood with confused looks on our faces, scratching our heads and saying "sorry, can you just go back over that again?". The truth is that there is something about God that is exotically mysterious. The Trinity will always be beyond us. Something that we could never possibly understand. But, as Jesus is stressing here, there is also something about God that is slap bang in our faces; touchable, visible, teaching us and caring for us. There is the Father, seen in the Son, known in the Holy Spirit. God is not distant and remote - he is here, calming our hearts, leading us in truth, giving us peace. It is quite rare for us to refer to Holy Spirit as the Counsellor; I've never heard anyone pray "Come, O Counsellor". And yet, in some ways that title emphasises the relational aspect of God more than the usual term does. Holy Spirit points to the "beyondness" of the Trinity. The Counsellor to the "here-ness" of the Trinity. To know the Trinity as Jesus discloses the Trinity is to know both the beyondness and the nearness. Simultaneously beyond knowledge and yet being known. Paradoxically "just right", calming and comforting us and yet "too much", stretching and astonishing us. As we've seen all through this gospel; growth comes when we press into both extremes - when the light shone in our hearts illuminates both friendship with God and fear of God; both bold faith-filled expectation of answered prayer and humble leaning on God's peace in times of trouble.

QUESTION FOR REFLECTION

Are you growing both in faith filled expectation and in humble dependence?

📖 JOHN 15

"It's so jolly sat here on this vine. The Father really deeply loves me and accepts me and I love him so, so much. It is like a perfect all-inclusive holiday just sat here soaking up his rays. I'm relaxing and munching on the free food from the bar and.... what!! What are you doing with those secateurs Jesus? You need to be careful with those; they could really hurt someone. What do you mean you are going to use them on me? When you said the Father was the gardener I thought you meant gardening like I do gardening - switching on the sprinkler once in a while and watching with casual interest to see how everything gets on? I didn't expect you to take pieces of me - things that I care about and have spent time investing in and growing - and to prune them and cut them off without even asking me if you can?" That (or something like it) is the inner-narrative of the disciple who finds herself experiencing some pain. And it is something we all need to grapple with if we want to become mature. The truth is that in recent years we have lost the idea that the Father is committed to working on us and not just through us. We love sharing testimonies of how God used us to heal someone but we think that God teaching us to obey him went out of fashion with Aaron's ephod. The biggest act of love from God to us is to prune us with pain. Now I know that sounds almost blasphemous to our modern ears but the ancient followers of Jesus, especially in the monastic tradition, saw challenging circumstances and trial as an essential and desirable element of their growing in the Lord. So, whether you are suffering right now or just want to learn how to suffer well in the future - hear this; wherever your suffering springs from (whether the devil, your own stupidity or judgement from God) God can and will use every instance of suffering to prune you for fruitfulness. God - the one who really loves you - the one who died for you - the one who is all wise - will always turn every instance of pain into your deliverance and glory, if you continue to remain in him. So we can pray for healing, and pray for freedom from pain, but even greater than those prayers we ask Him to help us remain in His love.

QUESTION FOR REFLECTION

How has the Father pruned you recently?

📖 JOHN 16

Jesus has been gradually unveiling himself to his disciples. He's dropped many clues and they know they are onto something... but they still aren't quite sure what. How encouraging. If we "read" the gospel properly - choosing to lay aside our preconceptions and put ourselves in the place of the disciples - then we will share their befuddlement. We know Jesus is Word Become Flesh, the Light who came to shine in our darkness. But what that all means for us - well, it still feels slightly elusive. It's like we've been climbing the spiral staircase inside the Tower in the Palace of Westminster. We can tell we are getting closer to Big Ben but we've also got slightly dizzy and exhausted, wondering whether we can make it at all. Now, in this chapter, we lay eyes on the Great Bell. Here Jesus begins to spell things out in clean, unambiguous language (he continues the "plain speaking" in chapter 17) - Jesus has come temporarily to release the Spirit to enable many people to come to know the Father. That we would Know the Father - this is the end game of Jesus' work. Ah. Our ears, our faces, our minds resound with the reverberating realisation that we barely know ourselves, let alone Almighty God. Can I, the real me, really know the Father? Really know him? God can feel so distant. Jesus can feel like he lived so long ago. Sometimes 'knowing God' can feel so depressingly ungraspable - like trying to hug Big Ben when it is wildly swinging back and forth. But that feeling ignores what Jesus said about the Counsellor. You see, knowing God is not about our efforts, it is not about us reaching out to touch the bell. It is about the ringing of the bell reverberating in us - the knowledge of God is received, not won. It is about His work, not our work. The Life of Faith is about being alert and being open to the Spirit of God who comes to us, convicting us of our sin, leading us into truth and making Jesus known to us. Oh what freedom there is in this truth. When you really understand it it changes EVERYTHING. It is not about us, except for how we respond. And so - in the words of Gordon Fee "the first imperative of the Christian Life is to be filled with the Spirit". We must go on being filled with the Spirit and to prioritise the knowing of our God who came to make himself known.

QUESTION FOR REFLECTION

What knowledge of himself has God put inside of you?

📖 JOHN 17

I can't believe Jesus prayed for me. I sort of knew he did but the hammering force of him actually doing it has only just hit me. My heart feels like it is charging around in my chest. That he would think to do that! It's staggering. But what he prayed for me is not what I expected. I would have expected him to pray for me what he prayed for the disciples - protection from the evil one, experience of the full measure of joy, sanctification - this is all good stuff that I long to see happening in my life. But instead Jesus prays that we will all be "one"? This needs some thought. As he reclines with a few guys in an upper room Jesus casts his genius mind forward to the billions scattered across every nation who would be swept into his sheepfold. And he sees the battleground will be fought over our "oneness". We'd be dumb not to dwell on this. Already - even with the few in the upper room - Jesus has seen the "oneness" begin to break apart as the devil entered Judas. The seed that leads to the scattering of the 11 has been sown. If Jesus' Kingdom was to be extended on earth the church would need to cling more closely to "oneness" than the disciples were currently doing. And that context - I believe - is the key to understanding what Jesus is praying for. It's not a pitch for a bland ecumenism. It's not a fuzzy smile and shoulder rub for anyone who says they believe in Jesus. The thrust of this prayer is for the church militant - hard pressed, outmanned, outgunned - holding the line, living as a band of brothers, working for the good of the sisterhood, not letting fault lines crack, lifting one another up in prayer, all for one and one for all. I'm remarkably unfussed about denominations and church titles. Doing joint projects with other churches is fine as far as it goes. That is not what Jesus is praying for here. What really matters is that whatever our title, whatever our project, we love the church. We love the whole of Jesus' church. We fight for them, mourn with them and rejoice with them. We hold them up in prayer and earnestly desire that they should know the Father. That they would be in the Spirit and in Christ just as Jesus was in the Father and the Father was in him. If that is where we get to, then we will really appear to be the body of Christ that God has made us. If that is where we get to, then it will be clear to all of creation that the Father is real and that he loves his world.

QUESTION FOR REFLECTION

Do you love the whole of Jesus' church?

📖 JOHN 18

We have it laid out here plainly - Jesus is a king. People bow to kings. People serve kings. People honour kings and cheer for kings. People look to kings for protection and they look to kings for provision. People look to kings for identity, for missions, for flags and for callings. Jesus is a king. We should treat him like a king. But Jesus' kingdom is not of this world and that is a less familiar concept. What could that mean? Jesus' next line is instructive: his kingdom is from another place; not 'in' another place but 'from' it. His kingdom is about testimony to truth, not taking of territory. Jesus' Kingdom is about faithful and fruitful witness to the Life of Heaven - to Lived Truth - that is going to be arriving on That Coming Day. Jesus is bringing a flavour of his kingdom to earth not to claim land but to point to a better land, not to plunder wealth but to use it to show to real wealth, not to build a reputation but to invite others to share in his everlasting honour and glory that will one day consume all the earth. No wonder Pilate was perplexed. He wanted things now. He wanted everything now because Now was his Truth. And so we see that Jesus' Kingdom is about one thing only in this time - it is about people. Jesus came to raise the dead; to bring true light to enlighten every man, woman and child. He calls us as his subjects to share his passions and his method - as exiles in this age. We are to bow and to serve to testify to the Lived Truth that is coming from another place. The Christendom Project - with its associated Crusades and Culture Wars - is ill conceived. It acts like the Kingdom (or the Millenium or whatever other word people want to use) can be established now by people by force. But Jesus' kingdom is not of the world. And it is His Kingdom to establish, not ours. If we are to be good subjects we will follow the ways of our King who is going to Come. Our task right now is to be faithful witnesses to Our Kingdom and His Kingdom. We gain resources to give them away. We give the best we have not to build our reputations but to salvage others. And we worship. Oh boy do we worship. As living worshippers we put on display the Lived Truth of the Kingdom from another place, that others may discover the better life for themselves. This led Jesus to the cross. Where is it leading you today?

QUESTION FOR REFLECTION

How could your life reflect the beauty and glory of the Kingdom from above?

📖 JOHN 19

The cross is so baffling. Every time I really come back to it I feel my ears ringing with silence. I feel my soul having the carpet pulled from under its feet. The cross undoes everything that is self-seeking and proud in me. The cross leaks away my silent assumption that I advance by being good enough, by winning, by the effort of my self. The cross shows us how our King wins... and that should baffle us. Most kings who are on crosses are pretty rubbish kings. Most kings on crosses are being proven to be failures. But this king on this cross at this particular moment is at the height of his powers. He is fulfilling scripture. That doesn't make sense. Not in 21st century London at least it doesn't. You can't lose in order to win - you need to fight to win. You can't die in order to gain - you need to beat others to gain. But the cross carves up all of that in me. It convicts it and smashes it and clears it all away. This has always been the way Our God wins in our world. This is how light penetrates darkness. Light penetrates darkness like a patient ferment; by the washing of feet, by weeping with the weepers, by unflinchingly speaking the truth, but doing it wrapped in love. Light offers up life in meekness and confidence, in surrender and assertion, in a defiant death that will probably end up being a victory, but which looks like a desolation on this day. This is how we fight our battles; through the cross... and that should baffle us. Don't move on in the bible until the cross grips you and tips your life on the floor. Don't move on from the cross until it feels like a jumbo jet that has landed in your garden. If we come away from the cross not thinking that everything is up for grabs then maybe we have not really come to the cross at all. We need to spend some time at the cross. We need to let the cross scar us and challenge us time and time and time again. For if we don't really come to the cross then we can't really come to the empty tomb either. If we try to win our way, we will never win at all... at least in the end. And winning in the end is what the cross enables us to receive.

QUESTION FOR REFLECTION

How has the cross affected you? How has it changed how you fight your battles?

📖 JOHN 20

Like the smell of freshly baked cookies this chapter is delicious to me. It reminds me of deep delight in the past. It excites me about pleasures yet to come. It wafts out of what happened in the gap between chapters 19 and 20; Jesus raised from the dead. I might have exploited the marvel of that a little longer, but John focuses on the cocktail of responses of the disciples - and how Jesus in sweet grace - leads each responder into life. First there is Mary who - in mourning and loss - has become an unnamed and confused woman. Jesus doesn't approach her directly. He comes from the side with gentleness. And then, with one word, he re-names her. With one word he turns her life. The word was only her name - nothing clever - but somehow the way Jesus uses it - the context into which he sets it - eclipses her dread with joy, swallows up her death with life. I've had those "unclever and yet life-shifting" encounters with Jesus. Have you? Oh they are so delicious. Next there is Thomas. Hurting. Isolated. Cynicism creeping into his considerations. Forever called "doubting" by the church. But not by Jesus. Jesus does not despise his agonised thoughts. Jesus doesn't directly deal with the response; he leaves Thomas a week to be haunted by his hurt (isn't that so much like Jesus...). But then he comes. He comes as one uninvited and unexpected. There is nothing "unclever" about this encounter; he offers Thomas very few words but a touch that goes beyond knowledge - to put your hands in a dead man who has come back to life. And Thomas - whether he manages the touch or not - is wrecked. And re-made. All in that moment. To him This Is Enough. And again, I remember those moments when Jesus' "Enough" has exploded into my dejected soul. But it is the central encounter and response that excites me the most - the breathing of the Spirit onto the disciples - the sending as the Father has sent. I've enjoyed receiving the Spirit. It's the greatest pleasure of my life to have Spirit living in me, whispering to me, encouraging me. He delights me. And yet I detect in this story untapped delights in the Spirit's desires for me. To be empowered to be sent as Jesus was sent. Oh Wow. I know it and yet I know there is more still to be enjoyed. Are you on the same page as me in this? Is this what you yearn for also? Why don't we eat these cookies together?

QUESTION FOR REFLECTION

What experiences have you had with the resurrected Jesus? Has he come to you with a word, or a touch, or a breath?

📖 JOHN 21

You get the impression that chapter 21 was added to the 20 chapters of John like the extra bit in a film as the credits are rolling. Why? What does it add? Well, I think it adds that extra bit of texture to our understanding of resurrection life. It's a texture we love. It is the texture of His Grace Being Sufficient and His Power being Made Perfect in our Weakness; if only we will Love. Back in chapter 20 we saw that Peter wasn't a very good runner (John beat him to the empty tomb). In this chapter we see that he was a truly rubbish swimmer and an ineffective fisherman. There is also the small thing about Peter denying Jesus three times and leaving him to be killed. But here - just a few weeks after that teeth-gnashing, insomnia-inducing betrayal - Peter is beckoned back to Jesus. They don't talk about the fish-finger breakfast. Jesus doesn't seem to care about the paucity of Peter's 'earthly talents'. And most shocking of all Jesus doesn't even bring up the "courtyard episode". All he wants to know is how much Peter could love. Three times he asks him about his capacity to love. To really love. I think sometimes I lose sight of that. I start thinking Jesus wants to inspect my sin in great detail and diagnose my latest dysfunctions. Or I get too focussed on perfecting human skills and overcoming my weaknesses. But Jesus talks to Peter about his love. Just his love. His mission is simple; "Take care of my sheep". Jesus says the same to all of us, I think. Life in him is about love. Love that is greater than what we are bad at or good at. Love that is greater than what we have failed at or succeeded at. Love that doesn't compare us to others or strive for status or need us to become functional. Just love; the love that washes and weeps and walks towards the cross. The Logos became flesh and he opened our eyes to love.

QUESTION FOR REFLECTION

What has Jesus done in you as you have read through the book of John?

📖 1 JOHN 1

Fellowship with God is the deep, hope-imbuing core of the faith. John's letter urges us on to the pulsating life-source of the Way; fellowship with the Father. Forget the slightly naff-sounding "personal relationship with Jesus". We are not talking about a daily 5 minute check-in to get an inspiring thought and confess the odd sin. We are talking about fellowship. Naked, intense, bonafide fellowship with the Father. Fellowship is inviting Him to look over every cell in our bodies and every fleeting thoughts in our minds. Fellowship is letting Him run his hands over every sweep of our emotions and every urge of our souls. Fellowship is us beholding Him and sitting with Him, chatting with Him and being silent with Him. Fellowship is us and God, naked, intense, bonafide. And you know if you have it. Because from fellowship everything else flows. Fellowship yields ecstasy. John calls it his "joy being complete". Fellowship with the Father opens new doors on the corridor of your soul, doors that lead to freshness and fancy. If you have never known unexpected delight - unconnected to your circumstances - simply a gift from the Father, then maybe you've been missing out on the fellowship He offers. Maybe you have been deceiving yourself? For fellowship leads us into the Way. The pleasure you are pursuing is picked up in the Presence. The pleasure you are pursuing is - shockingly - pick up in being pure; being whole; being entirely one with yourself and with your God. This purity, this oneness is also picked up in the Presence. Because in the presence your imperfections are exposed and then they are forgiven and they are washed. Sometimes this includes words. Sometimes this includes tears. But always - always - this includes the active presence of the Father; the deliberate drifting into devotion to him. Our fellowship is with the Father and with his Son, Jesus Christ. Is that true for you? Is the presence your pulsating life-source of your faith? Please make it so - it is the only way to really have eternal life.

QUESTION FOR REFLECTION
What does your fellowship with the Father look like?

📖 1 JOHN 2

This is where the antichrist language comes in. For John - as it was for all the authors of the New Testament - the End Times began at the death and resurrection of Jesus. We are now in the Time of the End and so we should expect a conflict of two Kingdoms to define our Age. The antichrist is the spiritual power who fights against the church. But the antichrist doesn't look like we might think. The biblical picture of the antichrist is not aggressively opposed to religion or to the idea of God or being "good". It doesn't have the theme-tune from the omen or paint itself red. At least, most of the time it doesn't. A front-on attack like that would be too easy for the saints to spot and snuff out before it snagged them. Instead this straying spirit smoothly steers us into seeing Jesus as a reflection of ourselves. It is very nice about it. Under its influence Jesus becomes an interesting person, but without power to make us change. God becomes a maker of the heavens but never close enough to touch. The antichrist deceives us into denying that Jesus really was God come to this very earth as a real human being. If the antichrist can detach our faith in Jesus from our daily life, then we can live a weak faith that never threatens the gates of hell. If we can become Christians who "believe" but never "do", who "chant" but never "change" then the antichrist has done its job; we've been taken out of the game. This is crucial if we are to understand the warfare we are in. We defeat the anti-christ through reminding ourselves that Jesus was God made flesh and that Jesus is our friend for this earth. Jesus brings heaven and earth together. And so we can never really love this world where the fragrance of the antichrist's master can be sniffed at every turn. Instead we act and love the world into becoming all that it will be when Jesus returns. We live the future reign of Jesus' Kingship now - through pressing into love and pressing away from sin. So as you commute today, or drop kids at school or work from home, or do your daily chores, look at the world differently. See it not as "home" but as contested territory, and choose to do all you do in a way that brings heaven and earth together, just like Jesus would do if he was living your life.

QUESTION FOR REFLECTION

How are you inviting God to fellowship with you in every single area of your life?

📖 1 JOHN 3

This is his command: to believe in the name of his Son, Jesus Christ, and to love one another as he commanded us (v23). Love one another. When we love other people our hearts can be at rest in God's presence. When we love one another we feel confident in our God. So I'd like to spend more of my energies on loving other people. I wonder if you feel the same? That means laying more things down. That means giving more stuff away. It sounds like a bit of a bummer but actually it is not. I've never had a material possession that has come close to the satisfaction of feeling confident in my God. Our new car (when it was new) felt pretty satisfying for a day or so but then it got a bit grubby and someone spilled food on it and I realised it actually wasn't that brilliant after all. Not compared to a heart permanently at rest with my God. I'm becoming increasingly convinced that there is nothing sweeter than expressing pure love to brothers and sisters in the faith. They are worth laying everything down for. To show them love just feels like the purest act that I could ever perform. That's why my wife and I have committed to spending as many Sundays at church as we can. That is why we lead a small group. That is why we have tried to organise our lives so we can lay down our lives for those around us. Because when we do that - when we love with actions and in truth - it feels like the most magnificent way to spend an hour (or two or three or four). Better than "seeking a blessing", better than "pursuing my dreams", better even than trying to "do evangelism" is expressing the pure love of Jesus to a person God loves. I wish we all prayed for that more. I wish we all wanted to love more. I wish we all wanted to give away more. When we really love one another we will look just like our Father who gave it all for us as an expression of pure love.

QUESTION FOR REFLECTION

Who do you really love? How are you doing that?

📖 1 JOHN 4

"We know and rely on the love God has for us." (v14). This is the wonderful voyage of our faith. There is always a fair wind behind us. Whenever we feel like we are just lolling around, going nowhere, lost at sea - we can come back to this. We can raise again the mighty mainsails of our faith, and let the fresh, reliable wind of God blow us back on course. The wind of his love always blows. It always blows strong - strong enough to carry your ship and mine all the way to the shore. The cross has assured us of this. The death of Jesus as an atoning sacrifice for our sins has assured us forever that the Father loves us strong. He loves us strong and He loves us now. He loves us in this moment. I think that takes time to accept. It takes even longer to understand. And the hardest thing of all is to rely on it. Imagine a life so convinced of the love of the Father that every single interaction, every single thought process was steered by his love. No more striving. No more insecurity. No need to win a fight or grasp for a prize. Imagine if we had the ability to take love-based risks for others and to give away stuff for their sake knowing we can never lose out. Mull a moment on the magnificence of that. If your soul becomes fueled and steered by a reliance on God's love then you could live in staggering goodness all of the time. This is what fellowship with the Father can give us. This is what the Anointing from the Holy One can rub into us. This is what it means to be set free from our sins. John sets the ethical bar of the believer so high not because he is unaware of our weaknesses but because he is so aware of God's love. The Father loves us and will set us free from our sins when we learn to rely on the love of our God.

QUESTION FOR REFLECTION

How could you push deeper into understanding the love of God, even becoming someone who relies on it in every way?

📖 1 JOHN 5

"He who has the Son has life" (5:12). Life is the shore that the love of God blows us towards. The early Christians didn't think the word 'life' summed up the sheer extravagance of what was on offer so they put the word "eternal" in front of it. It pimped up the idea like golden alloys on a Bentley. But today the phrase 'eternal life' seems a bit religious and dry. We need to think about it again. For John "eternal life" (or just "life") is the most exquisite and long-lasting pleasure available on this earth. It is life in all its fullness as you enter every single moment infused with the love of God. Eternal life is breakfasting in gladness for the provision of your creator who almost seems like he is sat at your table. Eternal life is having deep and vivid friendships where you give and see them grow. Eternal life is truly understanding who we are; knowing peace while standing in a train or overflowing with joy while sitting on the toilet. This God-fuelled life wafts us out into the world to see human potential and to give ourselves for its coming. This is what Jesus did and this is what we have in Jesus… as long as we remain in his presence. And that is what we need to fight for. There are so many voices eroding this vision of life. Some make Jesus seem dry, or aloof, or just... not quite… God. Other voices try to encourage you that "real life" is to be found in the pursuit of your passions. They tell us to idolise our comfort or our reputation or our progress. But those of us who know the Father see the falsehood in these claims. They are elevating trinkets above the treasure, they are denying the battle that is raging on the earth. We know that a life of love is not a burdensome command. It is a rich, vibrant and verdant life full of love. A life in God is an invitation to delight. And I think it would be rude if we refused to enjoy it.

QUESTION FOR REFLECTION

Do you enjoy God? Is your life with him rich and verdant?

📖 2 JOHN

This tiny little letter from an old bloke to a random lady (or is it a church?) has been preserved and prized because brevity brings clarity. The less you say, the more weighty your words. It's a bit like Yoda, in letter form. And so here we find a titan of the faith shrinking down to a few sentences our central call from Christ; This is love that we walk in obedience to his commandments. As you have heard from the beginning, his commandment is that you walk in love (v6). There is a fascinating circle formed by these two phrases. We are told that love is about obeying Jesus and that what Jesus told us to do is to walk in love. One keeps on flipping us back round into the other like a kid pushing herself around on a playground roundabout. As you push on obedience it brings you round to love. As you push on love it brings you back round to obedience. You love and you obey, you love and you obey. On and on with ever increasing strength. Except it doesn't make you dizzy. Instead it makes you "true". You know, the kind of truth that makes you feel connected to something eternal, that makes you feel so clean and so alive and like finally - after all this time - you have found your purpose and your goal. Truth or, as we might find more appealing today, living "true" is the most precious of commodities. And John tells us it is found in doing what Jesus said and then doing what Jesus said. We live the "truth" inside of us when we choose to obey and we choose to love. All of which brings me back to the brevity of John. This joy-filled generous old man had seen Jesus in the flesh and had an encyclopaedia of expertise in every area of faith. And yet he whittles it all down to obedience and love. Out of love for you and love for me he makes it all so simple and he makes it all so clean. It inspires me to obey; to choose to love and walk in love and to keep on loving until thievery end.

QUESTION FOR REFLECTION

What is loving and obeying looking like for you in this time?

📖 3 JOHN

I love this last letter of John. It exposes what the apostles had to deal with. Apostolic life wasn't a dramatic miracle followed by a dramatic miracle. Apostolic life was a dramatic miracle followed by someone slagging you off, followed by encouraging another believer, followed by dealing with someone who wants to be first, followed by a dramatic miracle. We can sometimes conjure up an image of being "anointed" that is so far removed from people's normal life. We can think that being anointed would mean being freed from the grubbiness of actually loving sinful people. It is a massive shame when we do so. We see that, for John, the greatest joy was not an eye-popping miracle nor a standing ovation when he preached. His greater joy was hearing that his children were walking in the truth. John had seen so much. He said there wouldn't be enough books in the world to write down all he had seen Jesus do. He'd watched as the fledgling Jesus-movement spread and was established in many countries around the Mediterranean. Yet he never tired of the simple joy of seeing one person doing well with Jesus. John never lost sight of the children of Jesus; each one precious, each one to be loved and celebrated and rejoiced over when doing well. Doesn't John's heart remind you of Jesus' heart? Doesn't his delight in people exude divine dignity, doesn't it glitter and glow like the goodness of God. I want to be like John. I want my greatest joy to be hearing someone rave about what Jesus is doing in their life. I want to whoop with wonder when someone tells me they are walking in the Word. So I'm going to go looking for it. I'm going joy hunting; taking chances to hear how others are doing and then grinning with gladness when they gabble about their God.

QUESTION FOR REFLECTION

Who do you know who is walking in the truth? How does that make you feel?

📖 JUDE

In his very forceful denunciation of false teachers Jude seems like he is playing bingo with every naughty bloke from the Old Testament; Sodom and Gomorrah, Korah, Balaam, Cain. Jude name-checks them. Bingo! Jude also deploys hyped up hyperbole when heaping holy hell upon the heretics. They are like bad clouds, bad trees, bad waves and bad stars. All of them bad things. All of them false. And that, I think, points to the primary thing we can take from this letter; that we should not be complacent about the threat of false teaching. We are going to need to contend for the faith. Let's try to pick our way through this minefield. None of us want to be the angry bloke who causes a church split over a misplaced comma. I think we realise it isn't helpful to constantly howl about heretics. But - if we are to trust the authority and wisdom of the New Testament - we must beware going too far in our desire to love and be generous, to "let things slide" and generally to be nice. The key seems to revolve around who we let preach; who we give ear to; perhaps who we follow on social media. False teaching is not a small thing. It is a massive threat. It has the worst of all consequences; it will eventually send people to destruction. Most commentators think Jude was a brother of Jesus. You know, one of the ones who initially called Jesus mad but then - after the resurrection - decided he was God. Jude knows what it is like to sit on the wrong side of Jesus, to fall off the cliff of faith, only to be snatched back by God's mercy before he hit the flames. He wants us all to avoid such a terrifying and ugly experience. And so he calls us to deliberately and repeatedly build ourselves up in the truth of the faith. He wants us to pray in the Spirit and to remain conscious of God's love. Essentially Jude wants us to keep his brother at the centre; to keep our Christianity about Christ. So here's the question. Are our conversations at small group keeping the main thing the main thing? Are the people who preach to us prioritising the Prince of Peace? When people ask questions about God and faith, does our answer make reference to who Jesus actually was and what Jesus actually did? Is our life putting Jesus on his throne and making his truth our own? If we aren't, let's come back to Him. Let's stick to the one who can keep us from stumbling. Let's refocus on the one who can keep us pure and keep us true. Then our future will be joy and we will live without fault forever more.

QUESTION FOR REFLECTION

How could you elevate Jesus even more in your faith?

📖 REVELATION 1

Wow. That is quite a start. It's like when you go bowling and your first throw is a strike. You stare in slight disbelief, a little tweak of a smile in the corner of your mouth. You begin to hope that this will be your night. So let us start by laying out just how awesome this book is. And to do that I think we need to get one thing straight right at the start - Revelation is not really a book about the future. Revelation is not really about the end of the world. Sure it does contain a good chunk of stuff about what is coming but the main thrust of this book focuses on the awesome victory of our God that has always been certain, was confirmed in the cross and will be consummated with Jesus' return. The adrenalin-pumping truth that is patient endurance is all the saints need to be rewarded with never-ended delight in a restored and perfected earth. Revelation gives us an eye on God and his counsel, right now, this very day, this very moment while you sit here reading. Revelation lets us squint with hands over our eyes at the unapproachable light, at the one whose face is like the sun shining in all its brilliance. We see God is massive. God is sovereign. God is strong. And in doing so we realise how teeny weeny we are. And - even - how light and momentary our troubles are... even if they roar like a beast. Revelation shows us that our perspective is too tiny, that our human-centred analysis has been grossly misplaced. Revelation reminds us again that there is only one Almighty. I am not Him. And nor is Caesar. Revelation even scorns our human obsession with time; with what is happening in the future; at what we're doing at 4.30pm. It lifts our chin to the Alpha and Omega who was and is and is to come - the one who watches clocks spin round like they are fake dials on a toy. He is no more dictated to by time than a builder is dictated to by his drill. He is the one who loves us. He is the one who has freed us. He is the one who has made us his kingdom and priests to serve him forever. Nothing can separate us from being swept into his glorious future... as long as we patiently endure. So let's fix our eyes on Him now and worship him now and fall as if dead before him now. He is the Living One. He is the firstborn from the dead. And he is the ruler of the kings of the earth who will bring us forever into his Kingdom that will never end.

QUESTION FOR REFLECTION

What does patient endurance look like for you in this time?

📖 REVELATION 2

This ferocious force in the heavens, this unstoppable time-bending warrior has eyes like blazing fire. He uses them to search every heart and mind. He is searching your heart right now. He uses his double edged sword to prize open every hidden thing that lives inside of you. That is true whether you choose to engage with it or not, whether you choose to think about it or not. God is searching your heart. And after he has searched it he speaks. His voice may be audible, it may be mediated through an Apostle like John who has written it in the scriptures, or his voice may be a "conviction within" that conforms to His Word. But he will speak. Because the God of the Heavens wants his earth back. And he is going to get it. His pattern of speaking is nearly always the same; "1) Hear me. Give attention to me. 2) You are doing well 3) But there is something that is not right. Repent from it 4) Have Hope! I will win this earth and when I win, I want you to share in the sweet and satisfying spoils" We see this format in each of the letters to the churches and, if we have ears to hear, we will recognise it in our lives. God invites us to lean towards Him. He takes the initiative in winning us back. He wants us to start by listening. If you are anything like me, that takes a moment to act upon. Actively listening to God is not something that I naturally do. But if we do it we will find Him lavishing us with such bewildering encouragement that we start to think that he has the wrong guy. And then, when we are safe in his arms, he begins to win every part of our beings. Like pulling grass-seeds out of a dog's ear God comforts us with his love as he works to pull our sins from our tangled souls. Our repentance is our 'yes' to him. With his forgiveness and his process of healing he continues to win every part of us. And after the repentance comes a further invitation to intimacy, a second request to be still. And He closes the conversation with an even greater promise, a sweeter kind of word, a yet more brilliant hope. The best is yet to come; what he is doing in us, he will do in all the world. Every fibre of creation will be won by God. The Mighty Warrior will win and heal and restore all things.

QUESTION FOR REFLECTION

Do you recognise the 4 aspects of how God speaks to the churches? Which of these aspects are you hearing? Are you also hearing the other 3?

📖 REVELATION 3

The thing that is getting me about these letters to the churches is the lavishness of what is to come. If we overcome - which doesn't sound too hard when we factor in the awesome power of the Spirit - we will be able to eat from the tree of life, we will not be hurt at all by the second death, we will have authority over all the nations, we will have our name acknowledged before the Father, we will be made pillars in the temple of our God. Isn't that just ridiculously remarkable? We will even sit with Jesus on his throne. Isn't it preposterous? There isn't an award ceremony on earth that could get close to giving us anything as incredible as even one of those things. There cannot be a person with such a mediocre record as mine who is even in the running for such a dazzling array of riches. And that is the point of Revelation. For a persecuted church, for a struggling church, for a marginalised and disempowered church a "mediocre record of success" can be so discouraging. It can pour cold water on your perseverance when Synagogues of Satan look so powerful and so permanent. And when they push you around and pressure you into compromising your stance it can be so easy to cede ground; to let discouragement make you lukewarm. Sometimes I go that way. I suspect you do too. But then we read Revelation. Then we hear the Word of our God. He will win all the earth. And he wants to win every part of us now. Stand firm. Strengthen what remains. Put salve on your eyes. See beyond the facade of fleeting forces. Buy gold from him. Let his rebuke and his love rework every thought. Don't look at your mediocrity. Just look at his love. See how great he really is. He will win. He is winning right now in a million hidden ways. And so lean into trust and lean into encounter. Open the door to the knocking King and eat of the food that he wants to share with you. It's a foretaste of the banquet that we will feast on for endless days.

QUESTION FOR REFLECTION

What would it look like for you to "buy gold" from God right now?

📖 REVELATION 4

Two mountainous truths that are so monstrous and so overwhelming that they feel like Everest and K2 appearing before my eyes. Everest is the inherent holiness, power and eternity of God. Holiness as a term seems to have lost a lot of its punch these days. It conjures up feelings of a trip to the dentist or having your hair de-nitted with one of those special combs. But the holiness of God is far from that. It is a storm with thunder and it is jewels of matchless price. The holiness of God is beautiful, it is worthy of all respect and all the accolades you can muster. And it always will be. For God is eternal. The truth about God is that at the end of our day, his day hasn't ended. In fact our whole concept of time itself - a concept that we are inherently incapable of seeing beyond - is just like a caterpillar crawling along the finger of God. He was. And He is. And He is to come. God's holiness, power and eternal nature mean that he will always rule, he can never be dethroned. No principality, no person and no concept could even enter the courts of God without his permission. God is unrivalled. Remember that when the persecution hits. Lean back on that when your earthly securities are crumbling in your hands. God is like Everest. But there's another mountain. K2 is God's ownership of the earth. The earth is God's; he made it, he's never given up on it and he will win it back. His eyes are always watching it like a creature who has eyes on every side. He is always visiting the earth, agile and mobile like a creature with six wings. And, as a symbol of the unbreakable connection between the Eternal One and his earth, there are 24 elders - 24 representatives of the earth - always before his throne. Think about this God. Cast your crowns before this God. He is the One who never forgets you. He is the one who will never overlook you. He is the one who will win us in the end. He is holy. He is powerful. He is eternal. He is our maker. He is our overseer and our helper. And, because of who he is, and who he will always be, there is not a shadow of a doubt that he will win the earth back in the end.

QUESTION FOR REFLECTION

"God will win his earth back in the end". What does that truth stir in you?

📖 REVELATION 5

The scroll represents God's plan and his authority. He will win back his earth and the scroll says how. But no one can open it. Angels are shouting, John is weeping and weeping and the elders are falling on their faces. But the One on the Throne sits serene and secure. He knows his plan is good. And he knows the one who will enact it. This is a vision of reality right here. Never mind Newsnight. Never mind I'm a Celebrity Get me Out of Here. If we really want to know where it is at, if we really want to get a glimpse of governmental power and authority then we need to flick off the television and get our face in Revelation 5. This is the future. And this is the present. And this is the past. God, on his throne, knowing. God on his throne serene and secure. The root of Jesse enacting his plan to win back his earth. Except there is a surprise in this passage. The surprise is why and how Jesus is worthy. The surprise is what that means for the church. This surprise defines the whole of the rest of the book. Are you ready? The worthiness of Jesus is due to his death. Jesus is worthy because he was slain for the sake of the world. No-one, not even the greatest of the saints was willing nor able to pay such a price. And it is for that reason - his willingness to die an obedient death of atonement - that Jesus is the worthy one. It is worth really dwelling on this point because the implications are massive. We see what it means to be in the Kingdom. A church who is seeing brothers burned alive by Nero or ripped apart by lions sees where victory and worthiness is found; it is found in humble obedience to the Father and sustained love for our neighbour. When we are persecuted we do not kick back nor fall back. We turn our cheek and love them back. We overcome evil with good. We stand firm, even to the point of death. And when it looks like we are losing we rejoice in our weaknesses. We aim for faithfulness. We take up our cross and emulate the lamb who was slain, choosing to enact the Father's plans no matter the cost.

QUESTION FOR REFLECTION

How are you emulating the lamb in the midst of your battles?

📖 REVELATION 6

The lamb begins to enact the plan. Is this future stuff? Or has it already happened? Or is it both?? There is much debate about that, but the passage doesn't major on it and nor should we. To try to pin these verses to specific years is to miss the inclination of the revelation. For the inclination of the revelation is the exaltation of the Hope of Nations. The Lamb - the hope of nations - opens six seals. He does it deliberately and easily. All eyes are on him. The Living Creatures follow his every whim. Vast spiritual horses advance at his flick of their bridle. Men receive judgement from him. Martyrs receive compassion from him. Neither can change his timetable or intentions. All the cosmic constants quake and change because he wants them to. The Lamb - the one who oversaw creation - now oversees decreation as if he were whipping up an omelette. He does what he wants. And no one can stop him. This is our God. Jesus may have died on the cross, his church may be being maligned and marginalised but this Lamb ain't weak and his stance ain't insecure. All the pretenders to the throne of the earth will eventually see that. They may have to suffer to see that, or they may see it up front. But in the end they will see it. This isn't a threat to the church. This is an encouragement to the church. It might seem right now that all the power - literally all the power and influence lies with the likes of President Putin or Lady Gaga or Elon Musk or even our boss at work. And it might seem that they can do whatever they want whenever they want and we just have to suck it up. But that appearance is false. In the end all of the "kings of the earth" are going to hide in the mountains in an attempt to escape the gaze of the Lamb. He was the only one who could open the scroll. And seal by seal he enacts the Father's plan. Everything will be shaken. Every single fallacy in creation will be unmasked and undone when Jesus wants it to be so. Everything will be de-created except the church of Jesus Christ (which might even include Lady Gaga). And so - Kingdom and Priests - we should honour the lamb. Let's keep our eyes fixed on him and stay faithful in our trials.

QUESTION FOR REFLECTION

How does this passage encourage you to hope more in Jesus?

📖 REVELATION 7

This section is like an advert break in the midst of the main show. In the hiatus between the six seals and the seventh seal we peer through a crack in the door of heaven to remember where all this woe is going. God is winning his earth back so saints from many cities can share the made-good earth forever with their God. All through Revelation we get little "advert breaks" which remind us of this. Each advert is drenched with adoration; diverse saints singing and dancing as they see the victory of God being unleashed by the Lamb. These 144,000 represent the martyrs. We shouldn't take the number literally (otherwise you'd have to feel quite sorry for the 12,001st martyr in the tribe of Naphtali. So close and yet so far!) The number 144,000 is what John hears announced. When he looks to see there is a huge multitude of every tribe and language. What is heard is a metaphorical description of the crowd he sees; 12 means 'perfection of government' and 10 refers to something being God's choice. So 12,000 refers to those who have been definitely and irrevocably chosen by God to carry out His perfect governance. The use of the names of the tribes of Israel shows how this vision is the culmination of the whole sweep of the biblical narrative from Genesis through to Jude. These symbolic representatives of all who have lived like the lamb - and been killed like the lamb - stand before the throne to celebrate the victory that the lamb is winning. Their standing and singing isn't a vision of the eternal destiny of these saints; we get to that in the closing chapters. Instead, they stand like cheerleaders on the touchline, beholding what the lamb is unfolding and - without the slightest doubt that he can and will win back the earth. And so we should bear these people in mind when we read the chapters on the woes. In South London, visions of God's wrath bringing decreation might seem rather unsettling; there is much in our way of life that we wouldn't want to come to an end. But the point is this; in this infected and corrupted earth great multitudes are being chewed up and spat out by the schemes of Satan. These people from many nations and tribes - Nigerians and North Koreans and Naphtalians and even South Londoners - have yearned for justice and have begged God for salvation. They died without consolation but now - from the vantage point of heaven - they are seeing the God of all creation winning back the earth to make it good again.

QUESTION FOR REFLECTION

How conscious are you of those who have died for their faith in Jesus? Do you hear the songs they are singing?

📖 REVELATION 8

The vision of the 7 trumpets seems too much for simple minds to comprehend. If you feel overwhelmed or confused; don't despair. Apocalyptic literature is intended to conceal and allude. It is meant to present the truth behind a veil which the faithful can lift through growing engagement with The Lamb. But even our wisest prayer warriors, with a lifetime imbued with the scriptures, still see the truth in Revelation as in a glass darkly; enough to advance but not so much that we get proud. A key method for these chapters is to focus on what you can understand, on what the Spirit highlights to you. Read the other bits but let them remain on the shelf to be considered "next time round". What am I "grabbing" today? Well, I'm drawn to see how all of God's de-creating work - crashing down cosmic constants, letting fire do its work - is in response to his people's prayers. God is doing what his people have been begging him to do for years. And so, I think that - if we follow the tone of their blasts - the trumpets should lead us to prayer and perseverance. Real prayer, proper prayer that fills the golden bowl of heaven. This prayer expresses a sickness with the prominence of pride. This prayer is pained by the posing of the Powers. Do we pray those prayers? Do we allow ourselves to express agonised dissatisfaction with the state of this earth? I, for one, am sick of all the pride and all the hate. I'm sick of humanities' sin that requires this kind of tragic response. In fact I'm sick of my own sin. Woe to us. Woe to me. Woe caused by me and my always-in-the-background, never-quite-quashed desire to do my own thing, to put two fingers up to God and choose to please myself. Woe to my flesh that keeps on dragging me down to my most base self. Now this woe must never become self-hatred (or other person hatred). With the woe we go to pray. We repent of our fallenness. We beg God to change things, to win his earth back in our days. And then, having prayed, we go. We go to living like the Lamb. We go to trusting in the God who always reigns, who always watches, who will never miss the tiniest act of faithfulness on our part. Yes, we go to faithful endurance. Most of all we go to faithful endurance. Knowing that life will be hard, that the decreation work of God against all that is evil will be robust; that the medicine will require a massive gulp. But we know that if we faithfully endure then all our prayers will be answered once the fire of God has done its work.

QUESTION FOR REFLECTION

What pained prayers are you praying about the state of the earth?

📖 REVELATION 9

A continuation of chaotic visions. The layering effect of the revelation adds intensity. The numbers convey certainty. But coming at it on this slightly weary morning, it all feels a bit baffling. Let's just recap on where we are; we're still watching the activity caused by the seventh seal. These are the seals that release God's great plan to win back the earth. The lamb is the only one who is worthy to open them, and he is doing so in fulfilment of the long-held prayers of his people. The trumpet blasts that accompany the opening of the seventh seal remind us of the walls of Jericho falling down. The locusts and the plagues remind us of the Exodus from Egypt. This thing we are reading is the climax of the victory of God. It may contain destruction. It may contain woe. But it is, in fact, a final act of liberation, a wilderness wandering coming to an end. For many of us, there may be a gag reflex at the idea that God - our God of love - is the cause of so much pain. We like to think that God is a bit coochie coochie. But the big picture of liberation helps us swallow and then digest this hearty meal. There is a huge evil force encamped upon the earth. He is a star fallen from heaven. He is the boss of the Abyss. His intention is dire and his power is grave. This beast - who we see in many forms in the next few chapters - is like Pharoah on steroids, like Philistines on a power up. His prime goal is to make people worship idols (v20). His power over people is to keep them feeling proud. They love the work of their own hands, they do what they want, how they want, when they want. And this pride makes them blind to the compassion and rule of God. And so - just like in Egypt - God releases plagues to expose the impotence of the idols. Each woe attacks a widely held idol; the lust of the eyes, the lust of the flesh, the pride of life. Each woe is measured and restrained; enough to expose the impotence but not so much that everything crashes down. It is all enacted by the lamb to achieve freedom for his people and to offer repentance to those "of the world". But tragically, very few repent. And that should steel us for these days. We need to pray for steel in our stomachs to stay humble before our God and to keep on keeping on when so many refuse to repent.

QUESTION FOR REFLECTION

How do you respond emotionally to this passage? How could you meet God in the midst of those emotions?

📖 REVELATION 10

Call me a coward, but if I saw an angel who had one foot on the sea and one foot on the land and who shouted like a roaring lion - if I saw that angel - and someone asked me to go up to him and take his scroll off him... I would leg it. But maybe I shouldn't. Maybe - if I really understood this section of Revelation - I would realise that these mighty angels are always around. Maybe I would realise that behind the sleepy-feeling days of this earth a crashing conflict is going on in the spiritual realms. Maybe I would then become more comfortable (if that could ever be the right word) with the idea of giant angels influencing every act upon this earth. This kind of talk is pretty much blasphemous to our modern "rational" ears. The disenchantment of the "enlightenment" makes most of us think spiritual stuff - if it exists at all - is "over there somewhere" while earthly stuff is "right here". This means many of us can love Jesus and try to follow Jesus without seeing the world remotely like he saw it. We can look at our problems and other people's power and we let them become the big story. If only we could get a new job, or have a bigger following, or get the government to do what we want them to do... then the stuff would be sorted. Let's google it and get the answer. We never imagine an angel needs to act, or some dark spiritual power needs to be undone. These passages show us that the unseen realm is where fates are decided. This doesn't diminish the seen realm at all. The vision of Revelation is that these two realms are constantly intersecting (the angel hand his feet on our earth and our sea) and - in the end - will become totally united when the unseen Kingdom of God becomes fully seen once Jesus has won back his earth. So faithful endurance - living like Kingdom and Priests - means we now live as if we "see" the "unseen". My prayer from this passage is that we become people who expect to see hulking angels holding scrolls. My prayer is that we pray and hear the words of heaven and see the visions God gives us. My prayer is that we find new ways to live like the unseen God is really Sovereign on the earth, trusting that his unseen power is actually something we can see and influence and release upon this earth.

QUESTION FOR REFLECTION

How much do you think you have a "disenchanted worldview"; where you only really think about "seen" things rather than "unseen" powers and forces?

📖 REVELATION 11

The stuff about the trumpets and the woes and the witnesses and the woes interlaces back and forth like a bowl of spaghetti. If we try to follow all the progress of the trumpets and the woes we might feel a bit dizzy. But there is a massive truth in here that we can suck up and be nourished by. It is the vocation and the vindication of the witnesses. The identity of the witnesses is widely accepted to be the church. Their vocation speaks into our vocation; God wants witnesses. A witness does not just speak whatever they want to speak. No, a witness shows and tells what they have seen. And that is the task of the church. Show and tell what you have seen. It is the simplest thing, as long as you have seen something. So have you seen something? Have you really seen God? That is Phrase 1 of our witness. "We give thanks to you, Lord God Almighty, the One who is and who was" (v17) Witnesses worship. But there is a Phrase 2 "because you have taken your great power and have begun to reign" (v17) or "The kingdom of the world has become the kingdom of our Lord and of his Messiah" (v15). Please note this; true witnesses are invited to declare not only that God is wonderful but also that he has already begun to reign. God has already acted in Jesus and his "unseen" power is already reforming this "seen" realm. Jesus has already begun to reign through his church. As we've said before - this isn't the most obvious thing you think when you look at the church. It looks a bit rubbish. It looks a bit beaten up, overpowered and killed. The church is something easy to mock. You could even send gifts to one another to celebrate its demise. But, just like the witnesses, in the end the church will be vindicated. The breath of God will fill the disempowered church, catching us up into the clouds, enabling us to live like we are walking in the heavenly counsel while others walk forward into awful judgement. God has already begun to reign through his church… and our stories and our gatherings must become witnesses of that truth. While it is great to read this book and to eat up this spaghetti, the real question is will we digest that truth? Will we become witnesses? Will we love all the body of Jesus Christ and celebrate how Jesus is reigning through them, even while others look on to mock and to gloat.

QUESTION FOR REFLECTION

How could you help the church live our vocation as witnesses?

📖 REVELATION 12

This seems to be a second look at the same situation as chapter 11. Rather than two witnesses, the church is now represented by a woman. The son - of course - is Jesus, born of the people of God and yet destined to rule us all. The dragon is the Devil. This vision calls the church to be alert to the prime plan of the Powers - to spew forth a torrent of accusations against them, causing them to drift away from Jesus' church. I wonder how you hear the steady stream of whispered thoughts and ideas that seem to pull you away from connection to Jesus' church? At times I've felt like a child in a rip-tide being washed out to sea. This chapter wants us to hear those thoughts as demonic devices determined to drag us away from our destiny. Notice that while God has stood secure, and sovereign all through this book, with his eyes constantly on his people, the devil acts in furious anger, insecure about his future, desperate to salvage stuff for himself. He couldn't even defeat an angel, let alone stand toe-to-toe with God. He is a Power who is weaker than we could ever believe, but more dangerous for it - as he lashes out with accusations that can really scar. And so we should help one another be ready to defeat his accusations. If thoughts come based in anger or insecurity or self-preservation they are likely to be spewed from the dragon's mouth. To listen to them and repeat them isn't "being real" or "just being honest"; it is idiotic foolishness, like licking your dirty pants. Understanding the Devil as Accuser helps us deal much better with the self-doubt and self-hatred that are the norm of our society. So often they are the Devil trying to use our minds as his weapon to destroy us. In those moments we don't need to go over and over the finest details of the thoughts. Instead we just keep on keeping on. We don't try to defeat the accusations; we can just forget them. In a bizarre but bracingly brilliant image we see all of creation opening its mouth to swallow the accusations of the enemy! And we see the great woman (us) being given wings by God and drawing us into his presence. So in summary, the truth behind this vision is the same as that of the whole of the Revelation - the church operates in a warzone and mighty powers are fighting it out, but God will easily win, and we will share in his victory if we faithfully endure and continue to live like the lamb.

QUESTION FOR REFLECTION

Are you prone to overthinking things? How might Jesus help you stop that?

📖 REVELATION 13

Revelation 13 isn't telling us to obsess over the mark of the beast, and it certainly doesn't equate that mark with a piece of body-borne technology. No, Revelation 13 is telling us about worship; it unambiguously asserts that people will either worship Satan or Jesus, and it urges us to worship the Son. This isn't quite as simple as it might appear; it calls for wisdom, so we don't get caught up with the crowd. It seems that Satan sneaks into our worship through human powers that have been distorted into beast-like beings reminiscent of the visions of Daniel. Almost certainly total devotion to Rome - worship of the Emperor, collaboration in their every agenda - was seen as worship of the devil. Almost certainly total devotion to capitalism, or to liberalism or to nationalism will cause us to bear the mark of the beast. The faithful will need to patiently endure in the midst of any culture; not to conform to the pattern of this world but to stand out, distinct, like those who hope in a different world. And so Revelation 13 should cause us to ask about our dreams and our hopes. Whatever we may sing about on a Sunday, it is what we yearn for and what we shoot for that shows what we worship. If you cut me open what would my ambition be shown to be? I'd like people to tell me I'm impressive. The odd applauding crowd would not go amiss. A little more acceptably I want to grow old with my wife and watch my grandchildren thrive in life. All of these things can be good, but what if the only way I can reach them is to compromise with my culture and calm my commitment to Christ? This "risky" environment is what the church is always in. The beast is so powerful and he can make his way of getting things look really good. Massive wisdom and endurance are required. Chapters like this can make faithfulness seem incredibly hard. And, when I think about it, so many of my friends seem to have fallen captive to the relentless assaults of the power-wielding dragon. But we must not lose heart. Chapter 14 shows us the resource we have to draw on when we need to endure; worship of the lamb. Honour of and glory of the One who has redeemed us from the dragon's power. If we want to endure and be blameless, it is worship of the Lamb that should be our battle-cry.

QUESTION FOR REFLECTION

If you were stop and audit your life, what would your use of your body suggest you are devoted to?

📖 REVELATION 14

I think this is the same content as Revelation 13, but presented through a different image. You know, like when Jesus spoke of himself as bread one minute and then a shepherd the next. None of us thought he had actually turned into a loaf of bread and then into a sheep-keeper; we understood them to be images conveying the same truth in different ways to pull out certain meanings. Here we have a vision of 144,000 men who have never had sex. Nowhere in the New Testament has having-it-off with your spouse been regarded as a defiling act. In fact the evidence has been massively to the contrary. (There has also been no suggestion in the New Testament that men are entitled to a higher level of heavenly dwelling than the womenfolk.) And so we embrace this image like we did Jesus as a bread roll; we understand the "144,000 men who kept themselves pure" as symbolic of something. They take us back to the wilderness wanderings of Israel where the women of Moab seduced God's people into worshipping their foreign gods. Or they take us back to Ezekiel and Hosea who again and again compared idolatry to sexual promiscuity. So we understand the 144,000 men not as a precise count of exalted males but rather as an image of God's faithful women and men, chosen by him (symbolised by the number 12x12) and perfect in number (symbolised by the number 10x10). Having understood this image it then tells us what action to take; to patiently endure, obeying God's commandments and remaining faithful to Jesus (v12). We do this like a husband waiting for his beloved wife to come back from a long trip. We do this like a wife waiting for her happy husband to come home. We do it knowing that we would be susceptible to seduction if we did some silly things but we don't want to do those silly things, because we love Him and we are his. We have been chosen by him and we have his name written on our heads. Blamelessness has become our birthright. Purity has become our preoccupation. And so we endure through the long and lonely nights and we endure through the difficult days when life feels a bit dull. We endure and we remain faithful because our spouse will return and, when he does, he will set all things right.

QUESTION FOR REFLECTION

How are you pursuing greater purity in this time?

📖 REVELATION 15

It has shocked me how much worship has gone on in Revelation. I knew the big passages like Revelation 4 and Revelation 19 were replete with crown-casting kings but I hadn't realised the praise-craze had soaked into every corner of this book. Most shocking, perhaps, is the fact that worship seems to lap right up and over all the most awkward bits about bowls of wrath and sharp-sickle-swinging angels. To me it feels a little hard to read about trampling the winepress until blood flowed out and then to say 'Great and marvellous are your deeds Lord God Almighty". But then again, I'm not yet on the right side of this view. I don't yet have the perspective of one who has been victorious over the beast. I have not yet been given a harp by my God. Revelation isn't God explaining himself to us, for us to find him more palatable. It isn't even about God making himself more understandable to us. It is about him showing us he is great. He is good. He has got Satan licked. He does everything well and must be trusted until the end. This takes us beyond anything that would be achieved were Revelation a chronology of the future. Then we might act like guests at a foreign language wedding trying to best-guess where we are in the Order of Service based on what seems to be happening in front of us. Then our eyes would be on something other than the Lamb. Instead Revelation embeds "advert breaks" of worship into multi-layered visions of angels and trumpets and woes and wonders. Revelation shows the cosmic crashing together of heaven and earth… and how the Alpha and Omega stands serene, secure and sovereign over it all. Revelation dares us to be destabilised and still to declare "who will not fear you, Lord". Revelation gives us a verbal volley akin to smoke and glory filling our minds, and urges us to admit "you are King of the Nations… just and true are your ways". Will you follow Revelation where it is trying to take you, even if it leaves you slightly paralysed by it all, like God's servants have often been?

QUESTION FOR REFLECTION

Is worship the constant "advert break" in your life?

📖 REVELATION 16

This ends the extended metaphor comparing the second beast to Pharaoh. Plagues have been used just like there were against Egypt. The enemy has been washed away in a sea the height of a horse's bridle (14:20), just like the Red Sea swallowed up the horse and riders of Egypt. The liberated ones have once again sung a song of deliverance (ch15) except somebody forgot to pack Miriam's tambourine. Here, through the symbol of seven bowls we see the same truth as the seven trumpets and the seven signs; and the same truth as we saw in the story of Moses - God has such commitment to setting his people free that he will even whip up a storm to bring it into being on the earth. What this letter told the christians getting ripped apart by the beastly rule of Rome was that God would bring them deliverance. What this letter has shouted to those ravaged by persecution, or smashed by oppression, or relentlessly looted of possessions was that they will be delivered by God and then they finally will be free. The imagery no-doubt sounds harsh to us - it is meant to. It points to the intransigent insufferability of living under the beast. There is massive corruption, hostility towards God, dehumanisation of whole classes of people, celebration of pride and greed. Human efforts are only scratching the service of these problems. The world needs to be shaken to root out every cause and consequence of evil. God will split into three parts the great city and he will end those who have got fat and brazen with their abuse of human power. God will win back his earth, and nothing can stand in his way. To really grasp this and accept it actually encourages us to show mercy to others trapped in this narrative. We know God's wrath will be a real storm felt by real people in real places. The recipients of God's judgement will be human beings, and the earth will feel it too. If we are like the lamb we will lovingly pray and urge others to flee from this; to come to Jesus and - like the Israelites on the brink of Exodus - to paint his blood around the doorway of their lives.

QUESTION FOR REFLECTION

What does the reality of God's coming wrath spark in you?

📖 REVELATION 17

I'm sitting in a coffee shop. I'm listening to the lovely twinkly Christmas music. I'm conscious that both the bible and the year are reaching their end. I'm looking at all the delicious treats on offer and I'm finding it hard to equate what I see with what I have just read. The passage tells me of great powers raging in this world. It tells of a grotesque and adulterous force that is intoxicating us with worship of false gods. It says that this force is violently opposed to me and my faith. It says that it wants my blood. But everything looks so jolly. Christmas is just so jolly... isn't it?? I think this is one of the areas of my faith that I struggle with more than anything else. In the affluent West we have grown so accustomed to things having the edge taken off them. Life is manicured around us; it has been declawed. I suppose there is nothing wrong with that except that it belies the truth of the vicious battle going on. I need passages like this so I can see through the fancy facade and remember the reality. I need to see that in their hearts - in their souls - people are haggard. People are on the brink. I need to look past the superficial "jolliness" and see the cancer and the divorce and the loss and the loneliness and the people struck by trains and the slander against Jesus and grasp that this is the work of a disgusting and despicable force. It is the work of THE MOTHER OF PROSTITUTES. In John's day that MOTHER was manifested in the idea of Rome. Today it is probably another manifestation that rules over the kings of the earth. It requires wisdom to recognise it because it is so easy to overlook. It is so easy to be serenaded by superficial and to miss the battle that is raging on this earth. We need to pray hard to see the foetid ugliness that hides behind what we call "normalness". Only then can we fight. Only then can we be sure we will overcome. The story of the book is coming to an end and it ends with a mighty battle and then the brilliance of a brand new dawn. We must not lose sight of that. We can enjoy the twinkly lights. We can enjoy the jolly stuff. But we must also see what lies beneath; being disgusted by the influence of greed and being delighted to be a follower of the Lord.

QUESTION FOR REFLECTION

What is the spiritual battle that Jesus is fighting in this city today?

📖 REVELATION 18

Babylon will be tortured. Babylon will weep in torment. These are the sections of Revelation I have always found hardest to like! But this time, as the sweep of the narrative is much clearer to me, I think it is winning me over. Babylon is a symbol of the great "idea" or the great "kingdom" of the day that scorns the creative order of God. God made the world for shalom, where all feed well and enjoy fellowship with God and men and women. But Babylon actively asserts itself over and above the Creator and then crashes around the earth snatching stuff intended for others. Babylon is evil. Despite clear and present warnings both in creation and from the Creator, Babylon advances in this greed with reckless abandon. She draws others into the pride and the plunder. It puts smoke in God's nostrils. God will bring them to ruin in just one hour. But before he does that he issues an invitation to his people. This is what Revelation is; one long invitation to the church to stand apart from the value-system of Babylon. The invitation is to reject the constant desire for accumulation; the constant need to have more than others. The boast of Babylon was that she was Queen; she was greater than others, richer than others, more powerful than others. Do we dream the dreams of Babylon? Do we judge ourselves comparative to our peers, only feeling happy when we get that phone, those clothes, that gadget that others have? What about shalom? What about God's intentions for his earth? What if the manufacture of your desired gadget ground the faces of the poor and denied their God-given dignity. Do you care? Babylon doesn't. But the people of God will care about these things. We see "excessive luxuries" as the rejection of God's shalom that they really are. Let's be clear about this; gold in itself is not evil. Gold is the pavement stone of heaven and a symbol of God's beauty. Buy presents for loved ones. Save up for your pension. Treat yourself every now and then. But beware merchants of Babylon. The love of gold leads to a yearning for accumulation, which will cause you to share in Babylon's sins. Instead let's come away from such things. Instead, in humility and in worship let's give allegiance to the Way of Heaven with what we say and what we want and what we spend. For the Way of Heaven will last forever, while Babylon will be overthrown in one night.

QUESTION FOR REFLECTION

What might it look like to live entirely unaffected by the desires of Babylon?

📖 REVELATION 19

Never again. That has been the refrain of the last few passages. Never again will Babylon be found. Never again will a lamp shine in her. Never again will she lead the nations astray. While much of the book of Revelation has been an open door into what is going on in heaven right now, what we are reading here is the True End of this world in its current form. This stuff hasn't happened yet. But it will. Yes it will. It is worth lingering a while on that. We get so used to the ugly head of the devil popping up in our lives that it can be hard to believe that a time is coming when it will never happen again. But what happens here really is a brand new reality being born. The Wedding will occur. The Banquet will begin. The birds of the air will gorge on the flesh of every demonic being. The beast and the false prophet will be thrown into the fiery lake. Lots of imagery points to the total destruction of all that is evil. Into the next chapter we see the wholesale destruction of every source of evil taking place. I say again that this is worth a linger; a sure and certain conviction that evil will be annihilated would be a good portion of our daily bread. To know that evil's days are numbered inspires us, emboldens us, helps us stand firm. And we can know that it is true because it is already happening. While the True End depicted here hasn't occurred yet, don't we already see The Rider on a White Horse already dressed in a robe that has been dipped in the blood? He put that on at the cross. Don't we already know that the KING OF KINGS AND LORD OF LORDS has started treading out the winepress. Every time we see an addiction overcome, every time we see a healing occur, every time we see someone forgiven of their sins or growing in love or standing firm in trial - we see the victory of Faithful and True, we see a glimmer of a foretaste of the downfall of evil. Jesus is doing his thing right now through his church when we continue in faithfulness and we live like the lamb. And so we worship now. Of course our worship then will be vaster, more roar-like, more "an ocean wave" than what we do now - as I said it is hard to comprehend life totally liberated from any trace of evil. But when we read these passages it shows us that we are on the right track and that our worship and our faithfulness and our "keeping on keeping on" is a clear witness about Jesus. Jesus will consummate the whole thing in the end. There will be a day when the devil is utterly destroyed and the world is utterly redeemed. What we taste in the now will become all things in all ways for all days without end..

QUESTION FOR REFLECTION

What would your life look like without any trace of any form of evil affecting it?

📖 REVELATION 20

People have defined their faith by what they think about the 1000 years. I still don't know where I land on it. Revelation is so replete with symbolism that the "millenium" could just be another example of communicating truth using numbers. But, even if the 1000 years are an actual stage in history, we should remember that it is only a stage, not the final destination. The primary point of the passage is what happens next; Satan is utterly, eternally defeated and every person stands before God's judgement. This is how we need to view judgement; it is God eradicating from creation every potential source of the devil's return. Judgement is not God subjecting us to an arbitrary exam. Judgement is not a public video of every bad thing you've ever done just to see how much you squirm. Instead, judgement is God's way of ensuring none of his future co-regents will do what Adam and Eve did. God is looking to establish a permanently pristine, eternally expanding, encyclopaedia of ecstasy for resurrected humanity. And he wants to entrust the stewardship of this new creation into the hands of his children. And so he picks his way through our lives, seeking out evidence that this is what we want as well. He is like an extremely generous, insanely optimistic conductor, holding auditions for a mighty orchestra to play with him in a symphony of symphonies. As long as you can hold the trombone and will commit to watching his instructions then you are in. If you've shown you'd refuse to follow his score, that you have no interest at all in trying to use your violin like he tells you to, then the evidence is clear that you would wreck God's new creation. Tragically for many, even this incredibly optimistic form of judgement will still find them out. With shock and horror that moment will prove they prefer their own agenda to Gods, that they prefer the dirge of Mog and Magog to God's symphony of extreme delight. We pray for those people and seek to lovingly witness to those people in this time. There will be a day when it will all be too late. But the thrust of this passage - as with the whole of Revelation - is to bring genuine hope and real motivation to those whose names are written in the book of life. All we need to do is keep trying to follow Jesus. We don't need to become a prodigy; we just need to show willing to follow Jesus' lead. And that means faithful endurance. Rather than waiting for a possible future Millenium, we see every moment as an opportunity to apprentice ourselves to becoming co-rulers with our God.

QUESTION FOR REFLECTION

How are you learning to co-rule with Jesus?

📖 REVELATION 21

This is our great hope. This is what we cry out for like a hot shower and our own bed after a week of soggy camping. The content of this chapter should be imagined and then reimagined to ensure our hope is real. Over and again I come across "bible people" who have no real imagination for what our hope will look like. Over and again I realise my understanding of "what it will look like" is too super-spiritual and vague to cause any change in my 9-5. In truth most communication about "heaven" sounds so much like an out-of-body floaty-sunny fantasy land that our minds cannot accept it. Revelation's images are far more "earthy" than many of us ever manage. In fact - get this shock - the hope of Revelation is not for us to go to heaven at all. Please do think about that. The hope of Revelation is not that we will float out of our bodies and out of this earth to some hovering utopia in the skies. No. The hope of Revelation comes down out of heaven. Twice in this passage we see our hope coming down "out of heaven". Both times it is the bride or the holy city that comes down "out of heaven" - where it has been paradising with Jesus while it waited for the New Earth to be made. The key phrase is that now, in this New Earth, God has come down to live with his people. All wrongs have been righted. The earth has been transformed; made perfect and fully redeemed in every way, but something that we could still only describe as 'earth'. It seems like this good and spotless place will have nations and kings and people who can make and bring things of splendour to the Lamb. It seems that the New Earth will be like Eden when it was "very good", except more populated, thriving, swirling, life-infested in every way. The garden will show signs of human cultivation, with every single good thing done in the body represented and remembered there in some way. It will be a city of joy. Brilliant and beautiful without a trace or threat of shame. So if you ever start to feel sick of camping, if you ever feel bored of feeling half-washed, then do not despair; the hope is coming. It is real, it is good, and if you have your name in Jesus' book you are guaranteed to make it there.

QUESTION FOR REFLECTION

Can you describe your vision of earth and heaven becoming one?

📖 REVELATION 22

The Fall is overcome. The river of life raises The City and its inhabitants way up above even the lofty heights of Eden. For now there is a throne and everyone is sitting on it. And they will reign for ever and ever without a pesky snake coming and wrecking it all up. Now there is no night or any temple because God is to be encountered everywhere, in every way, all the time. So unspeakably brilliant is this vision, so nostril-flaringly outstanding is this sight that John - even John who saw the transfigured Jesus and who ate the broiled fish with the risen Christ - even John can't help himself but fling his whole being down onto the dust and physically express his utter unworthiness to be around it. I can't remember the last time I felt such a depth of astonishment and conviction. I end this journey with a similar sense of trepidation to that with which I started it, except now I feel more aware of the sheer inadequacy of my knowledge, the meagre extent of my faith. This Jesus who I love, this Jesus who in my worst moment I feel I fully know - this Jesus is the same one who gave this vision to John. This Jesus is the same one who is called the Root, the Offspring of David and the Bright Morning Star. This Jesus has shown me Himself - he really, truly has - and so far all I've been able to look at is the nail of his little toe. What I've seen has been amazing. What I've seen nearly brings me to tears right now in this seat and yet it is just a whiff. It is just a tiny fragment of gold compared to all of Fort Knox. But there will be a day when I see it all. I pray I will keep seeing more and more until that day comes. But there will be a day when Jesus will come, where Jesus will come and claim his own and will reward for what's been done. And then I will see him as he is. Then his whole phenomenal, beyond-ordinary, beyond-temporary, beyond-constraint body will be unveiled before me. And I will fall face down and I will eat the dust. I can't wait for that day. Please come, Lord Jesus.

QUESTION FOR REFLECTION

What things has Jesus shown you in this journey through the New Testament?

"A New Testament Journey" has been developed by Croydon Vineyard Church to help all of our church engage with all of the New Testament, and in so doing, become a community formed by the word. We have other resources linked with this devotional available and explained at **www.croydonvineyard.org.uk**

Tom Thomspon is joint-Senior Pastor of Croydon Vineyard. After doing stints in the city and the government (he can't tell you about it or he'd have to kill you) Tom and his wife Lesley were sent by South West London Vineyard to plant Croydon Vineyard Church in 2013. In his spare time Tom loves trying to beat his four sons at sport and taking Fizz - his black Labrador - for walks.

Printed in Great Britain
by Amazon